TIBERIUS

Livia.   *Augustus.*   *Tiberius.*

Julia.

After Coins in the British Museum
Photo. by R. N. Haile.

TIBERIUS CÆSAR

Emperor of Rome

G. P. Baker

First Cooper Square Press edition 2001

This Cooper Square Press paperback edition of *Tiberius Caesar* is an unabridged republication of the edition first pulished in London in 1929.

Published by Cooper Square Press
An Imprint of the Rowman & Littlefield Publishing Group
150 Fifth Avenue, Suite 911
New York, New York 10011

Distributed by National Book Network

Library of Congress Cataloging-in-Publication Data

Baker G.P. (George Philip), 1879–1951.
  Tiberius Caesar : emperor of Rome / G.P. Baker.
    p. cm.
  Includes bibliographical references and index.
  ISBN 0-8154-1113-8 (pbk. : alk. paper)
    1. Tiberius, Emperor of Rome, 42 B.C.–37 A.D. 2. Rome— History— Augustus, 30
  B.C.–14 A.D. 3. Rome— History— Tiberius, 14–37. 4. Emperors— Rome— Biography. I.
  Title.

DG282 .B3 2000
937'.06'092— dc21
[B]
                                                                    00-063869

⊖™ The paper used in this publication meets the minimum requirements of
American National Standard for Information Sciences— Permanence of
Paper for Printed Library Materials, ANSI/NISO Z39.48–1992.
Manufactured in the United States of America.

HOC OPVS
GVLIELMO
GARTHWAITIO
DVNELMIAE
BARONETTO
EQVITI COR-
ONAE BELGICAE
INSCRIPTVM EST
QVI VT GRATIAS PATRIAE
SVAE AGAT SALVTEMQVE
COMMVNEM CIVITATIS
ADIUVET STVDIA HISTORIAE
GVBERNATIONIS ORIGINIS-
QVE ET AVCTVS DIGNITATIS
REGIAE FOVET.

PREFACE

The reign of Tiberius, the second of the Roman emperors, was a political battlefield on which great issues were lost and won. More were lost than were won. . . . They were issues not altogether unrelated to those that trouble us today.

The story of Tiberius does not afford any direct historical parallel with our own time. Its parallel—if it is to have one—lies a generation or two ahead of us. It is the tale of what happened to a Dictatorship when it was at last established. . . . The Dictatorship established by Gaius Julius Cæsar is the only one that ever permanently endured. It lasted, in effect, for eighteen hundred years. No Greek Dictatorship was ever permanent. It is only the successors of Cæsar who give us any illustration of what is likely to happen to a Dictatorship which permanently establishes itself. . . . And we see it necessarily transformed by degrees into a monarchy.

Tiberius was an active agent in giving the temporary rule of Cæsar, and the hazardous principate of Augustus, permanence as a reality hardly again to be shaken.

The nature of monarchy is not to be found by studying it exclusively in its later forms. We must wrestle with its problems while it was still new and fluid, and was being gradually given form by the impact of events. We need to apprehend what precise kind of force causes monarchy to become hereditary rather than elective or co-optative; what kind of necessity gives it perma-

nence; we need to see it in its first stages, gathering those
features which afterwards seem, through their familiarity, to be natural to it, but which were, of course,
acquired—or rather battered into it.

For this Roman monarchy which began with the
Dictatorship of Cæsar—or, we may truly say, with the
tribuneship of Gaius Gracchus, through the Dictatorship of Sulla—was the origin of modern European
monarchy. Its direct succession lasted until in 1453 the
Turks overthrew it. Its succession through the Holy
Roman Empire endured into the days of Napoleon. Its
derivatives, spreading through Marbod and Irmin,
founded the monarchies of England, France, Spain,
Russia and Scandinavia. Before Cæsar, Northern Europe
was ruled by chieftains such as still survive at the head
of the Scottish clans.

A concrete story is always better than a theoretical
dissertation. The reader can see for himself the current
and whirlpool of events. The real truth is after all never
entirely theoretical; more than half of it is a story which,
since mankind has written it, must perforce stand in
all its arbitrariness as the first part of the book which
we today have to continue, and later ages have to finish,
in accordance with the indicated plot. . . . If anyone
should complain that the story of Tiberius leaves a good
deal unfinished and undecided, he may be reminded that
it is part of a serial story which is continued in our next.

But the interest of Tiberius is not exclusively political. He has always been, and he remains, the greatest
psychological problem in history. He is Hamlet and
Lear and Othello rolled into one; and he is more than

this. We have a mass of evidence about Tiberius that for nearly nineteen hundred years baffled any attempt to understand him. We can easily construct two men out of the material, both of which are perfectly credible: one, a gruff, upright soldier-statesman, austere, just, capable; the other, a monster of cruelty and wickedness. It is when we have to consider him as he was, as one man, that the trouble begins. Some of the evidence can be read in more ways than one. . . . Hence, there probably always will be room for a certain amount of divergence of opinion concerning the real truth. . . . In that great library of perfectly frank confessions which doubtless exists in heaven, we shall find some reading which ought to compensate us for arduous perseverance in a sometimes trying world.

A good many things in this book are today, however, matters of course. It is no longer necessary to argue the question of the main moral accusations brought against Tiberius or of his general character. There have been a very large number of far worse men; and the modern student of Tacitus and Suetonius is much more disposed to lose himself in admiration of the most brilliant partisan pamphlet and the most amusing collection of gossip ever written in Latin than to congratulate those authors on the cold impartiality of their picture.

And as regards the story—apart from its function as a portion of the history of politics—if we can let it strike home to our own minds, so that we thoroughly grasp the nature of the lesson it implies, we shall at any rate make certain that whatsoever may happen to us, no such deadlock shall chance to modern civilization.

The noble legend of Jonah enshrines the eternal truth that the chief office of prophecy is not to anticipate the future, but to make sure that we shall not anticipate it. The truly successful prophet is a false prophet.

G. P. B.

Elmer, Sussex.

1928.

CONTENTS

ILLUSTRATION

Family Portrait: Augustus, Livia, Tiberius and Julia

Frontispiece

MAPS AND DIAGRAMS

CHAPTER I

THE TRIUMPH OF AUGUSTUS

I

ON the 13th of August, in the year 29 B. C., a car, drawn by four horses abreast, stood in the Italian sunshine just outside Rome. On the right-hand and the left-hand horses rode two young boys of fourteen and thirteen years old. One was the nephew of Augustus, the son of his sister Octavia—Marcus Marcellus. The other was his step-son, Tiberius Claudius Nero. . . . So Tiberius enters upon the stage of history—to what effect, there may have been speculation in the minds of onlookers, even then.

They were part of a tremendous procession which early that day—and for three whole days—began to urge its slow length along from the Campus Martius, through the Triumphal Gate, round the Palatine Hill, and up the Sacred Way,—flashing with gold and with silver, ablaze with rich oriental colour, fluttering with streamers— headed by ranks of stately senators, in purple-edged mantles, followed up by trumpeters sounding their yards of brass—rolling cars filled with trophies—white, garlanded oxen, golden-horned, and the guilds of priests carrying the sacred vessels—stalwart Illyrians, swarthy Egyptians, fair-haired Gauls—scarlet-clad lictors with fasces wreathed in laurel—bands of musicians and singers—in slow, measured march, with stately

The Triumph

1

pauses, massed ranks of glittering legionaries, bronzed with Egyptian suns and Cilician winds, among whom were borne the gilded military eagles. . . . And, at the front of these, standing in his four-horsed triumphal car, followed by the magistrates of the republic, the slender figure, pale bleak face, wistful eyes and almost girlish lips of Gaius Julius Cæsar Octavianus, the delicate main-spring of all this might. It was the Triumph of Augustus.

Its meaning

There was never another such Triumph as that of Augustus.[1] It was the golden dawn of a new age, after the stormy night of twenty years of civil war, during which the breath of great men had been blown away upon the blast. . . . Antony and Cleopatra would have been borne in chains in that procession, had they not seen to it that this should never be. The ship-prows of Actium, piled on their cars, and the modelled image of a queen, replaced the man and the woman who had fled from the struggle. And if any ghosts walked at mid-day in that procession, they were the ghosts of Brutus and Cassius, and Marcus Cato, and the sons of Pompeius and the grandsons of Sulla, wearing spiritual chains of defeat. And last of all, perhaps, invisible yet ever present, the vast wraith of Cæsar the Dictator, who had planned and organized and directed and brought to pass all the series of events which ended with the Triumph of Augustus. But all had gone, and Octavianus remained. It was he who rolled, behind the high-stepping milk-white horses, through crowded streets and packed Forum, past Vesta, past Castor, past

[1] It lasted three days—first the Illyrian procession, then that for the sea-fight at Actium, then, grandest of all, the Egyptian procession.

the bankers' offices that lined the Forum, past the temple of Saturn, to the Clivus Capitolinus, and the high-set fane of Dios Pater on the Capitoline Hill. . . . As the procession began to enter the Porta Triumphalis *Its route* it passed the building, still in course of erection, which a few years later Augustus was to dedicate to the dear memory of Marcellus. . . . As it swerved round the temple of Saturn to breast the Clivus Capitolinus, it passed the spot where, later yet, was to rise the Triumphal Arch of Tiberius.

When, clad in his purple tunic patterned over with flowers, and his gold-embroidered robe, Octavianus had dropped his bough of laurel upon the statue of the god; when the sacring was done, and the gifts devoted—such gifts as no man before had given—the fun of the fair began. The circuses and the theatres were open, the *The New World* actors—professional and amateur—the charioteers and the gladiators were ready; and the new world dawned.

II

Augustus—as he became two years later—must have been glad when the shows were over, and men could return to the serious, interesting business of life. He never cared much for the merely decorative. It must have given him pleasure when he superintended the closing of the temple of Janus. The Roman world was *The Temple of Janus closed* at peace. He can hardly have failed to inspect the doors of Janus with curiosity. If the hinges had been kept oiled, the Romans had certainly shown an optimism unequalled in human history. But the doors, whether oiled or rusty, were drawn to; and men could walk round the temple, and gaze upon something that the grandfathers of their grandfathers had never seen—a closed temple of Janus. War—for the time being—was ended.

III

A wave of hope and aspiration for the future was arising. When—in 27 B. C.—Augustus began in earnest to shape the constitutional outline of the monarchy, his thoughts were already dwelling upon the young Marcellus as the possible successor who should follow him. It was in this year that he celebrated the Troy Game, that ancient festival of the Roman youth which was believed to go back to the days of Æneas. The two youths chosen to lead it were Marcus Marcellus—and Tiberius Claudius Nero.

The Troy Game B. C. 27

In this same year, moreover, Augustus mentioned to Virgil that he would appreciate some expression of his powers. The great poet, with sympathetic imagination, understood the thoughts that were in the mind of Augustus. The work which he devised for him was nothing less than the *Æneid*, that banner of Roman patriotism and Roman faith. . . . Into the fifth book he introduced a description of this very Troy Game itself,[1] which

[1] *Æneid* v. 545–603. He draws a vivid picture of the ride-past of the youths, crowned with garlands, their necks clasped with torques of gold (the "twisted gold" famous in northern poetry, centuries later.) There were three parties, led by young Priam, by Atys (ancestor of the Atii from whom the maternal grandfather of Augustus was descended) and by Iulus (from whom came the Julians of his maternal grandmother's family.) The three parties each divide into two groups, which charge and retreat, and ride in intersecting circles, and finally blend again and ride in harmony,—a kind of mounted military dance which, it is easy to see, might be extremely graceful, and made, for its perfect success, great demands upon the boyish leaders who conducted it.

Marcellus and Tiberius captained—imaginatively disguised as a description of the occasion on which Æneas first held it in Italy; and through the tears of remembrance and hope for the future which their sons evoked in the exiled Troians, he expressed those same feelings as men felt them in this similar dawn of new days. Virgil describes the Troy Game

It was, of course, Virgil himself who imposed this touching symbolism upon the Troy Game held in the year in which Octavianus became Augustus; but his quick and half-prophetic sympathy expressed feelings which were real enough, and which certainly dwelt in the heart of Augustus. Such a re-founding, not only of the State, but of great families out of which alone a state can be built, was his deep ambition. . . . The choice of the leaders for the celebration of the Troy Game always bore a peculiar meaning. The appointment of Marcellus and Tiberius was equivalent to their selection as the two most promising young men of their day, of whom Augustus had the highest hopes, and for whom he marked out the greatest careers. . . . The tale told in this book is the story of what came of these hopes, and those careers. Marcellus and Tiberius

IV

Tiberius was the step-son of Augustus. He had been four years old when the divorce between his mother Livia Drusilla, and his father Tiberius Claudius Nero had been effected. Augustus had married Livia with such promptitude that her second son, Nero Claudius Drusus, was born after her re-marriage. There was, naturally, talk on this theme; and the suspicion that Drusus Augustus and Livia was Augustus's own son could hardly remain permanently unknown to Tiberius as he grew older. The surmise, whether right or not, seemed to gain in likelihood from the fondness which Augustus always showed for Drusus.

Besides his very unusual name, this somewhat questionable paternity and the special affection of Augustus, Drusus differed in a marked way from Tiberius in temperament and character. He had gifts of outward charm and facile accomplishment which might, indeed, have come from his mother's family, the men of which were distinguished by their high standard of manners and intelligence, but which might as easily have belonged to a son of Augustus. On the other hand, Drusus showed an ability which perhaps rose above the normal level of the Octavii, among whom Augustus stood out as an astonishing exception. All the undoubted descendants of Augustus were more or less fools of the true Octavian stamp. . . . Finally, Drusus certainly did carry the hereditary bad luck of the Livian men.[1] . . . Between these neatly balanced scales of probability, the paternity of Drusus will always remain uncertain.

Tiberius himself ran true to type. He was nine years old when his father died, and he was sent to his mother, and so passed under the care of Augustus. Nine years in the company of his father was enough to fix and emphasize the characteristics he had by nature and by descent. The lonely little boy who went from the human

Drusus

Youth
of
Tiberius

---

[1] Livia, however, was not of genuine Livian Drusian descent. Her father was a Claudius adopted into the Livian gens. None the less, the ill luck of the Drusi haunted the name; and out of all those who in one way or another came to bear it, few escaped violent or unfortunate deaths. The reader will find four different persons named Drusus in the present volume, and may judge for himself.

companionship of perhaps a commonplace father to that large, brilliant and by comparison inhuman world in which Livia and Augustus reigned was just old enough to feel the import of the change. He met his difficulties with the same sort of unbending, almost morose courage which in later life he habitually showed.

There were very obvious reasons why Augustus could not take charge of all the duties of his new ward towards the elder Tiberius. The nine-year-old boy had the strength of character to face an audience and himself to deliver the funeral oration for his father. The effort may not have been a masterpiece; but a boy of nine who can give any kind of public address on a formal occasion is very much out of the common run. He superintended his father's funeral games. Augustus and Livia saw to it that he had the money to do it well. . . . And this power of carrying out, without excess or defect, the work Augustus gave him to do, was the means by which he rose first to fame, and then to empire. *He becomes a ward of Augustus*

Though the first contact between Tiberius and Augustus was thus attended by that touch of the awkward which never quite left their relationship, we have no ground for thinking of Augustus as anything but the most conscientious of step-fathers. The young Tiberius received a sound education in all the subjects—literary, legal and military—appropriate to his future career. He was physically a fine youth, delicate of feature, white of skin, with the thickness of hair at the back of his head which was hereditary with the Claudians. He was sensitive, as most highly-bred men are. . . . He would have registered a rose-leaf under twelve

mattresses as swiftly as any princess in a fairy tale. . . .
Physical sensitiveness can be commanded by training,
and Tiberius grew up a robust man. The sensitiveness
of mind which goes with it is harder to manage, and he
scarcely received the kind of education which made the
best of him in that respect: he remained shy, a little
gauche, with the fastidiousness which shows itself in
apparently inconsistent ways, as a dislike of sentiment,
an appreciation of poetry, an intolerance of fools, a
sympathy with simplicity; he distinguished so accurately
between those opposites which men habitually confuse,
that he puzzled his critics. He knew the difference between courage and swagger, or between candour and
impertinence, and never made a mistake about them.
He put out few feelers for sympathy, and repelled rather
than welcomed advances. He was difficult to know. He
guarded himself with some care; and those who did not
care to penetrate the barrier, he allowed to remain outside.

His
Character

Tiberius had a spiritual Capri in his mind from the
first. He retired to his fastness at the least provocation.
He had a very strong sense of justice, an impartiality
which had no respect for persons—not even for himself. Therefore in turn he was exceptionally quick to
discern injustice to himself, and before it he withdrew
into aloofness. . . . These are the strange tricks which
sensitiveness plays with the soul of man.

Solid capacity, grounded on industry and good sense
rather than on brilliance—remoteness and individualism—acuteness of perception and impersonality of judg-

ment made him a good leader of men. To those who met him on this ground he was a cool, impartial, deliberate man, seeing things sanely and seeing them whole; just, exacting, an accurate judge, a generous but somewhat disagreeable chief; the kind of man who would give his shirt but not his sympathy. It was a character useful rather than decorative.

V

None of the oddities of Fate has been stranger than that which has overtaken the name Nero. It was the name of one of the greatest families of the noble Claudian house. Its repute was never tarnished by those who legitimately held it. The fame of Gaius Claudius Nero, who made that great march to the Metaurus which meant the downfall of Hasdrubal and the ultimate defeat of Hannibal, never died out. But all the fame of the Nerones has been overlaid and hidden by the infamy of a man who was not a Nero, nor a Claudius at all,— the emperor "Nero", whose true name was Lucius Domitius Ahenobarbus. And nothing that any man can now do will put that injustice right, nor restore to the family of Nero the honour of which it has been robbed by a Domitius. The emperor Nero was no Nero. But Tiberius was a Nero; he bore the name of right: in his veins flowed the blood of the consul who outwitted Hannibal and defeated Hasdrubal. And he too was a soldier and a statesman, touched with that intense and vivid character which haunted the Claudian name.

The family of the Claudian Nerones

VI

Augustus

Wise as Augustus was, there was a streak of shallowness in him. He owed to it his power and his prestige. Because of it he could endure a corresponding streak of shallowness in mankind at large, and could speak and feel with other men on their own ground without effort, and could manage them and make them work together. He expanded with the growth of his fortunes: but for all his increase in wisdom, he still lacked those last virtues which spring of ripe human quality, long in maturing, and bred in very old families. . . . He never pretended to like Tiberius. Himself a man who loved crowds, and conversation, and was spacious rather than deep, he did not sympathize with the narrower, deeper, more complex and eccentric character of his step-son. He viewed with some astonishment and repulsion the slow, brooding intelligence, the reticence, the fastidiousness, which always seemed to fall into the interstices of his own mind, and with an unaccountable accuracy to miss meeting it point to point.

His earlier marriages

Livia was the third wife of Augustus. The first had hardly counted; if he had ever lived with her the episode was short, and had left little trace behind. His second marriage, with Scribonia, had been a much more serious affair; but still it had been for the most part a diplomatic marriage. L. Scribonius Libo was the father-in-law and chief supporter of Sextus Pompeius, in the old days of the civil wars. Augustus—he had been only Octavianus then—had married his sister Scribonia in order to prevent young Pompeius from drifting into the arms of Marcus Antonius. A year later the necessity was over; and with a promptitude which must be counted against him, he divorced her on the very day on which was born his only child, Julia—of whom we shall hear in detail before the career of Tiberius is over. Under such cir- **Birth** cumstances as these Julia was conceived and brought **of** **Julia** into the world.

His marriage with Livia had been his real marriage— that with which his heart (and he had a heart) went; certainly that with which went his tastes, sympathies and personal affections. It was a genuine grief to Augustus that his marriage with Livia was childless. That was the point where his luck, otherwise inexhaustible, gave out. He would have liked to see a son of Livia and himself growing up to able and vigorous manhood to succeed him in the principate. But none was ever born.

Livia was a great lady of the old aristocratic stamp. She was a famous beauty, and a woman of dominating character. The great women of the aristocracy lasted **Character** longer than the great men: and Livia, who had only **of** **Livia** the mild and protected court of Augustus as a circle for her activities, was strong enough to have fought her way through the fierce competition of the late republican age when Cæsar was in his prime. In imperial Rome she dominated the social world as an eagle among the chickens. Under her vigorous rule, the fast and free life of the republican age went definitely out of fashion. She and Augustus set the example of a simple and faithful married life, undisturbed by scandal or agitation, between two people who consulted one another's feelings, and took trouble to work in harmony together.

Livia was of course powerful enough to have forced her two sons to the front. How far she exercised her power is one of the unsolved problems of history. If she relied on the normal course of events to work for them, she judged well; but some of that cool reasonableness and moderation of temper which surrounded Augustus himself like a soothing atmosphere, may have extended itself to Livia and quieted her energy. It was natural enough that Julia should take the first place in the thoughts of Augustus. Livia does not seem to have fought against this natural preference. Augustus reponded to her restraint with an equal consideration for her own affections. Though he hardly cared for Tiberius, he was sincerely fond of Drusus, and to both he was carefully just, and even generous. It is not improbable that he recognized their importance as a second string to his bow. If Julia died, they would be amongst his nearest heirs. It says much for the court of Augustus that for many years we can trace no savage intrigue, no desperate competition between the child of Scribonia and the children of Livia. It was, indeed, hard for anything savage or desperate to subsist near Augustus. He dissolved all human emotions into quiet and rational terms.

Attitude of Augustus towards his step-sons

VII

Julia was thus a person of importance. Round her revolved all the plans for the future which Augustus had in mind,—plans by no means a matter of barren ambition, but involving the fate of a great civilization. . . . There was, indeed, no possibility of a woman reigning in succession to Augustus; for whosoever stepped into his shoes would need to be head of that great military guild which controlled the Roman world; but it was almost sure that her husband and her children would reign.

Julia herself must have been acutely conscious of this side of the case. She would have been more than mortal if her thoughts had not dwelt a good deal upon her own sex and its significance. . . . She was ten years old in the year of Augustus' triumph. She was twelve when the Troy Game was held. She was only fourteen when Augustus formally adopted Marcellus as his heir and successor, and gave him Julia as the sign and seal of his elevation.

All this was too early and sweet a spring to last. . . . Augustus, of course, may have had his reasons, which we cannot now divine. The handsome young bridegroom, the son of Octavia, and the charming and clever young bride, the daughter of Augustus, were first cousins. Julia had been very carefully brought up. But the atmosphere was not quite healthy. Whatsoever the reasons of Augustus, the event seems to have been forced too early. Both the young people had a dangerous touch of precocity. All the brilliance of Marcellus cannot conceal the fact that Augustus' choice of a successor was an extraordinarily hazardous one,—a gamble with fortune. Not only was Marcellus quite untried, but there was nothing in his immediate ancestry to give any especial hope that he would be a remarkable man. Though the remoter Marcelli had produced many individuals of great ability, this was no reliable foundation on which

Julia

Her marriage to Marcus Marcellus B. C. 25

to build. . . . It is difficult to avoid the conclusion that a very great deal of domestic sentiment—perhaps too much—entered into the proceedings of Augustus.

Death of Marcellus B. C. 23

The golden dream lasted two years. Then, in spite of all the medical skill of the day, Marcellus died, and at sixteen Julia was left a very youthful widow. It was a great upset: but more of a family than of a political disaster. Augustus himself delivered the funeral oration. When the tactful Virgil read aloud his lines in praise of the young Marcellus, Octavia fainted. It was all very distressing. The succession to the principate, however, was a matter which would be fought out by grimmer methods than marriages and faintings. The angular Tiberius entered upon his first public office, the quæstorship, this year.

VIII

There is something characteristic and appropriate in the earliest work of Tiberius: it was mainly legal. He practised with success as an advocate in the imperial court, and before the Senate. He received two special

First steps of Tiberius

commissionerships which he seems to have conducted with equal success; one was an inquiry into the grain supply; the other an inspection of the slave-prisons. Reports had been received that the proprietors of these prisons were in the habit of kidnapping and detaining free persons, and also that they gave refuge to military deserters. . . . All of which, no doubt, was extremely dull, compared with the career of Marcellus: but probably Tiberius enjoyed it. It was the kind of work in which he would have been interested. He also had his first experience of military service in Spain, where the reduction of the Cantabrians was in progress. . . . While he was away in Spain, Augustus decided upon a fresh marriage for Julia: and the husband he selected for her was in rather remarkable contrast with Marcellus,— namely, the man who, next to himself, was the greatest Roman then alive: Marcus Vipsanius Agrippa, the victor of Actium. Agrippa was of the same age as Augustus—a vigorous man of forty-two; a stout country squire [1] rather than a man of fashion. . . . What Julia thought of it we have no means of knowing.

There was, no doubt, a very real difficulty in deciding upon any husband for Julia. The choice of Agrippa was not in all ways ill-judged.[2] He was strong enough and able enough to have formed an admirable successor to Augustus, had the necessity ever arisen. He was moreover a trustworthy man: and he might well have over-

B. C. 21 Julia married to Marcus Vipsanius Agrippa

Character of Agrippa

---

[1] "Vir rusticati proprior quam deliciis"—Plin. N. H. XXV. 26.

[2] Agrippa was one of the friends of Augustus' youth. He was of obscure descent, and ashamed of his common name "Vipsanius,"—which to a modern ear sounds distinguished enough. He was one of the most forceful characters of the age he lived in. He was not a man of creative genius, but he supplied exactly that element of vigorous promptitude and iron nerve which was perhaps lacking in Augustus himself. His two great sea-victories at Naulochus and Actium were decisive battles. He won them, not by generalship alone, but by his policy in naval architecture. His interest in architecture went beyond ships. The Pantheon was built under his direction, besides many other great works. He completed the great Survey of the World begun by Cæsar the Dictator, and from it had the great map made which, cut in marble, stood in the Porticus Pollæ on the eastern side of the Campus Martius, towards the Pincian Hill. The Vistula was included in this map,—a useful milestone in the progress of geographical knowledge. Agrippa stood in the direct tradition of those great engineering soldiers who were the glory of Rome, and in his strong character and practical interests was a very typical Roman. Grim as he was, he seems to have been a man of some taste and education.

There is a story—which sounds apocryphal—that Mæcenas told Augustus that Agrippa had become too powerful, and must either be co-opted into the succession or put out of the way.

awed and impressed a very young girl who was slightly intoxicated with her own position and excited with the memory of Marcellus. The deep streak of weakness in Julia scarcely showed while she was in the strong hands of Agrippa. And he was no laggard as a husband. Julia, —a long-nosed, large-eyed creature—developed into a Roman matron with five children. Her two elder sons, Lucius and Gaius, were unmistakably the true heirs of Augustus. There were also two daughters, Julia and Agrippina. Of the latter we shall hear a good deal more in due course.

The weakness of Julia's second marriage lay in the dangerous diversity of the elements which went to make it. In order that he might marry her, Agrippa's marriage with the young sister of Marcellus had been dissolved. Experience does not bear out the idea that human beings can be adequately matched in this cold-blooded way. The children illustrated, as they grew up, the instability of the blend; Lucius, Gaius and Julia seemed to reproduce their mother without any touch of their father, while Agrippina followed her father alone in a certain tight-bound obstinacy, and cold strength of temperament; and the youngest, Agrippa Postumus, combined to an alarming extent the selected weaknesses of both his parents. . . . There can have been just as little of a blend in their ordinary every-day relationships. The busy soldier and administrator could not possibly have discovered much common ground with his young wife. He was of the same age as her father. His memories, his work, his interests were all widely diverse from Julia's. He was much away. The Spanish and Il-

Julia's children

lyrian campaigns absorbed his attention and his time.
. . . Julia, as she developed under all these influences,
without any of those quietening satisfactions which
come of an equal companionship in marriage, grew
into a very striking personality poles apart from her
husband. She was a very beautiful woman, with a wit
that was famous. Her position gave her wide social opportunities. Before many years had gone, it was rumoured that she took full advantage of them, and found
ample means of obtaining the equal companionship
which she could not expect from her husband. . . .

It would have been unreasonable for Augustus to
feel surprise. Julia had been awakened and stimulated
and excited at a very early age. Her natural ardour of
temperament, in some respects over-excited and in some Julia's
too much repressed, was certain to grow a little dis- development
torted. . . . Augustus, a man of the world, may have
felt that the results of his policy were worth the risk,
and he may have been prepared to look steadfastly away
from some of the consequences, as long as the outward
conventions were observed. . . . If so, he considerably
over-rated his power to set a limit to Julia's proceedings,
once she was unleashed.

IX

In the mean time the career of Tiberius proceeded
on its dry and decorous way. His natural gift for getting through that unpopular thing, work, was steadily
developing; and no man with a taste for work is ever
unoccupied, even though he may be unrewarded. He Tiberius
in the
accompanied Augustus in a prolonged tour in the east. East

Augustus entrusted him with important missions. It was he who received the lost standards, taken by the Parthians from Crassus at the disaster of Carrhæ, which Augustus, by a little unspectacular negotiation, extracted from the Parthian Sultan. . . . The recovery of these standards was counted among the great achievements of Augustus. It was Tiberius also who, with humdrum efficiency, settled the Armenian question. The Armenians had applied for a new King, whom Tiberius duly conducted to the spot and duly crowned; returning without a battle and without bloodshed,—a depressing fact which did not escape adverse comment in Rome.

The date of Tiberius' marriage is unknown, but it must have taken place about this time. It was strictly dull and decorous,—in fact, it was an ordinary happy marriage of no interest to anyone save the parties concerned. Tiberius had for several years been engaged

to Vipsania, the daughter of Agrippa by a former marriage.[1] The marriage of Drusus was more impressive. He married Antonia, the daughter of the triumvir and of Octavia, Augustus' sister, and he thus became the nephew of Augustus. Although both were political marriages, they seem to have turned out well. The one would give the robust Agrippa a natural interest in his son-in-law: and the excellent military training which Tiberius undoubtedly received seems to indicate some such interest. The qualities of Tiberius as a soldier were sound rather than brilliant, and were very much in the tradition of Agrippa. If Vipsania resembled her robust

[1] Vipsania has some additional interest as the granddaughter of T. Pomponius Atticus, Cicero's friend and correspondent.

father and her gentle, cultured grandfather, she must
have been an ideal wife for a complex, introspective
man such as Tiberius: and the reluctance with which
he parted from her in later years seems to show that he
was attached to her by more than nominal bonds.

But the marriage of Drusus had about it that quality
which frequently belongs to acts of favouritism: it
was both more flattering in its personal aspect, and per- *Drusus*
haps ultimately much less profitable to him. To marry *marries*
the niece of Augustus brought Drusus right into the *Antonia*
innermost circle of the imperial family; and it is obvious that Augustus watched with care over the fortunes of their children, intervening, more than once,
to secure their interests even at the expense of Tiberius.
The latter raised no objection, even when the bias became somewhat noticeable: but he might be excused
for some feeling of bitterness at the continual preference given to qualities which (as he must have known)
were largely superficial. . . .

Drusus was a model husband. The strict moral tone
of the court of Augustus had no better exemplar than
he: and he certainly added to his prestige by a domestic
virtue which was equally admirable in the eyes of Livia
and Augustus, and in those of the army. The people
in all ages take a sentimental interest in the virtues of
their rulers. Whether the children of Drusus quite realized the hopes of Augustus is another and a more de-
batable matter.

Tiberius and Vipsania had one son, who was named
Drusus after his uncle, and who grew up a square-toed
youth, to end with the ill-luck of all the Drusi, as we

shall see in due course. For it was over these children that, in the height of his power, Tiberius was to stumble and fall. They formed at once the romance and the tragedy of the story.

X

The fairness of Augustus,—and possibly his caution, which Livia was near at hand to stimulate—took care to provide Tiberius and Drusus with that ample education in government which the public magistracies gave. Drusus, of course, could obtain almost any favour he liked: while the adequacy of Tiberius could extort it for himself. . . . They were both of them, though for opposite reasons, the kind of young man whom it is desirable to employ in serious work at as early an age as possible. Tiberius in particular had the peculiar and unusual gift which in all ages causes some men to be looked upon as fore-fated,—Men of Destiny— namely, the gift for reaching his end through any set of circumstances. There were no circumstances, apparently, that could succeed in bringing him permanent personal happiness. But there was none, however adverse, however hopeless, that did not in some strange way serve his end. . . . Life, for him, was one of those acrostics which, whether they are read up or down or across, read the same.

If Augustus had had no other reason, he might not improbably have employed and promoted Tiberius in the hope that by satisfying his passion for work he would divert him from ambition. The plan would have been well devised. Tiberius possessed the artist's interest

Promotion of Tiberius and Drusus

Reasons for their promotion

in the process rather than in the result; he had a dry, unsympathetic satisfaction in a piece of work well done; he enjoyed it for its own sake. Work, with men of this type, is a drug which renders them unconscious of the call of personal ambition. To keep Tiberius busy would provide the heirs of Augustus with an invaluable servant, and would keep the stage clear for them. . . . Hence all things conspired to push him forward along the path.

Tiberius was twenty-two years old when he held the prætorship: a grown man, rapidly maturing. It was in the year after his prætorship that the event occurred which, to a large extent, decided the direction in which his interests would, for the rest of his life, always lie. The conquest of Gaul by Cæsar the Dictator had given the North a peculiar, an almost romantic interest: it Gaul had extended the Roman frontier up to the Rhine and the borders of Germany, and given the Rhine some of the attraction which always belongs to wild, half-conquered hardly-held new lands,—the fascination that South Africa and Texas and Arizona have had in modern times, when men held a difficult and unexplored frontier by the armed hand. The most interesting problems of the contemporary Roman world lay along the Rhine and the coasts of the North Sea. To the more civilized type of Roman the social life and the immemorial civilization of the East offered a more sympathetic— perhaps a less wholesome—interest, but it was to the far northern frontier that the eyes of those who loved adventure and novelty were turned.

In 16 B. C. the Sicambrian tribesmen of the middle

Rhine organized, with the help of the Tencteri and the
Usipetes, a typical frontier raid of a highly sporting nature. They crossed the river and drove a plundering raid
right into the heart of the Roman province. There was
hard fighting and rough riding; they captured an eagle
of the Fifth Legion, and raised a hornet's nest of excitement. Augustus took so serious a view of the situation
that he went to Gaul in person, taking Tiberius with
him. And in Gaul Augustus remained four years.

Tiberius had been in Asia, and had served in Spain,
but this was his first sight of the world beyond the Alps.
He looked upon those vast mountains which Cæsar had
crossed and re-crossed, and over which Hannibal had
transported his elephants; he saw the immense rivers
and forests of Gaul, its tribes and hill-top cities, its florid
barbaric life, its tawny moustached horsemen, huge dogs
and vast spaces. The presence of Augustus quietened
the hornet's nest. The Sicambri and their friends were
pursued back across the Rhine by Roman troops and
Gaulish scouts, and matters were restored, after a
breathless interval, to the normal.

There was opportunity for Tiberius to look about
him and to acquire a little first-hand experience. It is
not likely that any preference which he himself may
have expressed would weigh with Augustus; but the romantic nature of Drusus, charmed with the wild and
healthy barbarism of the border, was more probably the
reason why Augustus retained his step-sons with him
in Gaul. Drusus was too young to be given a command
of importance. Tiberius, therefore,—a dour and reliable youth,—was entrusted with the governorship of

Tiberius
and Drusus
in Gaul

the Three Gauls,[1] and with a certain amount of responsibility for his brother. With Tiberius to look after him, Drusus could drink in adventure and romance to his heart's content: and, to judge by subsequent events, he drank his fill. It was a heady draught: but it does not seem to have affected Tiberius.

XI

The four years which Augustus spent in Gaul were of extraordinary importance. Whether the great raid of the Sicambri were the cause, or merely the occasion, he took in hand the great task of revising and reorganizing the northern frontier of Rome. Some important strategic adjustments of the frontier were carried out. After a year as governor, Tiberius was transferred, with Drusus, to a post in which they could gain experience on active service. They were given the command of the expeditionary forces which entered and reduced Rætia and Vindelicia. There was severe fighting in the course of the operations, including a naval battle on the Lake of Constance.

Tiberius was himself a very young man to be entrusted with a high command. If there were any quiet malice in the promotion, he stolidly survived it. He fell into no traps, and made no mistakes. He had, after all, but to hold his tongue and to consult the experience of the professional soldiers who knew the frontier as if it were their own garden. By the time that the operations were over, he had passed that most severe of tests,—the judgment of a professional army. He had not precisely

Conquest of Rætia B. C. 15

---

[1] I. e., the three divisions of the imperial province, excluding Southern Gaul.

won its love. Drusus was personally far more popular with the troops. But Tiberius had won its respect.

The conquest of Rætia and Vindelicia (together with that of Noricum, which was carried out by the Pannonian army) brought the entire northern slopes of the Alps into Roman hands, and allowed the frontier to be so continued that there was direct communication between the Rhine and the Danube armies. A troublesome source of minor danger, which, under certain circumstances, might have grown to serious dimensions, was removed; and the whole frontier was shifted clear from too great proximity to Italy. Strategic roads were surveyed and begun, so that access from Italy should be made rapid and easy.

Such steps as these—which permanently influenced the history of Europe—are not taken without very serious discussion and investigation, nor without consulting the commander who is entrusted with their execution. Tiberius must have become well acquainted with the detailed reasons which led to the annexation of Rætia and Vindelicia, and to the preparation of the new lines of communication. Nothing could have been more fitting than that the destined successor of Augustus should have full knowledge of the military policy involved. But that Tiberius was this destined successor can only have occurred to the minds of men as a remote and somewhat improbable contingency. . . . The man marked out by all the probabilities was the vigorous soldier who at this time had the decisive voice in every military question,—Agrippa. . . . And after Agrippa, the lives of no less than three of his sons stood between

Success of Tiberius

His position

Tiberius and the principate. . . . Nothing but a singular series of events could bring him into the position of a likely candidate; and over and above this, there was the question whether Augustus, whose decision was final, would even then accept him as such.

A certain doubt and suspicion, from which he could never free himself, hovered about the attitude of Augustus towards his elder step-son. He watched and superintended Tiberius during these years with great care. . . . It brought its own compensation. The very closeness with which he scrutinized the actions of Tiberius impressed him with a reluctant sense of approval. . . . On Tiberius lay the direct responsibility for seeing that the military measures taken were adequate, and were carried out with due attention to economy. . . . These were tasks in which Augustus was particularly exacting, and in which all the qualities of Tiberius showed at their best. He was good at the patient collection of intelligence and the rigid checking of accounts. His governorship of Gaul terminated not for military but for political reasons. . . . For now the first of the very improbable series of events came to pass, and the strange adventures of Tiberius began.

Death of Agrippa æt. 50

XII

In the year 12 B. C. Marcus Vipsanius Agrippa died.

CHAPTER II

THE CAUSES AND RESULTS OF THE WORLD-STATE

I

THE death of Agrippa had effects which troubled many men and many things. It involved changes in the fortunes of Tiberius. Augustus had never been one of those rulers whose government is remote and solitary. He was perhaps a great individual, but he was no individualist. He lived in an atmosphere of committees and discussions. He had started his career as one of a triumvirate, and something of the triumvir always clung to him. . . . Augustus looked about him for another Agrippa.

Conse-quences of Agrippa's death

There was, no doubt, some real difficulty in treating Tiberius with warm human feeling. He did not thaw to the pale geniality of Augustus; and Augustus did not possess the closer warmth which might have melted the reserve of his step-son. Yet Tiberius was indicated as the man who would naturally step into the place of Agrippa. Neither could Augustus stoop to those minor arts of ingratiation by which an inferior might have pretended to a warmth which he did not feel. He had the right to ask that any such placating pretences should be shown towards him, rather than by him. . . . Tiberius went home somewhat in the spirit of a mule who bitterly recognizes his own useful virtues.

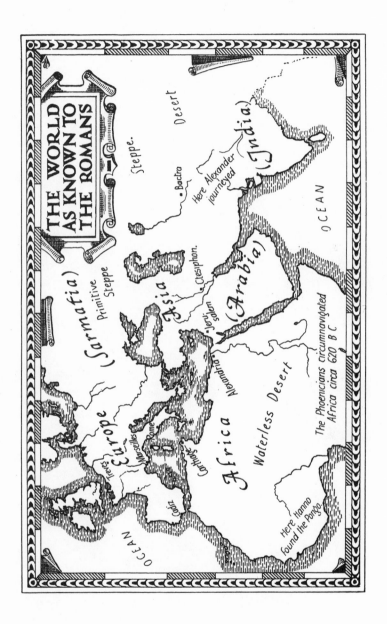

THE WORLD
AS KNOWN TO
THE ROMANS

Steppe.

Desert

•Bactra

Here Alexander
journeyed

(India)

Europe (Sarmatia)
Primitive
Steppe

Asia

Treves
Marseilles
Rome
Carthage
Cadiz

Jerusalem
•Ctesiphon.
Alexandria

(Arabia)

Africa

Waterless Desert

OCEAN

The Phoenicians circumnavigated
Africa circa 620 B C

OCEAN

Here Hanno
found the Ponto

That he had done well was undisputed. In the preceding year he had received the honour of the consulship—though with no one more important than Publius Quintilius Varus (of whom we shall hear again) as a colleague. He thus took rank as a consular, and entered the small but select company of those who had held the highest magistracy in the State. . . . Something else, perhaps more significant, was in the wind. Julia was once more a widow, and Augustus was revolving in his mind some of the deep considerations of policy which sprang from that fact.

Augustus had a great deal to think of. Being the man he was, he probably took advice, and if we knew of whom he took it we should be wiser than we are. He was certainly influenced by Livia, whether he knew it or not. It took him a year to make up his mind. A year was none too long a time in which to review the momentous project he had begun to entertain.

Tiberius Consul I.
B. C. 13
(aet. 29)

II

To follow the thoughts of Augustus, we may survey the considerations that weighed with him. He stood in a position to which no modern man has attained. Even though we see, as through a glass darkly, the gigantic possibility of the political union of the world, it is yet so far ahead of us that it enters very slightly into our practical decisions. But Augustus confronted the fact accomplished. The world he knew,—all the world he knew of,—was in actual fact united in one polity; and he himself was its head. He saw as a reality what we can see only as a perhaps impossible ideal: and here he pos-

Difficulties of Augustus

sessed an experience so far beyond ours that only by imaginative sympathy can we fully apprehend the astonishing truth. . . . And, as in all such cases, a measure of sobering disillusionment followed the fact. He could not romance idealistically about a beautiful dream, for it was no ideal dream. It was a very prosaic matter of fiscal account-keeping, assessments, judicial appeals, and all the rest of the drudgery which lies behind the more decorative aspects of government.

Augustus was not directly responsible for his own existence as supreme head of the world-state. He had been cast up to it by forces far beyond his own creation or control. Had he shrunk from the task presented to him, it was one which would have fallen in due course to Marcus Antonius,—a possibility from which any discerning mind might justifiably recoil. The question was merely of the person who should occupy a post which the logic of events had created: and if the issue were narrowed to this, Augustus had ample reason for entertaining a private conviction that the logic of events had also chosen the best man for the post. . . . These doubts being accordingly dismissed, all that remained was to decide the most suitable means of rendering this great monarchical control stable; for once it began to rock on its foundations, it would rack to pieces the world it controlled. The emperor did not conduct the processes of civilization. He merely regulated them, secured their peace and harmonized their action. . . . Peace, order and justice were the necessities which pressed upon the head of the Roman world. The most careful calculations of Augustus could have no objective other than the maintenance of these benefits. Mankind asked for nothing more.

His power and position were based on his ability to give men these gifts. If he failed, the forces which had made him would unmake him with ruthless certainty. He was no free agent—no despot ruling a crushed people by the Cossack. Those enormous forces of civilization—its torrential energies of industry and economic management, so easy to control while he consulted their course—would sweep him to death and limbo if he sought to fight against them. He depended upon public opinion and upon the support of those who trusted him. His range of discretion was thus limited and definite. He could, by ignorance or stupidity, wreck civilization; but it could even more easily wreck him. He depended upon an intelligent reciprocity. By a process of identifying his own interests with those of the world at large, he could secure both. . . . Perhaps he never distinguished them. A pilot needs no metaphysical distinctions between his own benefit and that of his ship. The identity of interest is too obvious to question, and distinctions are too subtle to be troubled about.

The stability of the principate was thus no mere question of personal ambition. It had its roots deep in impersonal ground, and the personal and impersonal considerations were twined too tight to be unravelled.

Its stability important

III

The causes of the world-state over which Augustus ruled lay in quite general laws which operate at all times and in all places. Human industry, together with its natural complement, commerce (for industry can exist and develop only through the exchange of products between men) has an inherent tendency to spread outward, and to enlarge itself in successive expanding rings. Its expansion breaks down the old isolated units of society and causes the formation of larger units. There is no point at which this process of expansion can be stopped. The development of commerce is a force occupying in the relationship of human life somewhat of the same position which in the relationship of inert matter is occupied by the forces of gravity and chemical affinity: and it is equally irresistible. Men can control and manipulate the one set of forces, just as they can the other; but in neither case can they get away from the forces themselves. . . . Hence in every age and in every country we see the same process steadily at work; industry implies commerce, and commerce implies a supersession of the small units of social life, and their reunion in progressively larger units until the whole of human society has been integrated into a single unit. The world-state is the natural result.

No human creation, however good, exactly fulfils the theoretical intention of its designers. A perfect thing, however small, would instantly become eternal, indestructible and unchangeable. The flaw in all things mortal is the starting point of the process by which they are transcended. Hence, there were many obvious defects in the world-state ruled by the Romans. It was not absolutely a world-state. The Romans had not explored the whole habitable globe, still less annexed it. They were not even aware of its size, nor that it was a

Causes of the World-State

Its limitations

globe; though a few elderly philosophers, in the seclusion of their lecture rooms, could produce recondite scientific evidence to show that the earth had a more or less spherical shape. . . . All that the Romans had really done was to unite in one political state all the various accessible human groups which belonged to a certain sort of industrial type. . . . This was a rough-and-ready sort of world-state: it served its practical ends; and we, looking back upon it, can see that it formed the indispensable basis for the subsequent processes by which it was broken up and reconstructed on new lines—a reconstruction still in progress. . . . And, in fact, surveying the course of history, as far as we know it, we might conclude that the evolution of society does not consist of the slow growth of one single organism, but in the creation and destruction of a series of organisms, each an advance upon the last, each embodying some element which its predecessors had been forced to omit.

IV

There remained, then, outside the circle of the world-state of Augustus' day, a ring of peoples who did not belong to it. In the east there was the Parthian state, and behind it a doubtful and unknown region which might or might not possess importance. North eastward were the tribes of the Danube hinterland, fierce and warlike races, backed by the dim cloud of Scythia,—an altogether incalculable factor, since the numbers of the Scythians, the extent of their country, and their customs and capacities were unascertainable. Northward

The Excluded Peoples

I. The Parthians

lay the Germans; and behind the Germans the more formidable fighting tribes of the Suabians; and behind these in turn, dim in the recesses of the north, men more fierce and formidable still,—the Angle, the Saxon, and the Langobard.

There are interests and curiosities in the minds of men which seem intuitive rather than rational. These tribes of the north drew the attention of the Romans as no others did. . . . The interest was partly romantic.

II.
The
Germans

The mere personality of the men of the north attracted a fascinated attention. The atmosphere they dwelt in was equally a matter for wonder. Cæsar himself had felt its lure. He had passed a tradition on to his successors: the legend of the dark and endless Hercynian wood, its elks, its aurochs, its fair-haired fighting champions, and the half-enchanted blue-eyed kings of the north.

For strategic reasons, the Parthian was not a serious danger to Roman dominion. His approach was so hemmed in by the Arabian desert, the Tigris and the Euphrates, and the Armenian mountains, that he could attack only along a limited and defensible front. The Scythian was partly a myth, mixed up with the old stories of the Cimmerians and the Amazons.[1] But the German was a real danger. It was a familiar fact of common knowledge that for hundreds of years, at least, the civilization of the south of Europe had walked in peril of the fighting men of the north. Little as the

---

[1] Any modern text-book will tell the reader that we know more than this; but the description in the text is an attempt to paint the picture that an intelligent Roman saw. The long pause in the ethnic movement from Asia had undoubtedly made the possibility of an Asiatic invasion seem very remote.

Roman might know of the Phrygian, the Achæan and
the Dorian, he knew only too well the tale of the battle
of the Allia; the siege of the Capitol, the cackling of
the sacred geese, and "Woe to the vanquished!" The
Cimbrian terror was not forgotten in the age of Augustus. The conquest of Gaul had been carried out partly
to prevent a repetition of those days when the two immense hosts of the Cimbri and the Teutones were striking, over hundreds of miles, at the eastern and the western gates of the Alps; and when Marius and his famous   Reality
"mules" stood as the sole salvation of a trembling world.   of the
German
On the other hand, the Germans really stood outside   danger
the Roman economic polity, which was compact of
social groups of approximately a similar type, all of
them advanced in industry and commerce: while the
German lingered in an earlier stage of culture. To bring
him within the Roman dominion would be a doubtful
experiment. It was impossible to judge whether he could
be civilized, and turned into a man living the same kind
of life as the Roman. The case was not analogous with
the cases of Gaul and Spain, which had for long centuries, before the Roman appeared upon the scene, been
slowly permeated by Greek and Semitic civilization.
. . . To conquer Germany might saddle the empire
with an acquisition which could not be assimilated,
but might remain for ever alien and a centre of dis-
ruptive forces. . . . And the serious problem remained,
whether Germany could, in actual fact, be conquered.
. . . Germany did not wither and pale before contact
with the civilized South. She flourished on it. . . . Germans were not like Polynesians, dying out before the

white man's drink and diseases. The Germans were an expanding race. . . . All these difficulties confronted the Roman world-state.

v

The Northern Frontier problem

The military problems of the defence of the world-state thus centred on the European frontier-line, not on the eastern, nor the African. The main doubt for Augustus was whether he could adequately defend the Roman dominion from the intrusion of a totally different and inferior type of culture, whose home was in Northern Europe, and whose heart was somewhere up in the Cimbric peninsula and the adjacent islands.

Behind the military problem—which involved a great fortified frontier line from the North Sea to the Euxine, and armies to man it—lay an even more serious problem on which all decisions respecting the former must ultimately depend: namely, the inward strength of the Roman dominion. Both in a military and in a political sense, Rome was as strong as ever she had been. The deep doubt, which had first called the empire into being, was whether Mediterranean civilization was sufficiently strong in the economic sense. The military and the political power alike were ultimately founded on the economic soundness of Mediterranean civilization,—its capacities, that is, for producing wealth and transmuting it into human life. . . . This doubt had haunted men since the days of Scipio Aemilianus and Tiberius Gracchus. Much of the wealth produced was consumed in luxury rather than in the creation of life. It produced a small number of unimportant rich men instead of a

Problem of internal strength

large number of important poor men. But even the wealth itself began to be a matter for care and caution. It was no longer possible to ignore consequences, and to let things run as they would. . . . The careful stewardship of Augustus, his attempts to enforce economy, to set an example of moderation in personal habits, to use wealth rightly, for good ends,—these were ultimately rooted in a sense of their necessity. He was no ardent idealist battling for a moral cause. He approached the subject rather as a business man who attempts to reduce costs, to economize on his unproductive expenditure, and to get more value for money. . . . Later ages were frank on the subject. They pointed out that the Roman dominion was ceasing to produce men: that Germany produced men on a bigger and more abundant scale. . . .

The policy of Augustus was to make no more new conquests. It was a sound policy from more than one point of view. The Roman dominion already included practically the whole of the groups which conformed to the economic standard. To go further, and to include groups belonging to a different type, would be to imperil the unity of the State,—unless, indeed, there were separate and important reasons of another nature for including them. In addition to this, it was only groups conforming to the economic standard which repaid the expenses of conquest. Egypt had far more than repaid the outlay involved. Gaul, which at first barely came under the standard, had repaid it, and was destined, in the long run, to prove a most valuable acquisition. But the conquest of groups which stood defi-

Difficulties of further extending the empire

nitely apart from the standard meant the expenditure of money which could never by any possibility be recouped. Hence further additions to the Roman dominion meant, as a rule, a dead loss: a prospect which no statesman enjoys. Such a loss could be justified only by special reasons. The annexation of Rætia and Vindelicia meant much unproductive expenditure: but it was urgent for military reasons. It added to the safety of the frontier.

The attitude of the Roman government to the outlying peoples of Northern Europe was thus, in general, an exclusive one. Augustus would have preferred to leave them alone. He was not free to leave them entirely alone; he could not restrict himself to a benevolent neutrality. When King Marbod, full of enthusiasm for the wonderful pattern of statecraft and civilization which he saw exhibited in the Roman world, began to found his own great central European realm, Augustus was not at liberty to look on with benevolent sympathy, and then, when the process of building was sufficiently advanced, annex the improvements. For the improvements of Marbod included a military establishment which might have enabled him to carry out a respectable amount of annexation himself. . . . The problem of the outlying peoples had thus a tendency to become locked in a vicious circle. They could neither be absorbed nor allowed to improve themselves. Their gradual rise in economic level, through long contact with southern civilization, could not be prevented; and when, four hundred years after Augustus, the economic level of the world-state was accidentally lowered to a point

Relation
of the
empire
to the
Germans

at which the two cultures met on something like equal
terms, the result was the disruption of the world-state,
and a chaos which ended in its reconstruction on totally
different lines.

VI

We may now turn to a different aspect of the situation, and ask ourselves to what degree the world-state
was a blessing to those who were supposed to enjoy its
advantages.

That it involved many disadvantages is obvious
enough. No man can look upon the degeneration and
collapse of the independent Greek cities without a mel- Disadvan-
ancholy sense that something was lost to the world which tages of
the world-
could hardly be replaced. We cannot pretend that the state
human level of Mediterranean civilization was higher
under the Roman world-state than it had been in the
days of the fighting, trading, manufacturing City-States
with their tremendous output of art, literature and
philosophy. But we may easily exaggerate the extent
of the difference; and we may even more easily mis-
state its nature. Most of the mischief was done under
the rule of the City-States themselves. Their cut throat
strife destroyed far more precious human flower than
was ever suppressed by the Roman emperors. . . . A
large part of the splendour of the earlier age was decorative. The material of art is not always found most
abundantly in the ages of human happiness and wisdom. Homer would have found Antoninus Pius poorer
stuff than Achilles for the purpose of an epic; but it
does not follow that mankind was either better or hap-

pier in the days of Achilles. . . . The dreams of mankind hover with pleasant regret over its fierce and romantic youth. It may be well that they should: but men would never have fought their way so determinedly out of those troublesome glories if they had not thought that there were better things ahead.

The peace and unity which descended upon the Mediterranean world with the accession of Augustus were like the superimposition of a new form of consciousness upon men. The latter had struggled through terrible and tragic days; they seemed to emerge meaner and poorer than they entered; but this was a seeming rather than a reality. In the dawn of the new era they saw themselves as they were, and not as they had seemed— gigantic and heroic shadows—in the gloom. Virgil and Livius wrote the story of the heroic shadows; Horace and Propertius, looking upon the actual world around them, were sad and satiric.

The sadness which accompanied that blinding light of peace and leisure penetrated to deeper levels than the Augustan poets revealed. In every class, and every portion of the Roman dominion, there was an awakening of thoughts which challenged, questioned and inquired into life. If the Augustan age ranks in this respect lower than the great era of Greek thought, it is largely because the movement which began under Augustus was wider, more diffused, less dramatically staged, less completely represented by a few picturesque personalities or a few coherent and systematic theories. It was less an intellectual movement than the Greek, and therefore it was less easy to formulate. . . . Merely to live

Its
moral
effect

in a world-state which is practically conterminous with civilization has a certain degree of effect upon the intellectual quality of a man, much as addressing a public meeting has. An element of cosiness and intimacy went out of human thought with the disappearance of those small independent states which had been like large families, full of the stinging spice of highly personal quarrels. Something larger, barer, bleaker, yet, if anything, more fundamental, replaced it: something that resembled the mind of Augustus himself. . . . Men were partly waiting, partly seeking, for explanations of a problem so immense that they did not altogether know what it was. . . . There is, in the Augustan age, none of that quick neat presentment of the question, and that definite (even if not conclusive) answer, which make Greek thought so bracing an intellectual stimulus. . . . Some time had to pass before, out of the tangle of things, men began to recognize what questions the world had asked, what answers had been given, and which was the question and which the answer.

VII

The age of Augustus brought together a variety of men, of traditions, of thoughts, of temperaments, of social experiences, such as no previous age had ever known: it brought into contact things which had never touched before; it faced men at large with the novel task, not of deducing from a neat coherent first principle a rational explanation of the universe, but of sorting and rationalizing a vast jumble, and of reducing it to simplicity. They accepted the task with a strange

Disillusionment

sense of humility,—even of humiliation. This sense of
being humbled is perhaps the secret of the whole process.
The confidence with which the Greeks had attacked
the problem of life had gone. A general feeling, which
was sometimes a conviction of sin, and sometimes a
profound scepticism, burdened the thinker. It was as if
some great and varied party, most of them strangers to
one another, had made difficult and perilous journeys to
meet together; and they had met,—and with infinitely
varied reasons and for infinitely varied motives, they
all realized that what they had hoped to see was not
there. . . . This vague and baffling sense of some indefinite frustration underlay the Augustan age.

But this was the beginning, not the end of the process. The spiritual activity of the age began to express
itself in a multitude of ways. Two or three of these
claim our attention. The Greek influence was directly
responsible for the philosophical method of approach.

Epicur-
eanism

Epicureanism appealed to those who found it sympathetic. Lucretius expressed an attitude which found
many followers, especially amongst the wealthy men
who, from their practical experience in the handling
of land and money, realized with force to how small a
degree any spiritual power intervened in the affairs of
mankind, how much depended upon intelligence and
good sense, and how little the results of human life
satisfied the hunger of the heart. This had its political
consequences. It effectually preserved those who held
it from any long views or profound policy. The permea-
tion of the wealthier classes with a materialistic philosophy profoundly affected the evolution of the Ro-

man world. It ensured that when—if ever—the call should come, they would not be able to meet it. And in fact the call, long afterwards, did come—and they were not able to meet it. They had made comfort and safety their gods: they had no clue to guide them when these gods departed.

But there were men of a tougher material than these. Stoicism, in the form it took during the Roman imperial period, was a composite product,—a Greek philosophic theory applied to the task of justifying and systematizing a traditional Roman attitude of mind. The philosophy of the Stoa was the refuge of men who saw in the pleasures of life no reward for its burdens, and who were so conscious of its tragedy, its disappointment and its lack of fulfilment, that they set themselves the task of living rightly without reward. As an ascetic theory of life, it produced a type of man which never fails to leave its mark upon the world,—the man who cares nothing for personal consequences.

Stoicism

All philosophical principles of action have a common fault. They are intellectual systems, and therefore are based upon only a portion of the total nature of a normal human being. An intellectual theory can never be an adequate guide to action because while it can guide the action, it can never provide a sufficient objective. There consequently never was any likelihood that the majority of men would turn to these philosophic forms of thought for help and guidance: nor did any statesman ever expect them to do so. But principles of conduct are important to the statesman for a very obvious reason,—to wit, that the conduct of mankind at large

Inadequacy of Philosophy

is the very material of the art with which he deals, and that therefore whatsoever affects this conduct deeply and extensively must enter into his calculations. . . . A statesman such as Augustus has a variety of interests in the question. He will prefer the principles of conduct to be of a widely accepted nature; it is convenient to rely upon the uniformity of large numbers of men. He will not, however, desire them to be too uniformly accepted. No secular statesman altogether relishes great rigid orthodoxies so united and disciplined that the priest wields more power than he does himself. A prudent ruler smiles upon a certain amount of convenient diversity of opinion. . . . Even a degree of the *odium theologicum* is not to him unpleasant. He will betray a benevolent interest in minorities.

These were the views which Augustus actually did entertain, if we judge him by his actions. They were views more or less traditional among Roman statesmen. He merely systematized and regulated the old policy of toleration of all local religions, and took steps to give this tolerated diversity a measure of common ground in the worship of the deified emperors and the genius of the Roman people. . . . He had not, however, travelled far beyond the old-fashioned conception of religion as practically a gentile—or at least a local —affair, so naturally entwined with the processes of the secular life, that it might be defined as a traditional method of political control. It presented itself to Augustus as a question of a certain ritual, a certain ceremonialism, by which elementary moral duties of a social nature were commemorated and emphasized. Anything

Theory of religious toleration

Religious policy of the world-state

more than this would class as philosophy. . . . Ancient religion, as it was known in the age of Augustus, had in fact separated into mere philosophy and mere ritualism. The religion which he probably anticipated as distinguishing the world-state would only be this ceremonialism applied to the purpose of celebrating the moral duties appropriate to the Great Political State.

Narrowness of the conception

VIII

Augustus and his circle missed, in this matter, truths of extraordinary importance and magnitude. The arrival of the world-state, with its tremendous organization of administration and law, its power of unification and consolidation, was to be paralleled by the advent of a no less tremendous world-faith, striking down roots right into the deepest and most obscure motives of men, with an apparatus of passion and thought and aspiration before which the philosophy and ceremonialism of the old traditional religion would pale and wither. The plenitude of ideas which was scattered among men by the free intercourse of the day fell on fertile soil. It accustomed men to the presence of a richness and fecundity of appeal. The eastern faiths were the missionaries of this process. With their disturbing emotionalism they opened a new view of religion to the European. It slowly became impossible for vigorous minds to rest content with conceptions which touched only a restricted area of their human nature. Men began to expect conceptions both rich in content and unified in principle. The image of a vast secular organization, infinitely varied in its parts and in its functions, yet harmonized into

The world-state proceeds to evolve its own religion

The Asiatic influence

one gigantic whole, irresistibly suggested the image of a faith which had a similar variety and unity.

Augustus had to expel the Egyptian propagandists from Rome. He did not approve of their methods. . . . The trouble was that the very existence of the world-state seemed to create in men an attitude of mind which rendered them dissatisfied with the crude doctrines and shallow formalism of traditional Roman religion. . . . The German threatened the empire with military invasion. The Asiatic threatened it with a spiritual invasion. . . . The essential feature of the case was that the citizens of a world-state were conscious of moral requirements on a correspondingly vast scale: and the government was uncomfortably conscious that this new sort of aspiration tended to weaken its hold on its subjects. . . . Nevertheless the mere fact of the world-state implied that men were brought into new relationships which could not be satisfactorily conducted on the old principles. The situation was still in its earlier stages. It had not yet developed to its maturity.

The new religious movements politically dangerous

IX

Let us return for a moment to the thoughts of Augustus.

To maintain the stability of the central power of the world-state involved, therefore, several considerations. It ought to be hereditary; not because of any theoretical beauty in the principle of hereditary succession, but because it was safer, and would exclude strife among ambitious candidates. The bare idea that the principate was open to competition would bring upon the scene just those possibilities of intrigue and violence which Augustus wished to exclude. His successor ought to be a soldier, and, above all, he should be a man capable of understanding and controlling the new forces which threatened to alter the incidence of power and to dissolve the old discipline. To fulfil both these conditions he should be a man of high aristocratic descent, trained in traditional sympathy with the old Roman institutions, and aware of their peculiar significance.

Qualifications of Augustus' successor

We are apt to speak and think too much as if the imperial family of the Cæsars were a reality. It was not a reality: it was a legal fiction based upon continuous adoption. Gaius Julius Cæsar, the Dictator, the conqueror of Gaul, was the last male of his house. Not one of the early emperors had more than the remotest connection with the family of Cæsar. Augustus was an Octavius, adopted by his grand-uncle; Tiberius was a Claudius Nero; Caligula the son of a Vipsanius Agrippa who had married the daughter of an Octavius; Claudius was a second Claudius Nero; "Nero" was a Domitius Ahenobarbus who had married a Claudian daughter. When, therefore, we speak of "Cæsar" we speak in a merely technical sense. After Gaius Julius, the family of Cæsar was extinct.

The imaginary "House of Cæsar"

But this fictitious and imaginary imperial house of Cæsar was not meaningless: above all, it was most certainly not the creation of self-seeking men trying to attach to themselves a credit they did not possess in their own right. It had far more serious meaning than this. It was an instrument by which the emperors attempted to keep control of the succession to the empire.

Gaius Julius, it is clear, thought long and deeply over the problem of monarchy, and would have been glad enough, for political reasons, to found a dynasty. For with all his intelligence, he could not invent any other method of putting the monarchy outside competition. He did not wish to see each reign prefaced by a civil war; yet that would have been the result of leaving the monarchy purely elective.

The trouble was due to two distinct causes. The emperor was at the head of what was practically a military guild. We know from familiar facts what usually occurred when the monarchy had to undergo a process of election. The quadruple war of Galba, Otho, Vitellius and Vespasian after the death of Nero; the struggle between Albinus, Niger and Severus after the death of Commodus, the later contests of the Illyrian emperors, show that Cæsar's foresight was accurate. The army had a tendency to split into three parties, corresponding to its three principal divisions on the Rhine, the Danube and the Euphrates. It could not be trusted with the task of peaceably electing its head. Every body of men, when it has to undertake such a task has a natural tendency to carry it out on lines dictated by its normal functions. A corporation of bankers who need to elect a chief will certainly turn a disputed election into a financial struggle. An army will as certainly turn it into a military struggle: and civil war is the death knell of civil government.

In addition to this difficulty, inherent in a military guild as such, there was a second difficulty. The first sign of serious dissension in the army over the election of its

Dangers of elective monarchy

head would have released all the forces which, among the senatorial party representing the old oligarchy, were but waiting their chance to regain power and influence. The position of a third party intervening in a struggle is always an advantageous one. Two or three disputed elections would have thrown power back into the hands of the senatorial party, and wiped out the principate. The reality of this danger is attested by the distinct rapprochement between the principate and the Senate after the death of Nero, and the attempt of the Senate, a hundred years later, to regain power—an attempt only terminated at the accession of Diocletian. *The Senatorial opposition*

Hence one of the main points of imperial policy was to avoid the necessity of elections. Here the ghosts of one or two social weaknesses haunted the scene. In the noble old days of large, robust and continuous families there would have been no difficulty in establishing a dynasty and securing stability in the succession to the principate. But Rome had come down to the days of small and incalculable families, when for some reason the wisest man might have a fool for a son, and the most robust man a weakling; and the trouble seemed to be to produce any children at all.

The natural resort, therefore, was to that strange combination of the gentile and the political principle which we see in the imperial house of Cæsar,—the maintenance of a family by the expedient of adoption. By this means the reigning princeps could exercise a real control over the succession: he could nominate and co-opt the man who was to follow him. The imperial Cæsars were themselves a species of guild rather than a family. *Co-optative monarchy*

Augustus ended by adopting Tiberius, his step-son; Tiberius adopted Germanicus, his nephew; the claims of Gaius were derived partly from being the great-grandson of Augustus and the son of Germanicus, and partly from being the heir of Tiberius; those of Nero, from being the great-grandson of Augustus' sister, and the grandson of Germanicus through his mother. These will seem to us, no doubt, claims of remarkable tenuity, if we regard them as examples of hereditary succession; but the accession of emperors on these hereditary claims was nothing more than a last resort when the more serious expedient of adoption had broken down.

The tragedy, the ultimate failure of the Cæsars, was due to the fact that it did break down. It we glance back at the foregoing catalogue, we shall see that Tiberius alone came to the supreme power by formal and explicit adoption. There must be some reason for this abrupt termination of the process; and there is such a reason. We shall come to it in its due place.

Now, Lucius and Gaius Cæsar, Julia's sons, were very young. They were not yet out of boyhood. It would be very unsafe to predict their future as a matter of course. Their succession, their adequacy to the succession, was no matter of course. A hundred accidents might prevent their succession. Augustus himself might die, leaving them too young to hold their own. They themselves might die. They might not prove able in any case to grapple with the difficulties of government. Had Agrippa lived, the case would have been changed; but as it was, all considerations pointed to the wisdom of marrying Julia again to a man who could be trusted

Problems before Augustus

to do his duty as step-father to the two young heirs of the empire, and who could be relied upon, if need arose, to step into the shoes of Augustus and carry on the task of government with firmness and competence.

Only one man fulfilled all the conditions,—and that man was Tiberius.

CHAPTER III

THE CONQUEST OF GERMANY

I

IF circumstances pointed to Tiberius as the predestined husband for Julia, it was certainly not Augustus who had brought them about. It is probable that he thoroughly disliked them. But the Logic of Events was at work. Tiberius, even if disagreeable, was trustworthy; he was a soldier; and he was discreet. Part of the dislike which Augustus felt for him may have been based on the almost unconscious hostility that one clever man naturally feels for another. Even Augustus may have been unable to exclude the uncomfortable feeling that behind the silence, the seriousness and the discretion of Tiberius lay a brain as astute as his own. Exactly how far he could be trusted was, of course, an unanswerable question, on which it was useless to speculate. All that could be said was that Tiberius deserved to be trusted, and had given some proof of his good faith. This had to suffice.

The personal problem for Augustus was even more delicate. He was proposing to give his only daughter to a man by no means distinguished for the more endearing human qualities. The experiment might or might not be successful. . . . At this point Julia herself, that alert dove of twenty-seven, fluttered into the fray. She had grown so accustomed to finding herself married

Circumstances point to Tiberius

The views of Julia

50

THE RHINE FRONTIER.

to the most important man of her father's circle,—first
to Marcellus and then to Agrippa,—that she seemed to
feel that some kind of *droit du seigneur* gave her a claim
upon the hand of Tiberius: his heart she was no doubt
confident of taking by assault. . . . Augustus, therefore, at last made his suggestion. He offered Tiberius
the opportunity of divorcing Vipsania and of marrying
Julia: and in doing this he may have admired his own
generosity.

If so, he might have saved himself the trouble. It
was Tiberius himself who raised the objections. He
had no desire to divorce Vipsania or to marry Julia. The
suggestion, however, was equivalent to a command.
. . . We do not know precisely what kind of pressure
was brought to bear upon Tiberius, nor what arguments   Vipsania
were put before him. Some of the most convincing   divorced
apparently came from Julia: and when Julia laid herself out to enchant, we have every reason to believe that
she could be very enchanting indeed. . . . Even Tiberius thawed before Julia's sunshine. . . . It is certain
that he had no wish to marry Julia: but it is certain that
he did.

He married Julia in the year 11 B. C. in the thirty-first Marriage
year of his age: one of the principal captives borne in   of
her triumphal procession.   Tiberius
                                                           and
                                                           Julia

II

In the considerations of Augustus there was one more
factor. The project for the marriage of Tiberius involved his recall from the Rhine frontier. It was necessary to replace him. The opening was the opportunity

for which Drusus had been waiting. He obtained the succession to the command which Tiberius vacated.

Augustus was no doubt willing to grant Drusus any favour within his power; but the decision to give him the Rhine command was one of more than usual importance. Tiberius was all his life opposed to gratuitous military operations beyond the Rhine, and he never willingly countenanced them. Drusus was the representative of a different school of military opinion, which must have been more influential than we are now able to trace. He was eager to attempt the conquest of Germany. The marriage of Tiberius to Julia thus involved not only a change in the Rhine command, but a change in the military policy of the empire. Drusus went to Gaul with full powers and with authorization to achieve the dream of his life. The army received him with enthusiasm.

Drusus succeeds to the Rhine command

The project which Drusus laid before Augustus would appear to have been a scheme to penetrate to the Elbe Valley, and to make it the new frontier in place of the Rhine. . . . This plan, if successfully carried out, would have several results: it would remove the constant threat of German invasion: it would shorten the actual length of frontier: and it would envelope the tribes of Central Europe in such a way that their power to make themselves dangerous would be greatly reduced. Augustus was swayed by these arguments. . . . Much depended on the "if"; for it still had to be demonstrated that the plan was practicable. It is true that it was no more difficult in itself than Cæsar's project for the conquest of Gaul; but then, Drusus was not Cæsar; and

Plan of Drusus

Cæsar had other motives for the conquest of Gaul. . . .
It may have struck Augustus,—as, by inference, we
may guess that it struck Tiberius,—that it was by no
means wise to dwell too much on the remembrance of
Cæsar,—for his other motives had been political. . . .
Augustus—and perhaps Tiberius—possibly saw that the
conqueror of Germany, like the conqueror of Gaul,
would come before his fellow-countrymen with a prestige which would secure his supremacy. . . . Augustus
seems to have consented. Whether Tiberius also agreed
is very doubtful.

The parallel with Cæsar

Trust and hostility were strangely mingled in the
policy of Augustus towards Tiberius. Having three years
before made Tiberius Governor of the Three Gauls in
the spirit of one who uses the most trustworthy and
adequate instrument to his hand, he yet would not leave
him to his own discretion. Augustus had remained to
watch, to check, and to assist. Tiberius was intelligent
enough to appreciate the very real help rendered him
by the presence of Augustus, which must have made
his task easier and his work more perfect; but he can
hardly have relished the hint of paternalism, the sense
of subordination, which, like a stone in a shoe, is an
irritant out of all proportion to its magnitude. . . . In
contact with the chiefs of the Rhine army, the emperor
no doubt heard all that they had to say. During those
years the slow pressure was brought to bear upon him
which in the end persuaded him to accept the military
program laid before him through Drusus. . . . And
when victory was won, and Drusus went to the Rhine
authorized to put that program into force, Augustus

Drusus given a free hand

underlined, carelessly or unconsciously, the attitude he had all along displayed. It may have been compliment; it may have been caution; but he left the field clear for Drusus in Gaul.

A certain inconsistency marked the conduct of Augustus in giving way to the persuasion of Drusus and his party. That the real weight of the arguments employed made it difficult to resist is possible enough. We might, indeed, ask ourselves why he did not choose his favourite Drusus as the husband of Julia,[1] and retain Tiberius, who shared his own views on the subject of Germany, as commander on the Rhine. . . . The fact remains that he did not adopt this course. He placed Tiberius in the direct line of succession to the empire; and then gave Drusus such a position that his success would endanger the power and prospects of Julia's husband.

Political dangers of the conquest of Germany

While to Drusus was committed the main work of conquering Germany and reaching the Elbe, Tiberius was given the task of bringing the Illyrian frontier up to the Danube, so that the new frontier might be continuous,—a task which he carried out during the years in which Drusus was conducting the German campaigns.

III

Drusus took over the command on the Rhine in the spring of the year 12 B. C. His plans were ready, and all the preliminary preparation had evidently been made before his arrival. Just as the history of Gaul begins with

Drusus on the Rhine 12 B. C.

[1] But see *ante.* pp. 5–6.

Julius Cæsar, so that of Germany begins with Drusus. It is worth our while, therefore, to have before our mind's eye some picture of the man who thus stands at the head of German history. Among the thoughts that occasionally flit through the mind of an onlooker is the reflection that both Gaul and Germany seemed, during the rest of their careers, to bear some strange, elusive stamp of the Roman soldiers who were first to tread their soil. The difference between modern France and modern Germany is the difference between Gaius Julius Cæsar and Nero Claudius Drusus.

Drusus was a man of great qualities, and these qualities were of a particular type. He was no mere curled darling. The affection—the devotion—which was felt for him by his friends and partisans, the enthusiasm with which they followed him, the intensity with which they remembered him, all had their source in the wonderful gifts he had for taking his part in the activity of great organizations. The greatness of Tiberius was contained within himself, and was expressed in his own actions; he was a great individual. But Drusus was not in the same sense of the words a great individual. We look in vain for any of the isolated actions, the definite quotable words, which neatly exemplify his quality. We should be left wondering whether his fame were not a popular delusion, had we not many examples in practical life of this kind of genius. His power was expressed in his relationships with other men. Not in what he did himself, but in what he could make other men do, lay the wonder that his friends adored. Every man felt great in the presence of Drusus; every man felt the electric

Character of Drusus

shock that passed when Drusus touched the chain of association.

This gift is no delusion. It is a very real thing. But it has its defects: and Tiberius himself was dryly aware of them. The quiet, unspoken criticism which the silence and policy of Tiberius all his life expressed towards Drusus and his son Germanicus was founded on the dangerous fact that they did not really lead men but followed them. The hold of Drusus over the Rhine army sprang from the aptitude with which he interpreted and expressed its public opinion. He contributed nothing to it. When we meet with this kind of gift in educated and persuasive persons we call them Representative Men; when we meet it in its coarser and less endearing form, we label it Demagogism. And Tiberius did not like it. He himself uncompromisingly acted on the principle that the duty of a leader is to command that which is to the common good, however distasteful,—not that which his followers wish him to command.

The qualities which Drusus possessed were thus practically very effective, without involving one spark of originality or moral power in the man who possessed them. But clearly there were awkward possibilities about such gifts. The army might have to decide the formidable problem whether it would obey the one type of man or the other. . . . And even an army of philosophers might have had difficulty in deciding such a point.

IV

The plans which had been prepared were on a great scale, and contemplated the complete conquest of Ger-

Political bearings of the character of Drusus

The Frisian campaign 12 B. C.

many. It is quite clear, from the proceedings of Drusus, that the ground had been carefully studied beforehand, the relationships and relative power of the German tribes had been taken into account, and a scheme evolved which was far more scientific and systematic than any that Cæsar the Dictator had put into force in Gaul.

The first year's campaign was directed against the North Sea coastal districts. It was made in great force. The preparations included a bridge across the Rhine, the collection of a great flotilla, and the digging of a canal to connect the Rhine with the Yssel, sufficiently deep to float sea-going ships. The engineers who constructed this canal (the Fossa Drusiana) not only knew their business, but knew the course of the Yssel and the topography of Frisia.

The entry of the legions into Lower Germany was a most formidable affair. Passing through the canal, the flotilla descended the Yssel into Lake Flevo, the eastern portion of what is now the Zuider Zee. The Batavians, always well-disposed towards Rome, did not contest the passage of the troops; the Frisians submitted. Reaching the sea through the northerly channel of Lake Flevo, and passing inside Texel, the fleet occupied Borkum at the mouth of the Ems. Although the Frisians had offered no resistance, the Bructeri, who controlled the valley of the Ems, prepared to fight. A sea battle at the mouth of the Ems, and the advance of the legions by land, resulted in the whole of Lower Germany falling into the hands of the Romans. *The Ems mouth occupied*

The Frisians [1] were the key of the situation. Their

[1] The civilization of Frisia was of very old standing. It had been, perhaps for hundreds of years, the commercial centre of north-western Europe, and the

commercial interests—as marked, though not as extensive as those of the Dutch today—not only predisposed them to peace, but made a friendly relation with the Romans much more to their profit than a very doubtful war would have been. Their passivity enabled Drusus to obtain control of the river-mouths. Once the coast was in Roman hands, the inland tribes were cut off from some of their most important resources.

The next year the scene of operations shifted up the river. Castra Vetera, the old military station which dominated the lower Rhine, was made the base. Setting out from Castra Vetera, Drusus marched up the valley of the Lippe,—which enters the Rhine almost at right angles—and proceeded to describe a tangent to the country he had secured during the campaign of the previous year. Following the Lippe, he passed behind the sources of the Ems and arrived on the banks of the Weser. This was the heart of central Germany—Westphalia, as it came to be called in later times—and the home of the tribal group which was the real centre of resistance: the Cherusci.

11. B. C.
The
Cherusci
reduced

The Cherusci called up their levy and retreated into the woods. It was late in the season when the Romans reached the Weser; supplies were short; so they turned back without attempting to force a passage. The reduction of the Cherusci was work enough for one cam-

point from which trade and communication radiated. The inland Germans seem to have been originally emigrants who came by sea: a good deal of help and support came to them by that channel—as the strategy of Drusus would clearly imply—and the closing of Frisia must have been a serious blow to them. What we know nowadays as "gun-running" is no modern invention. The Roman reports of the poverty and lack of effective weapons among the inland Germans are very likely due to such events as the occupation of Frisia or to the diplomatic alienation of their more civilized coastal neighbours.

paign. On their way back, they marched straight into
one of those ingenious woodland traps in the construction of which the Cherusci were expert. It was not
strong enough to hold Roman troops. After hard fighting they broke their way through. Drusus took the precaution of building an advanced post, Aliso, at the head   Aliso
of the Lippe valley, near the place where the rivers Alme   estab-
and Lippe join. Aliso became one of the most important   lished
means by which the Romans retained their hold on
Germany.

The third year's campaign saw the scene shifted yet
further up the Rhine. It was aimed at the Chatti, the
fierce and formidable fighting men of the Lahn valley.
The campaign against the Chatti was a particularly pun-
ishing war; but it completed the reduction of practically the whole of the middle Germany contained by
the Weser, which (with the exception of the land oc-   10 B. C.
cupied by the Saxon tribes of Chauci in the far north-   The Chatti
west) was effectively brought under the control of   reduced
Rome.

Augustus graciously gave encouragement. Drusus—
with Tiberius, whose Pannonian campaigns were proceeding at the same time—was granted the honorary title
of Imperator. In addition, Drusus received his first Consulship. So far, all had gone well: but the full justification of all these honours had still to come. Germany was
not yet conquered.

v

Drusus and his general staff carried out other work
quite as important as the actual fighting. During these

The
Rhine
fortified

operations the Rhine frontier was securely closed to the Germans by the foundation of the great chain of fortified towns which were to become famous in after ages. From Leyden and Nimeguen to Bonn (where he built a bridge) Bingen, Mainz, Spires, Worms and Strasburg the towns arose with their connecting web of strategic highways: and it was under the command of Drusus that they sprang into being. Cologne stands to the credit of another: but to Drusus belongs the honour of being the principal founder of the Rhine cities. As he began them, so they grew. Fifty fortified posts were established on the north bank.

And now, with honours already thick upon him, he moved yet further up the river, and prepared for a campaign greater still.

He set out from Mainz—the Moguntiacum which he had himself founded to serve as a base. Crossing the upper waters of the Weser, which now were near at hand, he struck north for the Elbe itself. The march was a long one, deep into country where no Roman army ever before had been. He reached the middle Elbe somewhere about Magdeburg. He was under instructions not to cross the Elbe, since Augustus thought it imprudent to raise unnecessarily the apprehensions of the tribes beyond the river. On the banks he built a trophy to mark his furthest north, and the establishment of the new boundary of the Roman dominion.

9 B. C.
The Elbe
Campaign

There was no possibility of completing in a single campaign the reduction of the whole of this large and wild land. Drusus was too prudent a commander to attempt more than he could accomplish. He began his return march. . . . Afterwards, a dark tale was told, and inauspicious omens were remembered. It was alleged that a giant woman appeared to him, saying: "Whither next, insatiable Drusus? Fate allows you no further. Go back!—for the end of your deeds and your life is at hand." . . . Men like Drusus were not superstitious, and did not share the beliefs they exploited as a helpful means of controlling the ignorant. If anything disturbed his thoughts, it is far more likely to have been a doubt lest, when so much effort was needed merely to reach the Elbe, there might be insufficient power in reserve to make good the conquest.

For all that, the luck of the Drusi fell upon him as the army returned from the Saal towards the Rhine. He was thrown from his horse, and his leg was broken. . . . Whatsoever the cause, the injury mortified. When the army emerged into the circle of civilization it was carrying with it a dying commander.

Accident to Drusus

Tiberius was at Ticinum, on the Po, south of Milan, when the news came. He got to horse and galloped for the Rhine. Ticinum was on the main post road. By Laumellium and Vercellæ he could cross the mountains to Vienne, whence he could strike the great Rhine road; and, travelling as he never travelled before or after, he reached his brother just before Drusus died.

Wolves howled around the camp. Two youths were seen riding through—doubtless the Great Twin Brethren. There was a sound of women lamenting, and stars fell from the sky.

Death of Drusus

VI

Man, though rational, is unreasonable. Some bitterness seems to have invaded the mind of Tiberius. He had lost a brother whom, in his disagreeable way, he loved —and a younger brother who had been his companion and friend. Younger brothers have a place in the hearts of the austere legion of elder sons which is not dependent on approval or agreement. Tiberius may have despised Drusus; he may have resented his habit of stealing away love and admiration; he may have been fatigued with the shallowness and insincerity which men at large adored; but children—and men are children of a larger growth—will weep for the beloved black doll which they have daily rebuked and placed in the corner. . . . How can man endure life without the dear objects of his disapproval?

And there were other things. The feet of Tiberius were set upon a road which led to an increasing isolation. As he rose in fame and importance his companions became fewer; as he rose farther, they would become fewer still. If, at last, he should rise to the highest, he would stand there alone, in a vast loneliness and isolation. . . . The passing of Drusus was not softened for him by his resentment against Drusus. There went, into the void, a man who was one of the few that inhabited the world of Tiberius Claudius Nero.

The marriage of Tiberius to Julia had been one of those experiments which would inevitably increase this
Relations of Tiberius and Julia sense of loneliness and isolation. In Augustus, that gift of sociability, that need for the presence and person and

intercourse of other human beings, which made him a successful organizer, was so balanced and steadied by his other qualities that it appears as a strength. In Julia the gift bred out pure; and like most pure and uncompensated qualities it was a tragic weakness. She was faced now with a problem as difficult as any that could have been presented to her: how to live with a cautious, reticent, complex man who cared little for conversation and nothing for society, and who was much swayed by considerations of the cold reasoning intelligence. He did not naturally love her. Any feeling he had for her was a fascination which she had herself created, and which might die away when she flagged. . . . Fate jested when she drew Tiberius and Julia together; but Augustus cannot be wholly absolved from folly. If he shut his eyes to the risk, he paid dearly for it in the end.

Julia was moreover married to a man who had preoccupations which prevented him from being completely fascinated. Throughout the years in which Drusus held the Rhine command Tiberius held that of the Illyrian army, a post hardly less important. His absences gave him time to think; and his work ensured that he should not lose the power of thinking.

Augustus had brought his daughter up very carefully. He had watched over her, guarded her from dangerous friends, and produced a model of the sweet domesticated maiden for which a later age, nearer our own, had so consuming a passion. But Julia was something more than a sweet maiden. She was a clever, fascinating and witty woman, born for a more strenuous

Julia's personality

life than Penelope's. Her temperament was one of those ardent temperaments which burn with an intense flame, and manifest themselves in an activity to which the physical and the mental worlds seem to offer a scope too narrow for their full effect. She had no control over her energies. Even before the death of Agrippa she had fallen into the hands of the man whose influence seems to have begun the mischief,—Tiberius Sempronius Gracchus.

Gracchus accompanied Julia into her new domestic circle. To marry a wife with a shadow is perhaps not a pleasant experience, though up to a point it may be an inspiring one. The imminence of Gracchus in the background may have combined with the charm of Julia to inspire Tiberius to hold his own, as he undoubtedly did during the first period of their life together. But marriage with Julia had certain drawbacks that were only visible to her husband. Both the young Marcellus and the burly Agrippa had come to untimely ends; and we can hardly feel wonder if Tiberius found himself confronted by the Hobson's Choice of following in their footsteps, or of condoning Julia's expanding passion for polyandry. His not unnatural objection to either alternative could only appear to Julia as an example of that lack of sympathy for which he was notorious. . . . But she could not maintain her power of fascination over a man acute enough to see whither it led, and sufficiently interested in other things to decline resolutely to be led thither. And she did not maintain it over Tiberius. He cooled rapidly.

Women of Julia's temperament become dangerous

Her "shadow," T. Sempronius Gracchus

Drawbacks of being Julia's husband

at this point. Tiberius had neither the leisure nor the
necessary disposition to maintain himself against the
competition of an unofficial lover who, by the testimony   Influence
of his contemporaries, was a gifted man with a tongue   of
which might have been put to better use. Gracchus suc-   Gracchus
ceeded admirably in the art of putting Tiberius in the
wrong. Julia was a great deal too conscious of her own
importance and her own charm: Gracchus carefully
fanned the flame of her feelings against her husband.
. . . When a woman in this state of mind is frustrated,
her line of action can be predicted with some certainty.
She will try to turn the tables. Julia proceeded to demonstrate her own virtues, and the satanic wickedness of
her husband, by turning the tables upon him.

She wrote a letter to her father full of complaints and   Julia's
accusations against Tiberius.[1] The terms of this letter   letter
have not come down to us;[2] but the gossip of Rome   to her
(which evidently knew more of the matter than it had   father
any right to know) alleged that it was drafted by

[1] The suggestion that the scandalous chapters of Suetonius were derived from
the memoirs of Julia's daughter Agrippina is well known. But it is conceivable
that their original source was this letter of Julia herself. This hypothesis would
explain far better than any other the subsequent course of events, and the attitude of Julia's children towards Tiberius.

[2] Tacitus tells us (*Ann.* I. 53.) that Julia looked down upon Tiberius as
beneath her. This is a somewhat extraordinary allegation. We are left wondering
in what sense to understand it. It has been suggested that it was due to her
consciousness of Julian blood. But Julia had no drop of Julian blood in her
veins nearer than her great-grandmother: and even if she had possessed any, it
would not have enabled her to look down upon the aristocratic descent of a
Claudius! . . . It is difficult not to interpret Tacitus' remark in the sense that
Julia took up an attitude of moral superiority. . . . But remembering Julia's
subsequent career, we may well ask ourselves on what such an attitude could
have been based. Obviously it must have been founded on some argument at-
tributing scandalous misconduct to Tiberius. This letter of Julia's is the first
suggestion of any such charge: and the circumstances under which it was
written are significant.

Gracchus. . . . Augustus seems to have put the letter aside: but it had some kind of effect. His feelings were no doubt mixed. He wished Julia on the one hand to be justified; and on the other he did not wish to believe any serious charge against Tiberius. In this unsatisfactory condition the affair remained.

To some extent it did not really matter. Julia had after all done her duty by producing Lucius and Gaius Cæsar, the heirs of the monarchy. No sons of Tiberius were in especial request to compete with them. . . . After his only child by Julia had died in its infancy they ceased to live together. . . . The daughter of Augustus was not likely to lack a circle of admirers, friends, flatterers and sycophants. She could have all she wanted; and she might indulge in her new excitements without damaging any serious interests—unless the dignity of Tiberius came under that description. . . . Here, too, he had reason for bitterness. A husband who can contemplate without personal humiliation the unfaithfulness of his wife must have private reasons for contentment which Tiberius does not seem to have possessed. . . . He saw Vipsania once after their separation and then he looked after her with a gaze of such intent emotion that he was never allowed to see her again.

Julia and Tiberius cease to live together

VII

It must have been from this time that the mysterious prejudice against Tiberius began to spread,—that private knowledge which so many of Julia's circle seemed to share, but which no one would put into words. When, years afterwards, those members of Julia's circle sought

Prejudice against Tiberius

to reveal their treasured knowledge, it proved remarkably varied and contradictory, not to say incoherent.
. . . But when Julia's own conduct was brought to
light, there was not much doubt about the definite nature of the charges in which she was involved. . . .
Tiberius must have known the facts from the very first.
He kept Julia's secret. It was perhaps difficult, after
all that had happened, to complain to Augustus; nor
could he have expected a sympathetic hearing if he
had done so. . . . A repentant and reformed Julia,
converted by the kind exhortations of her father, might
have been even more embarrassing than a wayward
Julia. The real truth was that Tiberius had never wanted
her. Once the mischief was done, and he was married
to her, his tongue was, for his own credit, tied. Augus-   Tiberius
holds his
tus remained in ignorance of the facts; or if he knew,   tongue
the knowledge came to him in so softened a form that it
may well have seemed to him hardly necessary to in-
terfere. His own views respecting the unnecessary seriousness and unsociability of Tiberius would have
explained to him any slight differences that might exist.
. . . Life is full of these savage ironies.

VIII

The death of Drusus added its full touch of unhap-
piness to these unhappy things. Tiberius conveyed the
body to Rome: and his biographer tells us that he walked
before it on foot, all the way thither. . . . After the
funeral pyre was burnt down, the ashes of Drusus were
laid in the Mausoleum of Augustus. Two commemora-   Funeral
of
tive orations were delivered: one by Tiberius in the   Drusus

Forum, and the other in the Flaminian Circus by Augustus himself.[1] . . . Augustus, in the course of a warm eulogy, had one or two remarks to make that may not have been wholly relished by all his hearers. He prayed that his grandsons Gaius and Lucius might prove such men as Drusus. He softened the implied criticism by expressing the wish that he might, when his time came, himself meet a death as glorious: and perhaps his audience realized, with a touch of discomfort, that both aspirations were equally unlikely.

The honorary title of *Germanicus* was given to Drusus and to his children. At Mainz, which he had founded and fortified, a cenotaph was erected, and a triumphal arch, to perpetuate for ever the deeds of the man who had founded the province of Germany.

The death of Drusus had consequences deeper and more permanent than any personal grief it gave. It was a blow to the party which still hoped for the restoration of senatorial government. Drusus, with his habit of taking the colour of his company, had more or less sincerely encouraged this political view. His tendency in this direction was no doubt over-rated; for although it was declared that he and Augustus in consequence disagreed, the wish that it might be so was probably the father to the thought. No such disagreement was ever visible. . . . There were issues still deeper and more lasting. The disappearance of Drusus, which left the conquest of Germany suspended, half complete, was a dramatic crisis in the history of Europe. How much

Augustus criticizes Julia's children

Death of Drusus a serious event

---

[1] Augustus moreover composed the memorial inscription, and wrote a memoir of Drusus. (Suet. *Div. Claud.* 1. 5.)

sprang from that unlucky fall from his horse, no man can fully estimate. The whole course of modern history would have been changed had he lived to complete his conquest: and even though, in due time, Othos and Fredericks might still have found an imperial Roman crown, it would have come to pass under very different conditions. . . . Hundreds of years of war, struggle and human suffering would have been avoided. The great "Folk-Wandering" might never have taken place: the Roman empire in the west might never have broken down; the German emperors would, like the earlier Illyrian, have succeeded to office without the long struggle which plunged Europe into the dark ages; and the great heathen power which resided in the Baltic would have been civilized before it had developed the sea-going sailing ship to the point of perfection which afterwards enabled it, not indeed to conquer Europe, but very nearly to destroy civilization.

Even at the time, men felt that some great and awful tragedy had befallen the world. The wisest could not foresee the results of failing to conquer and Romanize Germany. It was, indeed, not yet certain whether Germany could be subdued. The dispute over the military problem pursued its long-drawn-out course.

But in fact the death of Drusus meant the passing of the last man who had both the ability and the enthusiasm for the task. The means, the man and the opportunity were never again united.

Tiberius returned to Germany to take over the command. He was once more Governor of the Three Gauls and commander of the Rhine Army. Augustus, who had *Tiberius takes the Rhine command* left Drusus to his own untrammelled discretion, accompanied Tiberius. Much remained to be done. The conquests of Drusus needed to be organized, and the Germans needed to be convinced that they had not won the war. The Sicambri were still restless, and disposed to make a bid for fortune. The first necessity was to quieten these dangerous neighbours. One of the administrative tasks which Tiberius undertook was the transplanting of forty thousand people to the south side of the Rhine, where they could be kept under control.

The task of settling the new territories thus devolved, after all, upon Tiberius. It was a much more delicate
Pacifica- task than that of fighting, and it called for qualities
tion of of tact and sympathy which not every man possessed,
Germany and with which Tiberius is not commonly credited. That he performed it well is implied by the success which attended his arrangements. Little trouble was experienced with the Germans until a man of a very different stamp took charge of the province.

He made no attempt to force Roman institutions upon the German tribes. He left the presence of Roman government and Roman troops to produce their own effect in spreading a new consciousness of law and peace among tribes to whom both conceptions had some of the bright charm of novelty. But he imposed on them no new taxes and did not subject them to any compul-
German sory levy for the auxiliary service. There would be time
policy of enough for that when they began to enter into the idea
Tiberius of Rome, and to feel some pride in the share they could take in her activities.

Neither then nor at any other time does the person-

ality of the Germans seem to have failed to produce
its proper impression on their conquerors. But to appreciate their potentialities was not quite the same thing
as knowing how to handle them. Men of aristocratic
descent seem, by their mental build and mental habits,
to have been more successful than others in dealing with
the Germans.[1] No one ever handled them more successfully than Tiberius Claudius Nero. His discernment
may have been the cause of his opposition to the project of holding Germany by force at all. From the main
drift of his policy, we can see that Tiberius himself
would always have preferred to place reliance upon diplomacy rather than upon force: but since he had been
overborne, he made the best of the situation.

IX

Augustus was drawn nearer to Tiberius after the
death of Drusus. The invariable competence of the elder
brother made him the continual support of Augustus;
everything which Tiberius did was well done. The death
of Mæcenas, which happened in the following year,
must have increased Augustus' sense that his old colleagues were disappearing from his side. . . . Agrippa
had gone; Mæcenas had gone; Drusus, his favourite
amongst the younger men, had gone. . . . It was, indeed, some years since Mæcenas had played any part
in politics; still, he had dwelt serenely on the outskirts
of the world, pursuing his luxurious, cultivated life, and
it is likely enough that he and Augustus sometimes met.
His place was not easily to be filled.

Augustus and Tiberius drawn together

B. C. 8

[1] This is illustrated by the loss of Germany in A. D. 9, and the loss of Frisia in
A. D. 28.

But the patience and loyalty of Tiberius had been dangerously strained.

Reasons
for con-
ciliating
Tiberius

He had too long been put into a second place in the regard of Augustus; he had too long been watched, when he should have been trusted; he had too much been made to feel that the charm and social virtues of others counted for more than the real ability and effective work of a shy and silent man. More men are embittered by a sense of their disadvantage before superficial accomplishments than by real adversity and the cold blast of fortune. . . . His enforced parting from Vipsania and his marriage to Julia very clearly deepened this general embitterment. The loss of Drusus, though it may not have deepened it, must still have added emphasis to a position of rapidly growing isolation from the sympathies of his fellows. . . . Augustus, himself sensitive to the loss of friends, struggled awake into some belated fellow-feeling.

The important services of Tiberius were therefore recognized by a second consulship in company with a distinguished colleague, Gnæus Calpurnius Piso. Augustus made a serious effort to placate and encourage him. He may have realized, too, the ominously strained relations between Tiberius and Julia, even though he may not have known the precise reasons for it nor its full extent. To alienate the clever and able man whom he had intended to be the defence and the help of Julia's sons would have been disastrously to defeat his own ends. He accordingly proposed that Tiberius should receive the tribunician power for a period of five years.

Tiberius
Consul II.
B. C. 7
Aet. 35

The proposal was one that might well appeal to Tiberius, because it was a very real and serious political advancement. The tribunician power was one of the main constitutional bases on which the authority of the princeps was founded. Tiberius, in receiving it, would be lifted a considerable step higher towards the supreme power in the state, and it would enable him to undertake work otherwise impossible to him. The time limit only meant that he was not actually associated in the empire—and he could not expect that while Julia's sons lived. . . . Hence the advances of Augustus could be taken seriously: and Tiberius accepted the honour.

The tribunician power

X

It was just at this point that the explosion occurred.

CHAPTER IV

THE SURVIVAL OF JULIA'S THIRD HUSBAND

I

THE relations of Tiberius and Julia, always strained, reached an abrupt crisis. We do not know its exact nature; even Augustus did not, at that time, know the whole of it: but that it was serious can be seen easily enough from the consequences. Whatsoever it was that happened, Tiberius kept his own counsel, and Julia had certainly no object to achieve by revealing it. . . . Very suddenly, very definitely, Tiberius abandoned his career, resigned his employments, shook the dust of Rome off his shoes, and departed for Rhodes: and at Rhodes he remained for seven years.

He could not go without the emperor's consent: but on what terms that consent was wrung from the astonished and reluctant Augustus we can only speculate and imagine. It is certain that Tiberius did not confide his real reasons. He applied for leave of absence on the ground that he was over-strained with the burden of office, and needed rest. . . . Livia was called in to help; but Tiberius was immovable before her arguments and entreaties. Augustus expressed his own feelings publicly to the Senate: he felt that he was being abandoned by one on whose help he had relied. . . . Tiberius replied by going on hunger-strike. After four days, seeing that he was determined, they gave way. As

Crisis
in the
relations
of Julia
and
Tiberius

74

soon as he had the necessary permission, he hurried down Tiberius
to Ostia with very few farewells; and boarded a ship leaves
suddenly
without saying a single word to the doubtless much for
Rhodes
interested friends who saw him off.

The gossip of Rome never had any doubt that Julia
was at the root of it; [1] but even Roman gossip did not
venture to assert that he was to blame. It knew too
much, perhaps. . . . Tiberius himself, at a later time,
allowed it to be thought that he had taken a considered
and leisurely departure to Rhodes in order to avoid any
appearance of undesirable rivalry with Julia's sons. . . .
No one has ever believed this ingenuous explanation,
which leaves the violence of his exit conspicuously un-
explained.

II

He sailed from Ostia, pursued by the triumphant
hostility of Julia's friends. When he was off Campania,
he heard that Augustus was ill, and he stopped his journey. It was no doubt Julia's friends who spread the
genial suggestion that he was waiting for the good news
of Augustus' death. The slander is a straw which indi-
cates the direction in which the wind was blowing. It
caused him at once to continue his journey direct to
Rhodes.

[1] Suetonius: *Tib.* X. Tac. *Ann.* I. 53. The problem to be explained is that
Tiberius went to Rhodes almost immediately after receiving the tribunician power
for five years. He would scarcely have accepted the investiture if he had not
intended to remain in office. The change in his plans was very sudden and very
violent. If he had suddenly become aware of Julia's letter to her father, written
in the sense suggested *supra* p. 65 f. n., then at any rate we should have a
possible motive adequate to account for all the facts, which otherwise are
inexplicable.

His choice of Rhodes was a recollection of the pleasure he had felt on visiting it many years before, during the progress of Augustus through the eastern provinces. He settled down very much as any modern soldier or civil servant would do. He took a small town house, and, as Suetonius tells us, a country villa not much larger. He lived very simply, much as his neighbours did. He adopted the Greek dress, and took part in the social activities of the island.

Tiberius settles in Rhodes

Seven years is a long span in the life of a man. Tiberius spent his self-imposed retirement chiefly in study. He was a well-educated man, according to the standard of his age and social class; reading and writing Greek as familiarly as his native Latin. He regularly attended the lectures of the local philosophers; and during these days in Rhodes he picked up the interest in astrology which he retained for the rest of his life. The interest shows that he had scientific tastes; for astrology—however little store we may now set by it—was the astronomical science of the time, and included the strictly mathematical study which has grown into the modern science of astronomy. . . . He had his doubts concerning the prophetical aspect of it, but Thrasyllus, under whom he studied, was a very able man of some intellectual distinction, who became a life-long friend, and the personality of Thrasyllus was sufficient to smooth over any scepticism that Tiberius felt.

Occupies himself in study

Rhodes was a pleasant enough place in which to spend a voluntary retreat. It was an active commercial centre, near the great cities of Asia; it was in touch with Alexandria; it lay almost in the centre of a world fermenting with a new intellectual life far removed from the political struggles of Rome or the fierce life of the Rhine frontier. . . . Tiberius was in Rhodes when, southeast over the sea, Jesus the son of David was born at Bethlehem in Judæa. . . . Tiberius did not look up from his studies and his thoughts. No star guided him and Thrasyllus across the sea.

Since he was among people who had no interest in the political and personal rivalries of Rome, the stories that are preserved concerning the life of Tiberius in Rhodes are to some extent free from political colouring. The personality of Tiberius, when we catch a glimpse of it stripped of its official vestments, is interesting. He had the natural republicanism which was deeply bred in the old Roman aristocracy. We see him walking, unattended and without ceremony, exchanging courtesies on perfectly equal terms with those he meets. We see him deciding to visit the sick,[1]—an intention which it is worth while to remember when we are reading the story of his later life: and we see his intention misunderstood so that Tiberius, on leaving his house to carry out his mission, finds the sick assembled—carefully classified according to their medical cards—in a convenient portico for his inspection. We see him astonished at this unexpected sight: and then, recovering himself, proceeding to apologize personally to all the unfortunate patients in turn for the trouble inflicted upon them. We

Tiberius as a private individual

---

[1] We are not told the precise purpose for which Tiberius undertook these visits. It does not seem unreasonable to suggest that a man of the type of Tiberius would, even if his first object were sympathetic and charitable, probably combine with it a little useful medical study. There may be some connection between this story and the military ambulance service which Tiberius organized in Illyria some years later. Vell. Pat. I. cxiv. See post p. 104.

see him taking part in the very characteristic local philosophical debate. . . . His connection with this institution gave rise to the only occasion on which he remembered and exercised his dormant official authority. . . . Some excitable Greek lost his head, and Tiberius, when he ventured to intervene with an expression of his own views on the subject under discussion, was included within the scope of a picturesque wealth of language which broke up the orderliness of the proceedings as effectually as the remarks of Mr. Brown of Calaveras broke up those of a more modern society of a similar kind. . . . Tiberius retired to assume his authority and summon his servants, and the offending philosopher was stored away in gaol for purposes of quiet meditation,—a pleasing side-light upon the philosophical societies of the day!

III

But that which Tiberius concealed, Julia herself gave away. After his retirement to Rhodes, her descent was rapid and disastrous. Augustus was the last person who became acquainted with the truth. Long before he had heard the first hints which reached him, the conduct of Julia had become the richest and most outrageous scandal of the day. It was something which would have been talked of, had she been an ordinary person: that she was the daughter of Augustus gave it an unparalleled conspicuousness.

It could not possibly have continued indefinitely at the pitch it at last reached, and we can only wonder whether Julia herself realized as much, or whether she was intoxicated into a species of madness. . . . Livia Augusta was suspected of conveying the first hints which set the emperor inquiring. He had the power to enforce answers to his questions: and the answers to his questions led to stern examination which finally unravelled the whole facts. They could hardly have been blacker or more tangled had they been deliberately invented. To Augustus they were a shock from which he never perfectly recovered.

Augustus institutes inquiry

At least five men of high rank were involved in the scandal of Julia's conduct: Julus Antonius, the son of the triumvir, whom Augustus had pardoned and received with full forgetfulness of any enmity he may have borne towards his father: an Appius Claudius: a Scipio: the Gracchus who had been the beginning of the mischief: a certain Quintius Crispinus: and other persons of less degree—for Julia had been strikingly generous. . . . Moreover, the most notorious of the scandals had been public, and had taken place, not only in the Forum, but actually in the rostra, the elevated platform from which speakers addressed the Assembly. . . . The participants were probably drunk: but the probability was an added scandal. . . . And Augustus had other aspects of the case to consider, besides the scandalousness of the proceedings. To what extent were these men actuated by political motives? What were they really doing? . . . Of this side of the matter we know less. If Augustus gained any serious information, he kept it to himself. . . . Julus Antonius killed himself rather

The revelations

than face the consequences. Phœbe, Julia's confidential freedwoman, hanged herself. Everyone concerned was arrested.

The wrath of Augustus was terrible. He was a man who lost his temper with difficulty. He had none of that easy anger of the choleric man who can rapidly rid himself of the incubus of wrath. He was a cold, equable man, who took anger as if it were a sickness and was helpless in its grip. . . . Julia must have known well that there was no forgiveness. She had discredited her father. He could have tolerated a little harmless immorality. He was no plaster saint himself. But he could not tolerate what she had done. He even thought of inflicting on her the capital penalty. When he heard of Phœbe's suicide, he remarked: "I would rather have been Phœbe's father!" Julia did not take the hint.

Wrath of Augustus

As Rome already knew all, and a good deal more than all, there was to know, he addressed a message to the Senate setting out the facts, and communicating to it the penalties he intended to inflict on those concerned. It was read in his absence by a quæstor. For a long time he would see no one.

Julia sent to Pandataria 2 B. C.

Julia's lovers were executed or exiled. Julia herself was sent a close prisoner to the isle of Pandataria: and that was the end of Julia's career.

IV

Tiberius, when he heard the news of this serious business—which included, as one of its minor features, the service of a writ of divorce upon Julia in his name— wrote to intervene, and did his best to bring about some kind of reconciliation between his wife and her father. His efforts were useless. Augustus would listen to nothing: nor did he ever, at any time, listen to attempts to palliate or excuse the conduct of Julia. All that Tiberius could do was to confirm to her all gifts that he had made to her in the past. How large these may have been we have no means of knowing: but a man does not usually economize in gifts to a wife who is an emperor's daughter, so it is a fair surmise that they amounted to a reasonably great sum. . . . It is not recorded, in any case, that he got any thanks from Julia. . . .

Futile inter- vention of Tiberius

Her imprisonment at Pandataria was rigorous. She was not allowed wine, nor any form of luxury. A child was born to her after her removal thither, but Augustus refused to allow it to be recognized or reared. . . . No man was permitted to visit her without his express permission, and even then only after the most searching examination into his identity, which included the registration of his physical markings. Two men who formed a plan to rescue her were caught and executed. One of her freedmen was found in Augustus' bed-room with a knife. . . . She was as closely held as any state-prisoner in the Bastille. . . . Some of these precautions suggest that Augustus believed in the existence of a conspiracy which had employed her as an instrument. Pandataria was a pleasanter place of imprisonment than the Bastille, but it was quite as secure. Not until five years later was this severity relaxed; and that was after Tiberius had returned to Rome.

Julia a prisoner of state

The ramifications of the scandal of Julia spread somewhat wide, and went deep. They affected Tiberius far away in Rhodes. There was now no especial reason for him to continue in retirement. Moreover, his five years' enjoyment of the tribunician power was expiring and with it expired the personal immunity which it conferred. He requested permission to visit his relatives, giving, in support of his application, the reason that young Gaius and Lucius Cæsar were now grown up, and that it was unnecessary for him to avoid rivalry with them now that rivalry was out of the question. But he had not yet done with Julia and her friends. Augustus refused the request. Livia obtained for him the status of a legatus, and fortified with this rank, which gave him a legal position and legal protection, he remained in Rhodes, less willingly than before.

So far, therefore, from Tiberius gaining any advantage, it proved that the downfall of Julia was to be the starting point of fresh trouble for him. The legend that he was an abominable person, who had in some indefinable way been her enemy, and was continuing to be the enemy of the young Cæsars, grew, involved itself into ever-growing magnitude, and spread until his pleasant sojourn in Rhodes was changed into a difficult exile. Augustus, having made the young Cæsars his heirs and prospective successors, had no alternative but to consult their wishes. . . . Tiberius behaved with the utmost discretion. He avoided society, in order to prevent ill-natured gossip and misunderstandings: but every person of official importance who went to the east, drifted to Rhodes to call upon him, and it was impossible, without giving offence, to decline their visits.

Effect upon Tiberius

The cause of these difficulties became still more clear when Gaius Cæsar, who had received an appointment to Asia, passed through Samos. Tiberius did not fail to cross to Samos to pay a visit of courtesy. His reception was not encouraging. Gaius was accompanied by his tutor, Marcus Lollius, whom Tiberius had superseded as Governor of Gaul after the raid of the Sicambri when the eagle of the Fifth Legion was lost. Lollius made himself as unpleasant as possible. He had ample opportunities, and he poisoned the mind of young Gaius with those undefined slanders against Tiberius which were now the stock-in-trade of Julia's friends. *His interview with Julia's son*

It is easy to understand that Tiberius had never entertained any passionate admiration for the long-nosed progeny of the long-nosed Julia, who took after their Octavian mother much more than after their grim Vipsanian father. He must have known perfectly well that his young step-sons were never likely to develop into anything but commonplace men. Augustus himself had begun to perceive the fact. . . . But their very stupidity made them all the more dangerous. They already wielded an immense influence, without brains or character to guide them; and nothing is more dangerous than a fool in power. . . . When a definite charge was brought that Tiberius had received a visit from some centurions on leave, and through them had sent messages of a suspicious and seditious character to various friends,—Augustus referred the accusation to him for reply. Tiberius vehemently demanded that someone—he did not care of what rank—should be sent to observe *The young Cæsars* his words and actions. Augustus did not feel disposed to pay anyone a salary for so idle a task as this, and the observer was not sent.

Tiberius went to the length of giving up his riding exercise and his practice with arms, and of wearing exclusively the Greek civilian dress. But nothing that he could do would stop the rise of the flood. At Nimes [1] his statues were thrown down. Augustus himself began to be included in the stream of hatred and slander. The culminating point was reached when at a dinner party at which Gaius Cæsar was present, one of the guests, Cassius Patavinus, arose and expressed his readiness and willingness to stick a knife into Augustus, and finally offered to go to Rhodes and bring back the head of Tiberius if Gaius would only give the word.[2] . . . This drove Tiberius to write a letter of indignant remonstrance that such things should be said, and of earnest request that he might be allowed to return to Rome.

Augustus himself, who had never wanted Tiberius to leave Rome, was willing enough. . . . He wrote back in a very friendly, and slightly bantering spirit, bidding Tiberius (who was forty-two) not to be swept off his feet by the ardour of youth. It was good enough if they could prevent people from doing evil, since it was impossible to prevent them speaking it. . . . All the same, he visited Cassius with a sentence of banishment of the less severe sort.

But although Augustus did not miss much of these

Tiberius requests permission to return

Correspondence with Augustus

---

[1] Not in his old province of the Three Gauls, but in southern, Senatorial Gaul. The fact is worth noting as indicative of the current.

[2] Suetonius: *Div. Aug.* LI. *Tib.* XIII. These two stories seem to refer to the same incident.

things and their significance, he did not feel at liberty
to grant the request of Tiberius without the consent of
Gaius Cæsar; and the matter would have fallen through
but for a further series of events which once again
changed the face of affairs.

V

Lucius Cæsar died at Marseilles on his way into Spain,
and one of the hopes of Augustus disappeared.

The emperor bore the blow with a good deal more
fortitude than he might once have shown. But he was
sixty-five. He could not hope to last more than a few
years longer; and now the prospect of the succession had
dwindled to one grandchild, Gaius Cæsar, a very young,
quite inexperienced, and totally untried man, whose
promise did not altogether arouse the enthusiasm of
beholders, and who was none too robust in either body or
mind. Was it possible that Gaius could sustain the weight
of an empire which had taken all the diplomacy of
Augustus, all the worldly wisdom of Mæcenas, and all
the energy of Agrippa to win?—and which had needed
all their united strength, helped by the young abilities
of Tiberius and Drusus, to maintain? It seemed very
improbable. He would need very powerful backing if
he were to do it; such backing as he might have received
from the man whose head was to have been brought
back from Rhodes. . . . There, at any rate, dwelt a
man who had something of Agrippa's energy and of
Augustus' diplomacy: a man tried, and not found wanting. It was impossible to ignore the slow successive steps
by which Tiberius approached supreme power.

Death of Lucius Cæsar A. D. 2.

Weak position of Gaius Cæsar

He had made no effort to take it, nor to hasten the conclusion which he foresaw. . . . He had, indeed, actually left the field free to the young Cæsars, and had removed himself from any rivalry or suspicion of rivalry with them; and even though his purpose in so doing may have been to allow them to demonstrate their own uselessness, still he had acted legitimately and with discretion, and had refrained from exercising any influence upon the result. Augustus had thus none of the reasons which might have made him hesitate. He was willing to accept the help and promote the power of the one man who really possessed the force of character to succeed him in the principate. He could not avoid the inevitable trend of events. He never liked Tiberius. Even at the end he still regretted the necessity that Tiberius should follow him, and made that expression of sympathy, in part humorous, in part wondering, and in part sorrowful, for the unfortunate Romans who would be ground in the slow jaws of that strong and deliberate man.

Augustus favours the return of Tiberius

Augustus referred the question to young Gaius Cæsar. As it chanced, Gaius had fallen out with Marcus Lollius. Confronted with the question, undisturbed by the influence of Lollius, Gaius could only assure his grandfather that he had no objection to the return of Tiberius, on condition that he took no part in politics.

Gaius consents

VI

Tiberius, without enthusiasm or concession, returned. He had left Rome a man of thirty-six: he came back a man of forty-three. With disappointment and suppressed wrath heavy in his heart, with isolation widening around him, he had passed that great meridian, the age of forty, when for every man the process of spiritual evolution stops, and he goes on thenceforward working out to the end a character that has become fixed and unalterable.

This change had come to Tiberius. It was a more mature, more decisive man who came back from studying the stars at Rhodes to the politics and wars of Rome. He felt that he could afford to wait. He settled down to do so, and for two years confined himself to his own private affairs. Then events, perhaps not wholly unforeseen, began to happen rapidly. Gaius Cæsar, who had been wounded in Armenia, died in Lycia. *Tiberius in Rome A. D. 2*

The death of Gaius entirely altered the balance of affairs in Rome. It was followed by the removal of Julia from Pandataria. She was permitted to live at Rhegium, on the Straits of Messina, and was allowed the liberty of the city, but was forbidden to leave it. She could do no more harm to her sons; and Augustus softened somewhat. Most of his private hopes and ambitions had now gone. The one remaining son of Julia, Agrippa Postumus, should have his chance; but what kind of man would he prove to be? *Death of Gaius Cæsar A. D. 4*

The strongest and wisest man cannot struggle against fate. Whatsoever Augustus himself could do, he had successfully done; but some issues were determined by a power greater than his own. Tiberius moved towards power almost automatically. The eldest son of Drusus, the young Germanicus,[1] was nineteen years old, a very promising young man, who showed signs of fulfilling the hopes that had been entertained of his father. But he was still untried. The only son of Tiberius, named Drusus after his uncle, was about the same age: a youth much less attractive. . . . It seemed as if the imperial stage were to be occupied by descendants of the house of Claudius Nero.

In succession to Gaius and Lucius Cæsar, Augustus adopted Agrippa Postumus and Tiberius as his heirs,— **Tiberius adopted by Augustus** the former, because he was the surviving male representative, through Julia, of Augustus' own blood; the latter, because he was the only man who was competent to bear the burden of empire. He had no enthusiasm concerning either of them. Of Tiberius, he said frankly that he did it for the good of the State. The difference in his feelings was perhaps represented by a difference in the legal process by which the adoption was carried out. Lucius and Gaius he had taken to be his sons by the quaint intimate ceremony of the penny and the balance, buying them from their father by the archaic form of private sale. Agrippa and Tiberius, who were grown men, he adopted by the more formal procedure in the *curiæ*. . . . Yet for all that, Augustus did not break his heart over Gaius and Lucius. Since the scandal of Julia, he had seen the truth without any more rosy illusions.

It began to be clear enough, also, who would step into the shoes of Augustus. . . . Tiberius took up his

---

[1] This is the only name by which we know him; but it was of course a family title of honour rather than a personal name. He was born May 24, B.C. 15. (Furneaux: *Introd.* p. 173. Note 31.)

new duties with grim and impassive efficiency. . . . At
the age of forty-five he divested himself of his status
as head of the family of Claudius Nero, and assumed
that of a son of the house of Cæsar. Tiberius Cæsar he
was henceforth in the eye of the law. . . . As part of
the conditions on which he was adopted by Augustus,
he in turn adopted his nephew Germanicus as his son
and heir.

Agrippa Postumus soon betrayed faults that dismissed
him from the reckoning. His tastes were degenerate;
his temper violent. He was Julia's youngest child, born
after his father's death, and during the reign of Gracchus as her lover. . . . He grew worse and worse. At
last it became clear that he was mentally defective. The
episode of Agrippa's adoption as a possible heir to the
principate was at length terminated by strong measures on the part of Augustus himself. Agrippa was sent
away to the island of Planasia, and a decree of the Senate
was obtained to make his confinement perpetual.
Agrippa was insane.

This was the end of the hopes of Augustus. He could
hardly endure mention of Agrippa and Julia. . . .

So the descendants of Scribonia passed off the stage, and
the descendants of Livia occupied it.

And yet—not quite. Although Augustus' policy of
dynastic marriages had produced nothing but results
wholly evil and fruitless, he could not learn from experience. He was impelled to make one more anxious attempt to circumvent destiny and to contrive that his
own descendants should one day sit in his seat. . . .

While Tiberius was preoccupied with the German campaigns, Augustus arranged the marriage of Agrippina, Julia's daughter, to Germanicus; and in so doing he planted one of the most deadly of the dragon's teeth that in due time were to ripen to calamitous harvest.

The marriage possessed points of ostensible merits that seemed to justify it. Agrippina was by far the best and ablest of the children of Julia. . . . She was about nineteen years old, and untouched by any of the scandals that had blackened her mother's name. . . . Since omniscience is not one of the attributes of humanity, Tiberius raised no objection.

Marriage of Agrippina and Germanicus

VII

It was after his adoption by Augustus that Tiberius entered upon his second and greatest career as a soldier. He once more took over the command on the Rhine; and after long years of quiescence the Rhine Army welcomed with joy a trusted commander who was also the destined successor of Augustus.

Tiberius became available for employment on the Rhine at a particularly opportune moment. The events of the next few years indicate that serious and extensive designs were on foot among the military chiefs. His anxiety to get away from Rhodes may have been due much more to his knowledge that such plans were being discussed, than to any fear of personal violence from the friends of Julia.[1] The two blank years which had elapsed since his return were none too long for the discussions and preparations which would have been necessary. A

Tiberius returns to the Rhine command A. D. 4

[1] The Chauci and Cherusci were "out" that year, and remained out.

great military machine such as the Roman army in Augustus' day cannot be put into action without the most careful preparation, and is certainly never put into action without serious cause. . . . What was contemplated now was a question not of mere punitive raiding, but of completing the work which Drusus had begun for the rectification of the northern frontier,—a task of great magnitude.

Tiberius had had no share in the decisions which he was appointed to execute. The political reasons that lay behind the military activity were reported and argued by the men who were in touch with affairs in the north; for these reasons involved the whole problem of an Elbe frontier as against a Rhine frontier,—a controversy in which we definitely know the side taken by Augustus and Tiberius. Both were opposed to adventures beyond the Rhine: both were doubtful of the possibility and even of the expedience of a conquest of Germany. Their view had been overborne by Drusus and the Rhine army; and now Augustus was faced with the results of a policy which Drusus had been successful in forcing upon him. He was compelled to accept and to act upon advice the necessity of which, in the circumstances, he could not deny, though he would have preferred to avoid the circumstances that created the necessity.

German war projected

A commander of sufficient prestige and experience had, however, been lacking. . . . It was therefore doubly convenient for Augustus—a prudent and economical financier who had to find the money—that at this point Tiberius became available. Not only had Tiberius the ability and the status required for such a war, but he shared the views of Augustus, and would ensure that they were not forgotten.

VIII

The root of the matter was that the Germans, once aroused to the necessity of exercising some degree of intelligence upon the problem of their own situation, were picking up ideas and methods with something of the industrious rapidity which the Japanese showed some nineteen hundred years later. The danger of the Elbe policy had always been that it involved shaking the Germans out of the comfortable sleep of their ancient tribal institutions, and out of local separation and petty jealousies into larger views. This danger was being realized to an alarming degree.

It arose as the children who had seen the armies of Tiberius and Drusus grew to manhood. Among the young hostages who had been sent to Rome after the reduction of Rætia, Vindelicia and Noricum was a child named Marbod, of the royal blood of the Suabi. His intelligence and personality had interested Augustus, and the boy had received the education of a Roman of his own class. On his return home, he had proceeded to put into practice some of the knowledge he had gained. . . . What he had acquired was a knowledge of the theory and methods of political organization.

We are so accustomed to the political conception of social organization that it is difficult to put ourselves imaginatively into the position of men to whom these things came as novel and revolutionary ideas. They

Changes in Germany

Marbod

struck a German of the first century much as the analogous conceptions of modern European society struck an oriental of the nineteenth. By their aid society might be refounded and remodelled, and a people which had dropped behind in the march of progress might be protected from absorption by the competitors who had exploited to better purpose the lessons of experience. . . . And they aroused the same kind of opposition from adherents of the old established order which similar novel ideas in all ages provoke; and with the same justification.

Marbod was the first of the kings of the north to experiment with the political conception of social organization, as distinguished from the old tribal system. He was not to be the last. His success was at first considerable. He already held a supremacy over the Suabian Marcomanni of the upper Elbe; and from this starting point he began the creation of a great kingdom centred in that very ancient Bohemian land which was one of the oldest centres of civilization in northern Europe. Its southern frontier rested on the Danube from the Raab, where Regensburg stands today, to the borders of modern Hungary, and it stretched for some indefinite but considerable distance inland.

The size of this kingdom of Marbod was less important than the principles it embodied. He organized and disciplined, as nearly on the Roman model as was practicable, an army of some seventy-five thousand men, horse and foot. Marbod had moreover an accurate understanding of the means by which he could establish his realm as a genuine and permanent reality. He did not

Power of Marbod

intend it to be a romantic adventure, but a sober enterprise conducted on the strictest business principles. His army was a defensive army. He had sat at the feet of Augustus,[1] and had gathered some shrewd ideas concerning the functions of war and the significance of peace.

Military importance of Marbod's power

Had the kingdom of Marbod been sufficiently far from the Roman frontier, it might have interested the Roman observer as an instance of the civilizing effect of Roman example upon a lower culture. . . . Unfortunately it lay, as the military chiefs at once noted, in a position particularly awkward in its relation both to Pannonia and to the new province of Germany. The essential facts about it were first that it lay in the upper part of the Elbe valley, so that the project of extending the Roman frontier to the Elbe, and carrying it thence to the Danube, must either be abandoned, or brought about at the expense of Marbod; and secondly, that it jutted out as a salient into the midst of the Roman frontier, and unless driven in it would command both Germany and Pannonia. . . . The military chiefs were no doubt prepared to grant the peaceable intentions of Marbod, and his good faith; but they had their own professional duties to attend to, which included the suppression of dangerous military threats against the Roman frontier. . . . Marbod could not possibly guarantee the character or the policy of his successors. . . . The military chiefs had probably no great difficulty in demonstrating the irresistible force of these contentions. Augustus and Tiberius, little as they wished for ad-

[1] Compare Suetonius: *Div. Aug.* XXV. 4.

ventures in the north, could scarcely hold out against them.

IX

The main outline of the plans which were decided upon seems to have been determined by the view that the principal difficulty in dealing with Marbod lay in possible revolt in Germany or along the Danube. Either the Germans or the Pannonians—or both—might seize the advantageous moment afforded by the diversion of Roman troops against Marbod. Tiberius, therefore, as a preliminary move, took up the Rhine command.

Political considerations

He crossed the Weser in force in A. D. 4 and reduced the Cheruscan tribes dwelling between the Weser and the Elbe. The intention seems to have been to take up matters exactly where Drusus had left them. The principal strategic conceptions followed by Drusus were repeated with some differences of detail. But a more powerful intelligence was at work. The Cherusci were the strongest and most dangerous of the German peoples bordering upon the Weser. Their subjugation paralysed the German resistance, and at the same time fulfilled the purpose of blocking communication up the Elbe. Tiberius did not return to the Rhine. He wintered at Aliso, the advanced post which Drusus had founded. It was the first time that a Roman army had wintered north of the Rhine.

Reduction of the Cherusci A. D. 4

His second German campaign was the most remarkable ever carried out by a Roman commander. He entered the basin of the lower Elbe, and reached a limit not to be touched again until the days of Charles the

The Chauci reduced A. D. 5

Great, seven hundred and fifty years later. The Chauci, (who reappear in later history as members of the great confederation of Saxon tribes) were reduced; the Langobardi, the future conquerors of Italy, submitted. A fleet acted in co-operation with the army. The mouth of the Weser had been the limit of the naval operations of Drusus, sixteen years earlier. Tiberius entered the Elbe mouth and brought up supplies by sea for his land army. The fleet even passed the Elbe and touched the Cimbric peninsula—Jutland as we now call it. The tribes north of the Elbe sent their envoys to declare their friendly feelings—Charudes and Cimbri of the far North, and Semnones, the "Swæfe" whom the Angles in later times fought. . . . Of the Angles we hear nothing.

Tiberius on the Elbe

The fierce and irrepressible romanticism of the north, which in later ages was to fling the votaries over wider seas than Tiberius ever sailed, peeps out in one story of that campaign. An aged champion—some earlier Starkad—came over the Elbe alone in his boat, for the express purpose of shaking Tiberius by the hand. He shook it, and retired. . . . As a symbol of many things that might fill many volumes, the tale has its interest.

X

Tiberius was not, however, engaged in a conquest of Germany: his two German campaigns in A. D. 4 and A. D. 5 were cautionary demonstrations in force. As such, they achieved their aim. The tribes of the far north were evidently impressed without being seriously alarmed: they welcomed in a sporting spirit an interesting visitor whom they did not really expect to stay, and they remained indifferent spectators of the more serious war which now developed.

The preparation for the operations against Marbod far transcended those for the German campaigns. Twelve legions, with auxiliaries, were intended to be employed. Tiberius advanced from Carnuntum, near modern Vienna, while Gnæus Sentius Saturninus, starting from Mainz, led the German divisions up 'the valley of the Main, whence, striking eastward through the Hercynian Wood, he entered the borders of Marbod's territory, to effect his junction with the Pannonian troops of Tiberius. Such movements as these argue a much better acquaintance with the geography of central Europe than the fashionable writers of Rome were able to transmit to later ages.

The operations were countermanded before they had developed. Not Germany but Illyria revolted. The temptation had been too great to resist. The legions were away, and were presumably well occupied in the war against Marbod. An order that the Pannonians and Dalmatians should send contingents to the war was the excuse that started the trouble. Revolt spread, and Rome was involved in a war at the very gates of Italy itself.

The Illyrian revolt was just too early for its own success. Tiberius was not yet hopelessly committed to his campaign. Marbod, ever prudent, was perfectly willing to listen to proposals for accommodation.[1] He agreed

The campaign against Marbod

Illyrian revolt

---

[1] There seems to be no evidence to connect Marbod with the Illyrian revolt, and it is possible that he had nothing whatever to do with it. . . . If so, he was singularly fortunate in the event. It is certainly remarkable that it should

to the terms which Tiberius offered. The legions were withdrawn. Saturninus hastened back to the Rhine, there to keep watch, while Tiberius made the best of his way to the seat of trouble in Pannonia.

Marbod was destined never to fall to Roman arms. He was to play his experiment out to the end, and to suffer the fate which so often befalls pioneers.

have chanced at a moment so convenient to him, and at a moment when he had so much interest in creating unrest among his near neighbours. The two years of the German campaigns afforded ample time for propaganda. Had Marbod been a modern statesman, historians might have taken a severer view of the probabilities, if only because they are more intimately acquainted with the motives and habits of their contemporaries.

THE ILLYRIAN FRONTIER.

R. DANUBE

(Vienna.)

Pannonia

Aquileia
Nauportus.
Tergeste.
Siscia.
R. DRAVE
R. SAVE
Sirmium.

Dalmatia

Salonae.

Dacia

R. DANUBE

Moesia

Naissus.

Adriatic

Italy

Sea

Dyrrachium.

Macedonia

Neapolis.
Brundusium.
Capri.
Apollonio

Approx. Scale.
0   50   100
English ⊏⊏⊏⊏⊏⊏ Miles.

CHAPTER V

THE REVOLT OF THE NORTH

I

THE Illyrian rising was a matter before which even Marbod sank into insignificance. The Pannonians had for more than a generation been trained in Roman discipline. Their leaders had in many cases a Roman education, and even some literary culture. The rising was therefore planned on a scale, and with an intelligence, which made it formidable. And, as Velleius tells us, never did any people translate its plans into action with more vigour. The Romans were caught unprepared. They were dealing with a race which, two hundred and fifty years later, was to give a succession of famous military emperors to Rome: and the ancestors of Claudius Gothicus, Aurelian, Probus, Diocletian and Maximian were worthy of their descendants.

The Illyrian Revolt A. D. 6

The Roman citizens scattered on business or official duty throughout Illyria were massacred in detail. A body of troops stationed in a remote part of the country was isolated and had fallen long before help could reach it. Three armies took the field; of which one was given the task of clearing up the country, while another entered Macedonia, and the third advanced on Itaiy by the line Nauportum-Tergeste.

Now Tergeste was but a short distance from Aquileia; and once there, the Illyrians would be on the

Alarm in Italy

straight high-road into Italy. The panic that fell upon
Italy left no one unaffected. Even Augustus was disturbed. He was overheard to say in the Senate that unless adequate steps were taken, the enemy might be in
sight of Rome in ten days' time. The remark seems to
have been repeated from mouth to mouth. Men knew
that it was true.

Panic will lend men wings and wisdom. The outburst
of patriotic service which followed might have touched
a heart of stone. Levies were held, veterans recalled to
the standards; men and women not liable to military
service were compelled to send freedmen to join up.
Germanicus was given the command. The new elements
were more distinguished perhaps for fervent zeal than
for military training; but at least the will was there.
Augustus left for Ariminum, to be near the seat of
danger.

II

The Illyrian revolt was not quite so simultaneous nor
so unanimous as it appeared to a Roman observer. It had
its anatomy. The first rising was in Dalmatia, where
Bato, the chief of the Desidiates, led the way by marching on Salonæ, the great coastal port. He failed to take
the town, and was badly wounded by a sling-stone; but
his lieutenants entered Macedonia and won a battle at
Apollonia, south of Dyrrachium. As soon as the campaign was thoroughly on foot, others rose in turn under
Pinnes. The revolt fell so naturally into organized sec-
tions, each of which pursued a strategic plan of its own,
that it is clear that the proceedings must have been con-

The
three
insurgent
armies

certed beforehand. The Pannonian tribe of the Breuci, under another Bato, were the third centre of revolt. They marched on Sirmium, the great fortress of eastern Pannonia, near the junction of the Save and Danube. Pinnes advanced upon Italy.

While Salonæ continued successfully to hold out against Bato Dalmaticus, Aulus Cæcina Severus, the legate of Mœsia, made a dash to hold Sirmium. In a fierce battle fought beneath its walls the Pannonians were defeated, and the town saved. Tiberius was already on the march from the north, dispatching the legate of Illyricum, M. Valerius Messallinus, ahead, and following with the main body.

Bato Dalmaticus was the real heart and soul of the revolt. Wounded as he was, he hurried north to meet Messalinus. At the first contact the latter was defeated. He had but one legion—the twentieth—and that at half-strength. Although isolated and surrounded by the enemy, he managed to trap them into an ambuscade with such effect that he broke up a force five times his own numbers.

Tiberius now arrived on the scene with the legions, in time to throw himself between the enemy and Italy. By prudent and cautious operations he pressed back the insurgent armies. They retreated south-eastward down the valley of the Save. Bato Dalmaticus thus effected a junction with Bato Breucianus, and the united armies took up a position on a mountain named Alma, near Sirmium. They were kept there by the skirmishing cavalry of King Rhœmetalces the Thracian, who was acting with Cæcina; but Cæcina himself could do nothing

The insurgents masked from Italy

effective against them. Tiberius was short of supplies owing to his rapid march south, and the Dacians and Sarmatians were raiding Mœsia; the season was moreover late for military operations; so Cæcina withdrew into Mœsia, while Tiberius retreated upon Siscia. He was wise. The winter was a very severe one. At Siscia Tiberius remained through the winter, preparing for next year's campaign.

III

In the spring, Germanicus and the Italian levies, dispatched by Augustus, arrived to relieve the legions of duty at Siscia.[1] Germanicus was entrusted with the command of the expeditionary force which was to enter Dalmatia. Meanwhile, the Mœsian army, strengthened with detachments of the Syrian troops, and with a powerful force of Thracian cavalry, advanced up the valley of the Drave. Its first contact with the two Batos was disastrous. The camp was surprised, the Thracian cavalry, which lay outside the ramparts, was stampeded, and the auxiliary troops were driven off the field. The legionaries themselves began to waver. But discipline and tradition kept them steady, and in spite of the loss of many of their officers they charged home and wrested victory from what seemed foredoomed defeat.

When the junction of the Mœsian army with the army of Tiberius was effected, the latter found himself in control of the largest Roman force that had been as-

Campaign of A. D. 7

Cæcina enters Pannonia

---

[1] At least, so it is to be presumed. It is not very probable that an improvised levy of veterans and freedmen would be given the difficult task of undertaking military operations against the hill-fortresses of Dalmatia.

sembled since the time of the civil wars. It must have
been a hundred and fifty thousand strong. The insurgents recognized that they could not hope to meet this
force in the field with any chance of success. Their policy was to avoid pitched battles: and their mobility en- Cæcina's
abled them to reduce the Pannonian section of the war junction with
to a difficult business of raiding and harrying. The Tiberius
Romans were obliged to adapt themselves to these tactics, and to disperse their forces to control the raiding
parties.

The competence of Tiberius as a soldier could have
endured no more searching test than this trial of his
ability to command a really great army in the circum- The
stances of a difficult and distracting war, the nearest great army
modern parallel of which is perhaps the South African
War of 1899–1902. There was no scope for spectacular
display. It was the sort of war which needed a sound and
trained professional soldier with a gift for infinite
drudgery. . . . During these Illyrian campaigns, which
were the supreme military achievement of Tiberius, we
obtain one of the most vivid side-lights upon his personality.

G. Velleius Paterculus, a soldier who became a historian—as many soldiers have become, both before and
after his day—served through the Illyrian and German
campaigns under Tiberius, and left record of them.
The dithyrambs of Velleius have the advantage of being founded on personal experience, as against the mere
hearsay of Tacitus and Suetonius; and Velleius is very
dithyrambic indeed.

We see once more, though in very different circumstances, the sober and prosaic man who visited the sick in Rhodes. Not one man of any rank, says Velleius, with pardonable fervour, fell sick without having his welfare attended to as carefully as if Tiberius had nothing else to do. A horsed ambulance was ready for those who needed it. The private carriage of Tiberius was pressed into the service. Velleius records with pride that he himself rode in it. The personal physicians of Tiberius, his kitchen, his own bathing equipment, all were freely employed for the benefit of the sick. . . . Tiberius, alone of commanders, invariably travelled austerely on horse-back: he sat at table, when entertaining guests, instead of reclining. All of which Velleius thinks most pleasant as an experience, and remarkable for the kindness it showed.

Tiberius did not criticize those who took a different view of their responsibilities. He had, in matters of general discipline, that very great virtue in high commanders—a conveniently blind eye. He frequently advised, occasionally reproved, but rarely punished. . . . And this is a description which we meet, in one form or another, in all ages of the world's history; it is a portrait of the good officer.

Velleius bears testimony to another aspect also of the character of Tiberius. He was careful of the lives of his men. As a commander, his steady principle was safety first.

IV

The heavy work of Germanicus and the mountain expedition provided the main results of the year's campaigning. Dalmatia, the seat of the revolt, was gradually reduced. The Dalmatian mountain-fortresses were of great strength, well defended and well supplied. Their capture was an arduous task. At Rætinium the defenders set fire to the town in the hope of involving the Romans in its destruction. . . . Famine, naturally enough, began to spread throughout Illyricum. The land was being left uncultivated. Pestilence inevitably followed, and division of opinion began. Many of the insurgents wished to surrender. They were restrained by threats. A chief named Scenobardus, who had offered to surrender to Manius Ennius, the commander at Siscia, was so far intimidated that he withdrew his offer. . . . Famine seems to have prevailed even in Italy. . . . When, in the following spring, the important fortress of Arduba fell, there was a struggle within the walls between those who wished to surrender and those who refused all compromise. The former were defeated; and the women of the victorious party celebrated their triumph by leaping with their children into the flames that destroyed Arduba.

*Famine
A. D. 8*

The famine forced the issue. Pinnes and Bato Breucianus were driven to hazard a battle; and since the issue could hardly be in doubt, Bato Breucianus insured himself beforehand by entering into negotiations with Tiberius. The arrangement made was that he should surrender Pinnes, and in return should be confirmed in his position as chief of the Breuci. . . . The great battle of the Bathinus decided the fate of the Illyrian revolt.

*Battle
of the
Bathinus
Aug. 3rd.*

Germanicus himself was the messenger who carried the happy news to Augustus at Ariminum. . . . Augustus at length felt free to return to Rome, where his arrival was celebrated with enthusiasm.

V

But Bato Dalmaticus was of tougher metal, and he brought swift vengeance with him to Pannonia. Bato Breucianus, doubtful of his own position with his subject tribes, set out on a round of visits to take hostages from them for his own security. Bato Dalmaticus heard the news and set a trap for the traitor. Caught, kidnapped and brought to trial before an open-air court of Dalmatian fighting-men, Bato Breucianus was condemned to death, and the sentence was carried out on the spot. The Pannonians were stimulated to make another rising against the Romans. The legate Silvanus defeated the Breuci, and brought other tribes to submission by peaceable persuasion, until Bato Dalmaticus gave up the task and retired home. Harried by Silvanus, the Pannonians submitted. Nothing was left of the Pannonian revolt save a few desperate men who still kept to the hills.

Dalmatia remained: and it was the task of Tiberius to clear up the war in Dalmatia. Upon his arrival he found the troops in a restless mood, tired of the war, and much more anxious to finish it off at any cost than to see it drag on further. He therefore divided his forces. One corps was placed under Silvanus, another under Marcus Lepidus; the third, Tiberius commanded in person.

Velleius [1] has left us a graphic though brief record of

Reduction
of
Dalmatia
A. D. 9

---

[1] II. cxv. This Lepidus is to be carefully distinguished from Manius Aemilius Lepidus.

the sweeping movement conducted by M. Lepidus, "through the midst of tribes who were as yet uninfluenced and unweakened by the reverses of war, and therefore still ardent and aggressive; after struggles in which he had to contend against the difficulties of the country and the resistance of the enemy, and after inflicting heavy punishment on those who opposed him, by the devastation of fields, burning of houses, and slaying of inhabitants." The powerful tribes of Peristæ and Desidiates, in their almost impregnable strongholds among the narrow mountain ravines—expert fighters all—were at last reduced, though only by a process of very nearly exterminating them. . . . Silvanus also is recorded as having performed his work with success.

The corps of Tiberius and Germanicus took up the more difficult task of running Bato Dalmaticus to earth. He was now "on the run," and the pursuit led them over the whole country. He finally went to ground in the fortress of Andetrium, not far from Salonæ. It was a little difficult to distinguish between besiegers and besieged. Andetrium was built upon a rocky height, hard of access and encircled with deep ravines and mountain torrents. The town was well supplied, whereas the communications of Tiberius were precarious. He was in some doubt as to the prudent course to follow. *Pursuit of Bato Dalmaticus*

Bato, however, was by now feeling the strain. He sent to inquire after possible terms of surrender. The inquiry convinced Tiberius that the situation of those inside the fortress must be at least as uncomfortable as his own. He determined to assault.

The storming party climbed the mountain while

Siege
of
Andetrium

Tiberius, from a convenient perch, superintended the reserves. The defenders rolled down stones with great effect, but the storming party went on climbing until it got to hand-strokes. In the sub-ærial struggle which ensued—a skull-dragging contest of the most determined description—Tiberius fed in his reserves with such judgment that the defenders at last grew exhausted. Just as they had reached the right point of exhaustion, they were attacked in the rear by crag-climbers who had worked round the mountain paths during the battle. They could not retreat into the fortress. They fled, and were hunted down in detail among the woods and rocks. The exasperated legionaries gave no quarter.

Bato finally sent his son Sceuas to Tiberius, with an undertaking to surrender if his life were spared. Tiberius pledged his word. Bato came in during the night, and on the following day was brought before him. Bato asked nothing for himself. . . . He does not seem to have placed much reliance upon the promise made to him. But he spoke at length on behalf of his people, which would appear to have been the object of his surrender. Finally, he held out his head to receive the executioner's stroke.

Bato
surrenders
to
Tiberius

Tiberius only asked him why his people had revolted, and had fought so desperately against the Romans.

"It is your own doing," he replied. "To guard your flocks you Romans send not shepherds, nor even dogs, but wolves." [1]

---

[1] This phrase seems to have stuck in the mind of Tiberius, and may have been the origin of his dry message to the governor of Egypt, years later: "I want my sheep shorn, not flayed."

Tiberius sent him to Ravenna, where he dwelt until he died.

The Illyrian revolt was over. It had been a singularly expensive war. Very little booty was taken during the campaigns; there was very little to take; while the cost of maintaining the troops was immense. About fifteen legions and a large number of auxiliary troops had been employed. Some people thought it the hardest war fought by the Romans since the war of Hannibal; and though all comparisons of this kind are easy to make and difficult to sustain, there may be a certain truth in it. . . . Never, at least, were so many honours bestowed. Tiberius was granted a triumph; he and Germanicus were saluted with the title Imperator, and besides other honours had two triumphal arches erected to them in Pannonia. Augustus would not allow more. Most of the divisional generals—Lepidus and Messalinus among them—received the triumphal ornaments. . . . But the triumph of Tiberius was not destined to be celebrated just yet.

VI

The secondary effects of such catastrophes as the Illyrian war are often more serious than the primary. The repercussion of the events set going by Bato Dalmaticus went echoing through the northern frontiers of Rome, and did not die down until, many years later, Septimius Severus died at York; perhaps they have not died out yet. While the revolt was at its height, and Tiberius was fully occupied in dealing with it, a decision fraught with the most momentous consequences

Effects of the Illyrian Revolt

was taken at Rome. Publius Quintilius Varus was appointed to the governorship of Germany, and sent to the Rhine commissioned to begin the task of Romanizing the Germans.

The instructions of Varus seem to have authorized him to introduce into Germany such arrangements as would bring the new dependency up to the normal standard of a Roman province. It was, to say the least, a dangerous decision to make while the Illyrian revolt—itself due to a premature attempt to lift the province to the normal level of taxation—was still undecided. The drain on the resources of the imperial fisc certainly required that every possible expedient should be employed to raise taxation wheresoever it could safely be imposed; but no money so acquired could compensate for the danger involved.

Change of Policy in Germany

The appointment of Varus meant a departure from the principles which had hitherto marked the dealings of Augustus with the Germans, and a reversal of the policy of Tiberius, who had been responsible for the settlement of the province after the death of Drusus. On its personal side, moreover, it was an extraordinary lapse of judgment. Varus was no soldier; and he was given the most important and difficult military command in the empire. He was an easy-going man, none too sound on the side of honesty; [1] somewhat of a blockhead and somewhat of a shark; and he was sent to manage men who, whatever their virtues might be, were

P. Quintilius Varus

---

[1] He had been governor of Syria; and it was said of him that when he arrived there Syria was rich and he was poor, and when he left it, Syria was poor and he was rich.

then, as they are today, singularly astute, prompt and ruthless, and swift to resent the presence of a man whom they did not respect. . . . They seem, after a slight pause, to have welcomed him with sinister pleasure and false smiles. The conversations which precede a conspiracy were at once set on foot. The opportunity was too good to miss.

The head of this movement was Irmin, one of the younger chiefs of the Cherusci.

VII

Irmin was of the same generation and apparently of the same age as Marbod; and like the young Suabian Irmin he was deeply influenced by the new ideas which contact with Rome was spreading throughout Germany. But he was a very different type of man, and perhaps a more typical German. He did not share the cautious temperament of Marbod. He was more of a fighting man and more of an intriguer, thinking and acting with a stronger sense of nationality, viewing matters from a less purely political and more distinctly gentile standpoint, and more interested than Marbod in preserving German independence and German tradition. The only common ground he shared with Marbod was a disposition to turn to new methods. His father-in-law, Segestes, was irreconcilably opposed to him, and firmly upheld the principle of friendship with Rome; but the motive of Segestes seems to have been the wish to keep the old tribal system intact, and to avoid the risk of its destruction by war. Irmin was prepared, like Marbod, to adopt a new system inspired by Roman models, and to sacrifice the old system in order to preserve the living reality of independence.

If the conquest of Germany by Drusus did nothing else, it destroyed the prestige of the old tribal system which had failed to withstand him in the field, and it impelled the younger men to learn the political conceptions which seemed to create so infinitely more powerful a social organism. Marbod represented one form of the new movement. He would have been willing to found a new state without regard for the gentile link. Irmin represented another form. He wished to found a political state while still recognizing and preserving the gentile link; that is to say, he was feeling his way towards the principle of nationality.

The New Movement in Germany

Both Irmin and Marbod were men who adventured boldly along new paths. The paths were to prove longer than they thought; many a generation was to pass before the ideas which they mooted became established, and were proved sound in practice; far worse and weaker men succeeded where they failed; but their especial interest to us is that they stand at the distant fountain head of a process which transformed the old local tribalism of northern Europe into the nationalism of today.

VIII

The efforts of the conspirators to lull Varus into a false sense of security were admirably successful. They judged their man well, and indulged his personal vanity and official pride to the full of its appetite. He proceeded

to civilize the conquered barbarians with a firm hand.
He assessed the province for taxation; his judicial decisions as governor ignored local usage and tribal law,
to the fury and stupefaction of men who, knowing no
other law, thought that they were being denied the
benefit of law altogether; and the conspirators saw to
it that neither party should be disillusioned. It took two
years to bring the mass of the Germans to the breaking
point; but by that time Irmin and his friends had not
only the Cherusci, but the fighting Chatti, the Marsi
and the Bructeri ready to leave the mark as soon as the
word should be given. It was necessary to hasten, for
the Illyrian revolt was dying slowly out, and before long
the legions would once more be free.

The governor's summer progress brought him, with
three legions, to quarters on the Weser, somewhere up
near Minden. The principal conspirators were present
in his camp, on the best of terms with him, and con-
stantly dining at his table. Their conversation gave him
a conviction of security against which the warnings of
others were in vain. The summer was late when, in accordance with his regular program, he made ready
for his return to the Rhine. There was no difficulty
before him. His line of communication with Aliso, at
the head of the valley of the Lippe, secured his line of
march; and from Aliso the way was easy to Castra
Vetera. The conspirators had their plan ready. At the
last moment before he started a message was brought
that a tribe, well off the line of march, had risen. An
experienced soldier might have scented danger. Not so
Varus. He was persuaded that he could make a circuit

to include this rising on his way home. He was definitely warned by Segestes, the Cheruscan chief. Varus dismissed the warning. He had confidence in his friends.

Having now made sure that he should have no excuse whatever in the event of mishap, he set out on his march.

The calculations of the conspirators worked out to perfection. All the preparations had been made. They accompanied Varus sufficiently far upon his way to make certain that he was walking into the trap. Then they excused themselves upon the ground that they had better collect their own levies in order to give him support. Even then Varus does not seem to have suspected their good faith. Their levies were as a matter of fact close at hand. The word was passed. While the auxiliary troops garrisoning the tribal districts were massacred by a simultaneous concerted rising, the main body of the Germans pressed after Varus.

The German Revolt A. D. 9

At some point between the Ems and the Lippe, north east of Aliso, the legions, engaged on their wild-goose chase, were struggling through a rough and trackless country of hill and forest and marsh, where, encumbered with a heavy baggage train and many noncombatants, including women and children, they were obliged to cut their way forward, felling the great forest trees, laying down roads, bridging ravines as they went. The column of route, disordered and strung out by this necessity, straggled still more when bad weather broke in violent gale and rain; the ground became a slippery quagmire; falling branches added to the confusion.

And now the Germans, expected as friends, fell upon them as foes. The attack came from all sides. Familiar with the ground, the Germans had no difficulty in striking where they would, at first with missile weapons, and then, encouraged by the feeble resistance, hand to hand. The column was hopelessly disordered by the first unexpected attack. It was never adequately pulled together. The legionaries, the non-combatants and the wagons were inextricably mixed; and the legionaries were in no position to concentrate against their assailants.

It was just such a march as General Braddock (a far abler soldier than Publius Quintilius Varus) found too much for him. The best place possible, considering the circumstances, was chosen for a camp that night, and an effort was made to get the column into proper order. In the morning most of the wagons were either burned or abandoned, together with all baggage that was not absolutely indispensable. The second day's march was therefore begun in more promising circumstances. The column forced its way temporarily out of the forest-land into open country. It was necessary, however, to fight a way through another forest; and here the worst losses were incurred. The troops were penned into narrow ground where any kind of concerted manœuvring was difficult. The column marched all night, for in the morning it was still advancing. A fresh downpour of rain and a high gale came with the dawn. Progress became impossible; even foot-hold was difficult. Rain-drenched weapons could scarcely be handled; the bull's-hide shields of the legionaries were soaked, with

The
March
of
Varus

consequences that can easily be guessed. Few positions could be more pitiable than that of Italians lost in a North European forest in such weather. The Germans naturally suffered much less, and could choose their ground. Their numbers also had greatly increased. The news of success and the prospect of plunder were bringing up all who had at first hung back. . . . The legionaries made an attempt to dig an entrenchment. It was destined never to be finished. The end was clearly enough at hand. Varus, wounded and hopeless, killed himself. His principal officers followed his example, rather than fall alive into the hands of the Germans. Vala Numonius, the prefect of the cavalry, abandoned the column with all his remaining men, and left the infantry to their own resources. He was probably himself wounded, for he died during his march to the Rhine, but his troopers made good their escape.

Disaster of Teutoberg

The exhausted survivors, thus abandoned, and without leaders, gave up the struggle. Many were butchered without resistance; some fell on their own weapons; a few were captured. Twenty thousand men, and three legionary eagles (those of the XVIIth, XVIIIth and XIXth legions) were lost in the so-called "Battle of Teutoberg." Only the cavalry and a small number of foot-soldiers escaped and reached the Roman lines. The whole of the lands between the Rhine and the Elbe, which Drusus had with such difficulty and at such expense conquered, was lost by the Romans.

Destruction of the Roman Army

The fate of the prisoners was terrible. Many were crucified or buried alive, or offered up as blood offerings to the dark gods of the German groves. Some were

Germany lost

afterwards ransomed by their friends. Roman discipline
was not mild towards men who allowed themselves to
become prisoners of war, but as an act of grace the
imperial government permitted the ransoms to be paid,
with the proviso that the men concerned should not
return to Italy.

IX

The worst possibilities of the battle of Teutoberg
were avoided. The fall of Varus had left Castra Vetera The
open to the enemy. As soon as he heard the news, Lucius Rhine
held
Nonius Asprenas at Mainz made a rapid march to the
point of danger, and reached it not only in time to save
the town, but also to save Lucius Cædicius who was shut
up in Aliso. Cædicius, in turn, held Aliso until it was
too late for the Germans to gain Castra Vetera before
the arrival of Asprenas. They could not take a fortified
place, and they suffered heavy losses from the archers
who defended Aliso. When at last they realized their
mistake, the lost time could not be made good. But the
diversion drew off most of the German force. A blockading detachment was left to watch the Romans.

The position of Cædicius, isolated, with many women Cædicius
and children, nearly a hundred miles from the Rhine, isolated
in
was disquieting. He kept close within the fortifications, Aliso
and waited for relief. The blockading force, confident
that he could not hold out indefinitely, waited for him
to make the inevitable break-away. Though the Germans were invisible, their pickets watched the roads.
The supplies gradually diminished and gave out, and no
relieving army appeared. Cædicius was obliged to make

the resolution which the Germans were patiently await-
ing.

He spun out the time until the move could be made
under favourable conditions. The garrison was pinched
with hunger before a dark and stormy night afforded
the circumstances required. Then the Roman column

He runs the blockade crept forth on its perilous attempt. The troops who
led the way and brought up the rear were greatly out-
numbered by the non-combatant civilians and the
women and children in the centre of the column. . . .
They got past the first and the second pickets without
mishap; but when they reached the third, the trouble
began. The women and children, hungry, tired and cold,
and frightened at the dark and at the disappearance of
the soldiers in front of them,[1] lifted up agonized voices
and called for them to come back. The alarm was instantly given, and the Germans descended upon them

The column caught by the Germans with promptitude. Though the historian Dion Cassius
does not actually say so, the story necessarily implies
that the Germans arrived with torches and flares which
enabled them to see what they were doing. All would
have been lost if they had not immediately rushed for
the baggage—the only pay they were ever likely to
get for their trouble. This gave everyone the chance
to bolt into the darkness without being followed.

On realizing the situation of affairs, some genius
among the soldiers—possibly Cædicius himself, for the

---

[1] A noble story of adventure is evidently lost behind the brief phrases of
Dion Cassius. One would like to know the precise means by which the pickets
were passed! The tales of this escape from Aliso brings a modern man far nearer
to the ancient Roman than all the tales of high politics and full-dress battles
that have come down to us.

order must have been given by an officer—directed the trumpeter to sound the double-quick-march. The two-edged ruse was successful. . . . Recognizing the signal, and convinced that Asprenas himself must be at hand, the Germans stood to their arms and made no attempt to follow, while the Roman column rallied to the sound, and resumed its march. Before the Germans could realize the truth, communication had been established with Castra Vetera; a relief force sent by Asprenas was really at hand, and the column was struggling safely home.[1]

The garrison of Aliso was saved, and the Rhine frontier remained intact. The people of Gaul could sleep in their beds.

Escape of the Romans

X

The suicide of Varus had been well advised. The loss of the province of Germany was an indiscretion which might have been excused, but to throw away twenty thousand men of a long-service army was a crime for which, save death, there was no secular expiation. For Augustus the blow was doubly severe. All the efforts he had made—frequently against his better judgment—had been rendered useless, and to the actual loss, serious as it was, disgrace was added. He, who had been so proud of recovering the standards which Crassus had lost at Carrhæ, had himself lost three! . . . He had some kind of nervous breakdown. It was rumoured that for months the cold, self-contained man cut neither his hair nor his beard, and had struck his head against

Feelings of Augustus

---

[1] One hopes that Cædicius got an appropriate crown for this! Asprenas rose to be Governor of Africa and doubtless deserved it.

a door, crying: "Varus! give back those legions!" . . .
This was only gossip.[1] . . . But Augustus had every
reason for taking it hard. The worst of it was that he
could not absolve himself from blame.

Rome at large, fatigued by its exertions over the Illyrian revolt, was somewhat indifferent. It is unlikely
that anyone had money invested in Germany, and
in such cases men are liable to take an optimistic view
of the misfortunes of others. Augustus ordered recruits
to be at once enrolled. They came forward very slowly.
A mixed assortment of reinforcements, including retired veterans and ambitious freedmen, was hastily
drafted to the Rhine.

Reinforcements rushed to the Rhine *(margin note)*

The rapidity of Asprenas and the skill of Cædicius
had, however, saved the day. What the consequences
might have been if, with the legions concentrated in
Illyricum and the revolt barely quelled, the Germans
had broken the Rhine frontier, no man can say.[2] It
was an opportunity such as seldom falls to the lot of
earnest men. . . . But when, the body of Varus having
been mutilated and partly burned by the Germans, his
head was sent to Marbod, the latter dispatched it on to
Augustus, who had it decently buried in the family
tomb. . . . Marbod to some extent held the key of
the situation; and he very definitely refused to act with
Irmin.

Marbod remains neutral *(margin note)*

It was, of course, Tiberius (the universal resort in
time of trouble) who was called upon to clear up the

---

[1] Suetonius (*Div. Aug.* XXIII). Beside, Augustus was notoriously irregular in
his patronage of the barber.

[2] Simultaneous action between the Germans and the Illyrians had been the
prospect to fear. (Suetonius *Tib.* XVII.)

damage. In the following spring he proceeded to the Rhine, and spent the year in reorganizing the frontier, and in restoring the discipline and *moral* of the army. He was known as a man of independent judgment, who consulted his own sense of fitness rather than public opinion; but he showed, on this occasion, more than customary interest in the views and opinions of others. He took the advice of a board of counsellors, whose recommendations he adopted. . . . On matters of ordinary military routine he is little likely to have needed its help. This board had another significance. He was examining into the whole problem of the north-western frontier; and the conclusions which he drew, and reported to Augustus, were revealed later.

Tiberius sent to report
A. D. 10

He was joined, next year, by Germanicus, who was introduced to the country and the army in which his father had run that brief but immortal career which men still vividly remembered. There was a hint of augury in the advent, at this moment, of Germanicus. He might be the man destined to carry on to its end the work of Drusus. . . . Tiberius made a demonstration in force across the Rhine, with the object of creating a moral impression among the tribesmen, and possibly of giving Germanicus a little experience of the country.

A vivid glimpse of Tiberius as a soldier has survived from this campaign. We see him personally inspecting the loads of the transport wagons, to make sure that the restrictions he had ordered were observed; cashiering the legate of a legion, for sending soldiers across the Rhine to protect his freedmen on a hunting expedition;

Campaign of Tiberius in Germany
A. D. 11

sleeping in the open; taking his meals on the ground. He issued his orders for the day in writing, on the previous evening, and any officer in doubt of their meaning was invited to consult him personally at any time, night or day. . . . The good omen in which he placed his chief reliance was to see his lamp burn out at night as he worked. . . . He dryly observed that his Claudian ancestors had found it reliable. . . . It was a very Claudian kind of portent!

Impending changes

But a change of times and days was impending. If the work of Drusus were to be restored, Tiberius could not be the man to do it. . . . The report he had made to Augustus on the question of the Rhine was not yet known: but in any case his work began to lie decisively elsewhere. The Illyrian war was his last great campaign. . . . Augustus was rapidly ageing, and began to make definite preparations for his own departure from the stage. Germanicus returned to Rome to take up the consulship, which detained him there throughout A. D. 12. He was then duly qualified to relieve Tiberius of the command on the Rhine. Early in A. D. 13 he arrived to take over the command, and Tiberius, turning his back for ever upon the northern frontier, left for Italy, which he was never again to leave.

Germanicus takes the Rhine command

Germanicus was inactive during his first year in the command. Perhaps he was feeling his way, ascertaining what he had to deal with, and learning what others had to tell him. . . . Perhaps the verdict of Tiberius on the Rhine problem was having its effect. . . . There is a hint in the tension of the air that everyone was waiting upon the fragile old statesman, so frail yet so long-lived, so wonderful and so famous, who was gathering together his papers and making ready to abandon his task to younger men.

CHAPTER VI

TIBERIUS CÆSAR

I

TIBERIUS had reached a dividing ridge in his life, and from this time onward all his rivers began to flow another way. His career as a soldier lay definitely behind him. He was never again to see the sword drawn in war: never again to see the great mountains or the open road. He came from the disciplined, orderly, open-air life of armies and frontiers to the crowded and competitive life of the great metropolis. For many years now his absence from this latter had been the rule; his presence in it the exception. . . . He cannot have enjoyed the change. A man who has grown used to the effortless wheels of command and obedience seldom enjoys the heavy friction of civil life. To return again to a world in which the effort of mental readjustment to others is a continuous unbroken process, without cessation or holiday, does not make for increased happiness. There is no reason to suppose that Tiberius was conscious of any increase.

The prospect of friction was not diminished by the terms on which Augustus had adopted Tiberius and by that means co-opted him as his successor in the principate. Whether the reason were the family sentiment of Augustus or whether there were deeper reasons, the stipulation was that Tiberius should pass over his own son Drusus, and adopt Germanicus, who was married to Julia's daughter. The condition was a hard one. Tiberius had accepted it. With that impartiality which throughout his life he showed in most things, he never pushed Drusus unnecessarily forward. . . . But the plan had its obvious disadvantages. It would direct the suspicion of enemies and half-friends continually against Tiberius. If his own anticipations were confirmed, he would be accused of having created the facts he anticipated. If ill hap should chance to Germanicus, he would be accused of complicity. If any wild combination of circumstances arose to the injury of Germanicus—and human life is full of wild combinations of circumstances—the eyes of mankind would instantly be turned upon Tiberius. All this was certain beforehand. It needed no preternatural astuteness to foresee it. We shall see how far this prospect was fulfilled.

Prospects of the future

During the year of the first consulship of Germanicus, Augustus gave his formal intimation of the arrangements that had been made. He addressed a letter to the Senate, recommending Germanicus to its protection, and itself to the protection of Tiberius. This year, too, the Triumph of Tiberius was celebrated. He was accompanied by all the divisional generals of his Illyrian campaigns, who had been awarded the triumphal ornaments. Augustus and the Senate met him at the Porta Triumphalis, and Tiberius fell at the feet of his nominal father before entering the city. It was a generous triumph. Bato Dalmaticus, after treading that road which for so many foes of Rome ended in the Tullianum, was dispatched to Ravenna, handsomely pen-

Triumph of Tiberius A. D. 12

sioned, there to meditate over his remarkable discovery of a man who kept his word. The people were feasted at a thousand tables. A gratuity of three hundred sesterces was paid to each of the men who had fought in the Illyrian and German wars. . . . As a further mark of thanks Tiberius restored and re-dedicated the temple of Concord and the temple of Castor and Pollux the divine Twin Brethren, in the joint names of himself and his brother Drusus.

When, after he had surrendered the Rhine command to Germanicus, Tiberius arrived in Rome, the serious business was begun. The two principal bases on which the authority of the princeps was founded were the proconsular imperium and the tribunician power. The former gave him his administrative control in the provinces, while the latter gave him his political power in Rome. The emperor could delegate his imperium. Augustus had already done so: but the validity of such a delegation of course expired at his own death. He therefore caused a formal measure to be passed through the Senate bestowing on Tiberius the full proconsular imperium, equal to and co-ordinate with his own. Tiberius was at the same time invested with the tribunician power for life. By this means it was ensured that the authority of Tiberius should not be affected by the death of Augustus. As soon as the latter should pass away, Tiberius would step forward equipped to take his place. There would be no real interregnum. . . . Tiberius was also appointed chairman of the senatorial committee which, during the last six months of Augustus' life, when he

Process of Co-optation

was more or less of an invalid, met at his house and transacted business in the Senate's name. His first experience of the actual exercise of his future office was thus acquired under the guidance of Augustus himself.

It had moreover been arranged that a census, the periodical scrutiny of qualifications (which was practically the issue of a writ of *Quo Warranto* to every individual in the Roman dominions) should be held by Augustus and Tiberius conjointly. This gave them the opportunity of making a thorough review together of the whole state of the empire, and of every important person in it. A full account of their conferences, if we possessed it, would make remarkably interesting reading. . . . No emperor ever entered upon power more carefully coached, more thoroughly trained or more completely in possession of the counsel of his predecessor, than did Tiberius; and yet there hung about the proceedings of Augustus a vague hint of the same distrust which had made him stay in Gaul during the governorship of Tiberius, though he left it during the governorship of Drusus. It was never possible to distinguish between the paternal care and the personal distrust of Augustus. To the last it remained baffling and puzzling.

The margin note: The conjoint censorial review

The census having been held, Tiberius proceeded on his way to Pannonia, where he was to take up the general command. He never reached it. Augustus had parted from him at Beneventum, and had then taken the road to the milder air and sunshine of Campania. Messen-

The margin note: Last illness of Augustus

gers overtook Tiberius. The emperor was attacked by dysentery and lay dying. Tiberius raced back to Nola. Time was all-important. He arrived just in time [1] to receive the last words of the man who was the first, and remained the greatest, of all the Roman emperors.

Augustus was tired. After Tiberius had left him, he made one of his half-bantering comments. He did not envy the unlucky Roman people who would have to deal with that very solid and deliberate man.[2] . . .

Death of Augustus A. D. 14

He died at Nola on the nineteenth day of August—his own month—in the year A. D. 14.

II

Tiberius acted with promptitude. He was fully equipped with the power necessary to deal with the situation. He at once, in virtue of his tribunician power, **Tiberius assumes power** summoned a meeting of the Senate; in virtue of his proconsular power he gave the countersign to the Prætorian guard, and sent out the dispatches communicating the news to the Army. He acted as though he were already emperor and princeps—and in actual fact he was. He still had to pass the critical test of gaining the authoritative assent and acceptance of the Senate.

Quick as he was, there were foes who were no less quick. He had acted promptly from instinct: he did not at first realize the full range of the battle he was about

---

[1] The importance of this point is that on it depends the question whether or not he received any communications from Augustus just before the latter died. There were various matters which Augustus would probably hold back until the very last.

[2] Subsequent events gave the particular phrase used by Augustus a meaning which he can never consciously have intended it to bear. His remark was only the kind of comment which King Charles might have made after an interview with a particularly dour specimen of the Elect.

to fight. No sooner was Augustus dead, than a ship had set sail for Planasia to secure possession of Agrippa Postumus, the only surviving son of Julia. He was at once slain by his gaoler. . . . When the officer who was responsible arrived to report his action, Tiberius replied that no such order had been issued by him, and that the matter must be referred to the Senate. . . . It was the first of those mysteries of ambiguous and conflicting evidence which were to haunt his reign. The matter was never referred to the Senate. Tacitus tells us that Sallustius Crispus sent the letter which authorized the deed, and that he now went to Livia and expostulated with her at the idea of consulting the Senate at all on such a question. Tacitus does not tell us by whose authority Sallustius sent the order, nor when it was sent; but he leaves us to imagine that either Livia or Tiberius was responsible, or that both were. . . . In any case, the matter was allowed to drop, for by degrees the meaning of the attempt to seize the person of Agrippa became formidably clear.[1] . . . Suetonius says that it was not known who really authorized the death of Agrippa: the officer certainly received a letter, but whether it was written by Augustus before his death, or whether Livia afterwards wrote it in his name, and whether Tiberius was cognizant of it, were never discovered.[2]

Murder of Agrippa Postumus

The mystery unravelled

[1] See *post*, p. 211.

[2] The story is told in the text as Tacitus (*Ann* I. 6.) and Suetonius (*Tiberius* XXII) relate it; but it can be "restored" with some probability of achieving the truth. The officer had a standing order of Augustus, issued to him for his protection in case of necessity, authorizing him, in the event of attempted rescue, to slay Agrippa. The officer acted on this order. But when Tiberius, a legally minded man, was confronted with it, he saw it to be inadequate. An

The death of Agrippa removed Julia's last hope of reigning in the person of one of her sons. There was still Agrippina; but the reign of Agrippina could never mean so much to Julia, and it was still too remote a prospect to have much meaning for her. Julia seems from this time

Death of Julia

to have fallen into a decline. Her partisans declared that Tiberius allowed her to starve to death. The fact seems to have been that Tiberius steadily and completely ignored her existence; and her partisans, although they inveighed against Tiberius, did not go to the length of subscribing on Julia's behalf anything more solid than indignation.

But there was another person, whose existence Tiberius was far from ignoring. T. Sempronius Gracchus, the author of more catastrophe than most men can claim the credit of starting, had been for fourteen years in exile on the island of Cercina, near the African coast.

Execution of Gracchus

He does not seem to have been greatly surprised—nor need we be—that a party of soldiers was not long in

order of Augustus might create rather awkward precedents unless he himself endorsed it; but as Agrippa had been incarcerated on a commitment by the Senate, it was doubtful if his own endorsement could give it any legal validity. Sallustius went to Livia and pointed out that this way of regarding the case was pure destruction for them all; for their hands would be hopelessly tied by such a formal legal view. When Augustus obtained the decree of the Senate, he had never meant it to tie his own hands. Livia, who could answer for the genuineness of the order, therefore went to Tiberius and insisted on his endorsement being given to it. Tiberius was unwilling to accept responsibility for a deed he had not done and could not legally justify; he was very anxious, for reasons that appear in the sequel, not to alienate the Senate by disregarding its constitutional position; so, as the arguments of Sallustius were on their own ground unanswerable, the matter simply dropped, and the real truth remained in convenient obscurity. This would fully account for the statements of Tacitus and those of Suetonius.

arriving from Julia's husband.[1] They found Gracchus on a cliff, in a not unreasonable state of deep depression of spirits. He merely requested time to write to his wife; and then he died with more dignity than he had lived.

We may notice that all three incidents, varying in the directness with which they were connected with Tiberius, were somehow related to his marriage with Julia. These auspices were not to be misleading. That marriage pursued him. He had done Julia no injury, and he had received much; but he was to receive much more, and he was never to be free from the avenging furies which pursued him with punishment for the crime of having been Julia's husband.

III

The funeral of Augustus was the first public appearance of the new Cæsar. It was an occasion of great solemnity, on which men at large might well review and sum up their thoughts of a great historic figure and all that it had meant.

Funeral of Augustus

The funeral pyre was in the Campus Martius. The ashes of Augustus were deposited in the mausoleum he had built between the Via Flaminia and the Tiber, north of Rome, and had surrounded with gardens. Tiberius himself and his son Drusus delivered the funeral orations. The senate solemnly decreed Augustus —like Julius—to be numbered among the gods. His cult

---

[1] Tacitus (*Ann.* I. 53) is careful to inform us that according to one account they came from Asprenas,—this being of course an insinuation that Tiberius was trying to hide behind Asprenas. But we may doubt if any husband would have denied himself the luxury of taking the centre of the stage on such an occasion as this.

was officially instituted: temples and priests were authorized. . . . This process of deification had been designed as a calculated step towards isolating the holders of the imperial dignity from the common run of men. It tended to invest them with a more awful prestige, and to add a degree of moral force to the barriers which excluded the principate from the political dangers of open competition. While it did not absolutely fail of this effect, it did not completely achieve it; and in the case of Augustus it somewhat overshot its mark. . . .

Political effects
To many men it seemed rather to close a door for ever upon Augustus and his power, and to draw a dividing line below his name. The immensity of his success was equivalent to failure. . . . Many men left that mighty ceremony persuaded that a great episode had come by natural steps to its due end. There could never be another Augustus: there was no man remaining who could fill his place. . . . Tomorrow the Roman world would return to the normal, and, strengthened by the care of its temporary master, would go back to its ancient republican constitution.

Not all men thought so, or wished it so; there were powerful currents of material interest which conflicted with any such return. But even Tiberius himself went home impressed with a sense that the mantle of Augustus was too great for him to wear. . . . It was nevertheless his solemn duty to drape it round his shoulders, and to lift up his small and unpopular voice in a claim to the overwhelming laurels and gigantic fasces of that divine man.

IV

The first meeting of the Senate, convoked after the accession of Tiberius, had been preoccupied exclusively with business relating to the funeral of Augustus. The second meeting, held when Augustus was at last definitely out of the way, was the serious field of contest.

The task of Tiberius was to secure his own confirmation in the principate. In carrying out this task he worked under definite limitations. He was already, in gross material fact, the holder of all the powers Augustus had wielded; but by the rules of the game which had been founded by Augustus he was not permitted to mention the actual fact, nor to invite the Senate openly to invest him with the supreme power in the state. In order to carry the matter through in the prescribed form, with proper respect towards a constitution still republican in principle, he had to induce the Senate freely to offer him various titles and privileges, and even to press them upon him. The consuls had the draft of a bill ready to lay before the house. It was part of the etiquette of his position that Tiberius should hesitate, decline, and finally deplore the necessity which forced him to accept its terms.

Meeting of the Senate

He evidently felt very much like doing so in earnest. He faced a senate which was in some ways a little uncertain of itself. He also was a little uncertain of himself. The death of Augustus was an event of tremendous magnitude. . . . The prestige of Augustus, his personal influence, coming down from the almost legendary time of the civil wars, had made him a man apart, surrounded with a halo of romantic splendour which overawed the Roman world. Most men had been born into a world in which Augustus exercised this magical power; they had never questioned it; they had taken it as a matter of course. . . . Even his official deification was not quite a mere question of policy. It represented an impression of which all men were acutely aware. . . .

But now a successor to Augustus stood before them, and they realized that he, at any rate, was no matter of course. . . . He was about to ask for a ratification of his claim to the supreme power—though no such phrase as "supreme power" was permissible in anyone's mouth. How far had they the power to decline? How far had they the right to decline? How far did they wish to decline? The whole problem was suddenly re-opened: and yet they were not sure how far they could take seriously the conception that it was re-opened.

Tiberius himself understood his difficulties. He certainly had enough sense of humour to feel some embarrassment at asking for a grant in law of powers which he already possessed in fact. He had not himself originated this system of masking realities under polite pretences. It laid him open to possible rebuffs—even to insults—which he can hardly have enjoyed in prospect. More than this, he may have felt what every man is liable to feel in great moments—a very real sense of personal inadequacy. He was a shy and disagreeable man. No sensitive man in such a moment needs any hypocrisy to help him to refer to his own unworthiness. He will do so, if only to disarm criticism in face of the dangers and difficulties he foresees.

He was aware that a large, if indefinite, party among the Senators believed in the possibility of a republican restoration, and even believed that Germanicus, like his father Drusus, might lend himself to the idea. Julia's party would not hesitate to wreck a dignity which they could not enjoy—though it was no doing of his that they could not enjoy it. There were some who were prepared to plunge the world into a new civil war. . . . And with all these under-currents he was limited (not by his own will) to certain indirect methods of requesting them to offer him freely a supremacy which must not be named, and which they probably did not wish to offer anyone, least of all himself.

v

The debate which followed the introduction of the bill was more difficult than perhaps even Tiberius had anticipated. In opening it, he spoke of the vastness of the empire, and of his want of confidence in himself. No mind (he said) but that of the Divine Augustus was capable of dealing with a task so great as the government of the Roman dominion. Having been himself invited to share in the responsibilities and the decisions of that great man, he had learned by experience how arduous and how precarious was the task of government that required to satisfy so many diverse needs. A state which contained so many men of distinction ought not to place all power in the hands of one man. Government

The debate

would be an easier process if it were divided among several partners.

In all this he was speaking strictly by the book. He said nothing that was not in a general sense perfectly true; and probably, up to a certain point beyond which it was not his province to go, it represented his real opinion. It provoked the appropriate answer of tears, prayers, protestations, and a general mental gesture of vague emotion from the assembled house. Practical business was then begun.

The will of Augustus, which had been filed, as was usual, in the custody of the guild of Vestal Virgins, was brought forward and read. Two thirds of his private fortune were bequeathed to Tiberius. But in addition to his personal will he had drawn up a political testament (the *Brevarium Imperii*) which was now produced. It contained not only a general report on the state of the empire and the public resources, but a series of recommendations for the guidance of future statesmen, in which Augustus gave certain policies more definiteness and binding force than could have been obtained by the mere private expression of his wishes. He advised restriction in the free admission of provincials to Roman citizenship; he laid down the maxim that the Roman frontiers should not be extended further; and he counselled the policy of employing men in the work of the State on the ground of merit alone.

These were very remarkable counsels. They were indeed rather more than counsels. They were expressions of opinion which had all the weight of formal and official declarations. It is very probable that at the first

The
*Brevarium
Imperii*

reading of the text their full import did not reach the minds of all who heard. As we know by familiar modern experience, it is necessary to possess a copy of such documents and to study the words at leisure, before the meaning of a carefully drafted instrument can be grasped. We will leave ourselves for the moment in the same state of doubt as the Senators, and return to the *Brevarium Imperii* when its significance had perfectly dawned upon them.

Tiberius then said that although unequal to the burden of government in its entirety, he was willing to undertake the charge of any part that might be entrusted to him.

Asinius Gallus (the second husband of Vipsania) expressed a hope that in this case Cæsar would let them know which part of the government he desired to have entrusted to him.

A. Gallus
Saloninus

Now the opening gambit of Tiberius had been perfectly correct: and the correct reply to it was, of course, that the Senate could not bear to be deprived of the full benefit of the services of Cæsar: and that it implored him on its knees with tears still to devote himself to the patriotic defence of the State. The actual answer of Gallus was therefore rather startling in its impertinence. It was certainly a breach of courtesy to pretend to take literally a statement which everyone knew to be a polite form designed to save the dignity of the Senate.

Tiberius (after a distinct pause) said that it would not become him, diffident as he was concerning his powers, to select or decline any part of a responsibility which he would prefer to avoid altogether.

Asinius Gallus (seeing that Tiberius was considerably offended, and hastening now to take a line rather closer to that which he ought to have adopted before) explained that he had not put his question with the purpose of dividing a government which was indivisible, but in order to convince Cæsar out of his own mouth that the state had but one body and must be governed by a single mind.

(*Lauds Augustus and recalls the distinguished career of Tiberius in civil office.*)

L. Arruntius

L. Arruntius spoke similarly.

These ingenious efforts to explain away the offensive remarks were, however, somewhat spoiled by

Q. Haterius

Q. Haterius, who inquired how long Cæsar would suffer the state to remain without a head?

This was a downright insult. Tiberius had said nothing offensive—nothing that in any way departed from the decorum of the form he was going through: and the remark of Haterius was an oblique way of implying that Tiberius was in some manner intending to usurp a position of despotic power which both parties tacitly agreed did not exist and was not to be mentioned. Tiberius probably showed that he resented this entirely uncalled-for insinuation that he proposed to go outside the recognized and agreed conventions of his office, for the next speaker, who possibly had intended to be equally unpleasant, modified his tone without wholly taking the sting out of his words.

M. Scaurus

Mamercus Scaurus entertained the hope that the Senate's prayer would not be in vain, since Cæsar had not imposed his tribunician veto on the motion of the consuls.

This recalled the house to the point, although the reference to the tribunician veto was an unnecessary gibe. No one supposed that Tiberius was going to decline the powers ratified in the bill. Still, Scaurus had reminded the Senators that the bill was before them.[1]

Part of the unpleasantness may have arisen from the terms of the bill. It certainly differed from the practice of Augustus in one important respect. No time-limit was stated in the draft prepared for the Senate's approval. The appointment was neither for life nor for a fixed term of years, but was left indeterminate. Tiberius explained this by the remark that it was to last until it might seem right to the Senate to grant an old man some repose.[2]

The bill was passed: and Tiberius stepped formally into the principate, the first man to succeed peacefully, with all the normal legal procedure, to an authority founded amid civil war. This in itself was somewhat of an achievement.

VI

The achievement may have been none too welcome to the Senate: for it exercised a little more unpleasant- The Imperial titles

---

[1] The reader will appreciate that the report of the proceedings given by Tacitus (*Ann.* I. 11–13) is a highly condensed summary of a debate that occupied some time. Still, the gist is his own version, and is not invented by any modern apologist for Tiberius.

[2] If this hint is possible abdication was seriously intended (and the reception of Tiberius so far had not been encouraging) circumstances ultimately put it beyond the bounds of possibility. Sulla's prophecy had come true, when he

ness before its opportunity was over. The imperial titles were discussed. This opened up questions of some interest and importance. Among these was the question of Livia.

Livia had always been a woman of dominating personality: somewhat of a lioness, with the faults as well as the virtues of a lioness. Like most women of her type, she seems to have cared a great deal more for immediate and concrete things than for those romantic abstractions, such as glory and honour and posthumous fame, after which, for some unaccountable reason, men ardently strive. She had profoundly influenced the policy of Augustus—but it had been his family and domestic policy which she influenced, not that which dealt with matters of general statesmanship. She dealt with persons, rather than with principles. It is just because of this typically feminine materialism that her influence is hard to trace.

Livia naturally was not eager to lose the power she had wielded. She was particularly anxious to keep her hand upon the career of Tiberius. If Augustus had shown a vein of paternal distrust for Tiberius, this was the mother-lode. . . . The maternal feeling of such a woman as Livia is hardly a form of affection. It may be a form of passion—but it is scarcely a form of love. Perhaps it is best described as a "craze." It would be difficult to detect between her and Tiberius any kind of tenderness. That rosy glow with which modern Europe—and still more modern America—has surrounded

**Livia's
position**

referred to the young man who would "prevent any future holder of such power as mine from laying it down again."

the relationship of mother and son, was conspicuously lacking. Nothing could better illustrate the truth that the relationship is at root independent of any sentimental content.

The expedient which Livia had adopted was the plan of persuading Augustus to create her a perpetual Augusta. It would be hard to define, in a way satisfying to a jurist, precisely what constitutional position an Augusta occupied, or what functions she was supposed to fulfil. But Augustus had given her what she wanted, and his testament included the provision that Livia should be Augusta—whatsoever that might mean —while she lived.

It was this situation which the Senate now surveyed, with some appreciation of its possibilities. The title of Augusta was ratified. Various senators then proceeded to embroider the occasion with a little juridical humour. *Livia is made perpetual Augusta*

Since Augustus had been *pater patriæ* it would be reasonable to bestow the same title on Tiberius. The proposal was also made to give Livia the title *mater patriæ*. The alternative *parens patriæ* was suggested by someone who perhaps felt the former to be a little too daring. Tiberius declined all these suggestions. Finally, it was proposed to add the title *Filius Juliæ* [1] to his own title, after *Cæsar*.

It would have been difficult to imply more plainly that the Senate was inclined to treat the new emperor with contempt. But the element of personal ridicule (and it was very certainly present in these proposals) was not the only aspect to be considered. Such titles

[1] I. e. Livia, who became a Julian by adoption.

tended to bring the principate itself into contempt. The fifty-five-year-old son of Livia did not intend to be tied to his aged mother's apron-strings; and he could not miss the truth—of which the Senate itself was aware —that the creation of a perpetual Augusta with these undefined rights of vague interference was a distinct threat to the principle of personal monarchy. . . . Livia was imperilling her relations with her son when she brought this uncomfortable episode, objectionable both with respect to principle, and with respect to personal dignity, upon him. He had a duty towards the office he held which he was not likely to forget or forego. Tiberius rejected the whole series of proposals.

He told the house that there must be some limit to the honours bestowed upon women,[1] and that he intended to exercise a similar moderation in his own titles. He refused to allow a lictor to be appointed to attend Livia. On a proposal to erect an altar to her he put his veto.

The meeting concluded by conferring the proconsular imperium on Germanicus, and by voting a special delegation to convey it to him, together with official condolences on the death of Augustus.

VII

Tiberius had emerged with success from an ordeal that might well have shaken the nerve of a weaker man. He had obtained what he wanted, and had taken the opportunity to emphasize the principles according to

---

[1] I. e. honorary titles bestowed on those who fulfilled no actual political function.

which he intended to guide his conduct. . . . It would Meaning of Tiberius' success
have been very easy for the principate of Augustus to
have perished as did the autocracy of Dionysius of Syra-
cuse, and for some of the same reasons. If it survived,
it was largely due to the steadiness and patience of the
man who guided it into a haven of legal and constitutional precedent which made it a permanent thing. It
was this first accession which counted. The difficulties
ahead (and they were more serious, looking forward
to them, than they seem to us, looking back) could be
grappled with as they came. The first step had been
made. . . . But the undercurrent of hostility, with its
ominous presage, was not to be mistaken.

This hostility showed itself partly because the Senate
was up to this time still imperfectly acquainted with
the man it had elected to treat so lightly. An impression
existed among the Senators that Tiberius was a mere
tool—and as such none too well trusted—of Augustus; Revulsion of feeling
a somewhat eccentric figure whom Augustus had
adopted as his successor in the absence of a more suitable
candidate. Though doubtless some had an interest in
spreading such an impression, it was one that began to
fade as soon as Senators had enjoyed a little leisure for
reflection. One of the first to see matters in a truer light
was Quintus Haterius.

Haterius seems to have repented of his unpleasantness
with Cæsar, and to have hurried off to the Palatine to
apologize. He was, however, rather more ardent in his
repentance than was altogether comfortable to its object; for he fell on his knees to embrace those of Cæsar,
according to the demonstrative—but perhaps then new

—custom of the day. Tiberius, in the spirit of an Eng-
lishman being kissed by a Frenchman, furiously repudi-
ated this servile and new-fangled proceeding; but as

Haterius had him round the knees, he unfortunately
came down backwards with a crash. The Prætorians,
seeing Cæsar struggling on the ground with a man hang-
ing on to him, rushed to the rescue. The life of Haterius
was in danger, and Livia had to be summoned to mediate. . . . The Latin language was perhaps inadequate
to express the feelings Tiberius must have experienced;
but as he knew Greek well—a much more expressive
tongue for some rhetorical purposes—he may have employed that. Haterius doubtless retired feeling life indeed a heavy burden.

VIII

Any doubt and dawning apprehension which the senatorial oligarchy entertained with respect to the personality of Tiberius became strengthened by a more thorough appreciation of the meaning of the *Brevarium
Imperii*. The opinions of Augustus (even from beyond
the grave) still had the power to influence the views and
the conduct of that large majority of men who had admired him while he lived, and had looked to him for
guidance and leading. The oligarchy had to realize that
the monarchy under which they lived possessed rather
more continuity than they had given it credit for possessing. Though Augustus was dead, his power survived.

It is unnecessary to suppose that the armies were
quicker to appreciate the meaning of the *Brevarium*

than the Senatorial oligarchy at Rome. Only among the armies could any action originate. If Augustus had foreseen, and sought to provide against danger in this respect, he would have drawn up just such a document as the *Brevarium*. He would have added his own endorsement to the policies which he knew Tiberius intended to adopt.

Importance of the *Brevarium*

The tendency of the *Brevarium Imperii* is so peculiar that it may very well have been drawn up in consultation with Tiberius, and even at his request. It gave the authority of Augustus to principles which it is clear enough Tiberius shared. Augustus himself had not always observed them. Their embodiment in a definite memorandum shows that he had recognized the necessity of protecting Tiberius from the suspicions which might follow a change of policy upon the Rhine. The provincials whose admission was to be restricted were the Germans; the frontiers which should not be extended were the German frontiers; and Augustus clearly contemplated the possibility that his successor might find himself embarrassed by claims which were not founded solely upon the fitness of the claimant. . . . He couched his recommendation in general terms; but general terms very conveniently include the particular.

The counsels of the *Brevarium Imperii* summarized, therefore, in all probability, the report which Tiberius had made after his examination of the situation in the North, and they represented a victory over the policy of the military chiefs on the Rhine which he had won in the counsels of the government during the last days of Augustus' life.

It involves a change of policy

CHAPTER VII

THE MILITARY MUTINIES

I

MILITARY revolt on the Rhine and the Danube was prompt. It is not quite clear to a modern observer why the military chiefs found so sudden a difficulty in controlling the expression of opinion among the troops under their command. The armies knew Tiberius well. He was not likely to be intimidated by mutiny: and he was even less likely than Augustus to grant demands which they had not cared to ask of the latter. If they thought that the accession of a new emperor, conscious of his newness, was a favourable moment for compelling attention to grievances, they showed a political astuteness which was singularly lacking in their subsequent conduct.

The mutinies on the Rhine and the Danube deserve to be described in some detail, not only as part of the history of the reign of Tiberius, but as an interesting and almost unique glimpse into the life and personality of the rank and file of the Roman armies. That luxuriant—almost too luxuriant—comedy of character, in which the common people of all ages far excel their masters, runs through the story in a rich vein of unconscious humour. Tacitus tells a tale which might have come out of the pages of Charles Lever or Captain Marryat.

II

The Pannonian Mutiny was the first to break out.[1]
Three Pannonian legions (the VIIIth. Augusta, IXth.   Pannonia
Hispana and XVth. Apollinaris) were encamped in
summer quarters together. On hearing of the death
of Augustus their commander, Junius Blæsus, suspended
the ordinary work of the camp in recognition of the
solemn occasion. During this period of idleness, while
the men had time on their hands, the trouble began.

The first mischief centred round a man named Percennius, whose antecedents are of an interesting nature.
He had formerly been an organizer employed to ar-
range and lead theatrical claques. Those party divisions
in the world of sport which, centuries later, showed
themselves in the wars of the Blues and Greens, and the
famous "Nikë" sedition at Constantinople, were already
in flourishing existence at Rome. This Percennius was
an expert agitator or publicity-agent whose job in life
had been to organize popular successes or failures. . . .
He had subsequently enlisted in the army. We are not   Ante-
favoured with the interesting reasons which induced   cedents
him to take this rather remarkable step; but it is not   of
                                                          Percennius
unreasonable to surmise that some benevolent paymaster
had made it worth his while.

This man was soon at work among the troops, who,
during the long unoccupied evenings, had nothing to do

---

[1] As Tacitus informs us (*Ann*. I. 16) that there was no particular reason
for it except that the death of an emperor seemed to offer an opportunity for
licence, civil war, and all the gains that might accrue, we may deduce that
he felt it urgent to establish an alibi on behalf of his friends.

but to listen. The more steady and respectable men kept away; but he soon had a following among the fools and the bad characters. The speech which Tacitus puts into his mouth as an example of his methods is exhilarating in its familiarity. It is to the life just such a speech as a modern Hyde Park orator might make. It very decidedly is not the kind of speech a reputable labour leader would make. Reading it, we are hardly able to doubt what Percennius was, or what kind of world he sprang from. . . . The identity of his possible paymasters is a question which must be left in the obscurity that from the first surrounded it.

There were doubtless excellent reasons why Junius Blæsus did not at once terminate these proceedings by the arrest of Percennius, and the prompt employment of the troops in useful occupation. The modernity of the speeches of Percennius is matched by modernity of the remarks of Blæsus, when at last he intervened. . . . "Better dip your hands in my blood than become traitors to your emperor." . . . He said, in fact, exactly what any modern officer would say. Riot and mutiny (he told them) were not the proper method of bringing their grievances to Cæsar's ears. Never, in the old days, had soldiers pressed such demands upon their commanders. The beginning of a new reign was not the right time for adding to the difficulties of their ruler. He invited them, finally, to appoint a deputation, and to instruct the delegates in his presence.

The amateur mutineers—who were not particularly *intransigeant*—did not imbrue their hands in the blood of Blæsus. With remarkable amiability they adopted the

Intervention of Junius Blæsus

useful suggestion of a deputation. A tribune, the son of Blæsus, was chosen to go to Rome to demand, on their behalf, discharge after sixteen years' service. Further instructions would be sent when this concession had been granted.

Demands of the mutineers

Nothing could more vividly illustrate the unreality of the mutiny than this promise of "further instructions." These very mild mutineers evidently entertained the notion that their mutiny would last peaceably for a long time, and that they could send their demands—when they had thought of them—one by one to Rome, there to be granted by a subdued emperor. They were so new to mutiny that they did not know what it was, or how it was conducted.

III

The efforts of Percennius, however, were cast into the shade by a more vigorous colleague. While these things were happening in the summer camp, the troops at Nauportus broke out, and proceeded to celebrate the occasion by looting the villas in the neighbourhood. The attempts of their centurions to restrain their ardour led to high words and then to violence. The particular object of their animus was Aufidienus Rufus, a ranker who had risen to the post of commandant of the camp, in which he combined the modern offices of adjutant and quartermaster. Aufidienus was a man who, having worked hard all his life, made others work too. They seized Aufidienus, loaded him with baggage, and drove him on before them, asking him facetiously how he liked heavy loads and long marches. . . . Aufidienus

Violence at Nauportus

was the first of a number of victims among the centurions, who illustrate where the friction really arose. If
there were any genuine grievance, it lay in the strict-
ness of the discipline, not in the conditions of service.

The arrival of these men in camp destroyed the results achieved by the diplomacy of Blæsus. The example
of looting began to spread. The gentleness of Blæsus'
methods had been from choice, not from necessity. As
soon as he realized that matters were assuming this more
serious aspect, he adopted vigorous action. The centurions and the best of the men were still loyal. The chief
offenders were promptly arrested, flogged and gaoled.
These steps came a little too late. The victims called on
their friends for help, and were instantly released by
force.

Vibulenus   The mutiny now began to take a dangerous turn. The
man who was chiefly responsible for the trouble—a certain Vibulenus—sprang to the front and made a very
emotional Italian speech in which he singled out Blæsus for personal denunciation. . . . According to the
statements of Vibulenus, his brother had been dispatched
on business by the mutineers to carry news and messages
to the German legions. This messenger—engaged in the
work of the mutiny—had been murdered by the gladiators of Blæsus.

The outbreak of feeling which followed swept away
the authority of the commander. The mutineers had
the gladiators arrested and thrown into irons, while they
searched for the body of the murdered man. No body
was found; and on the gladiators being examined under
torture, they unanimously denied having murdered any-

body. Finally, it transpired that the indignant Vibule-nus had never had a brother. . . . This trifling fact, however, was of no importance. The mischief had been done.

For meanwhile, everyone had been committed waist-deep in active rebellion against authority, in which blood had been shed. The officers had been driven out of camp, and their quarters sacked. One—the centurion Lucil-ius [1]—had been murdered. The others found safety in concealment. Clemens Julius, however, was caught and retained as a possible spokesman. The episode showed signs of culminating in general bloodshed, for the VIIIth. legion Augusta demanded a certain centurion named Sirpicus, whom the XVth. legion Apollinaris re-fused to surrender. Only the intervention of the IXth. legion Hispana prevented an armed conflict. . . . Vib-ulenus had certainly proved a more expert organizer than Percennius!

The attack on the centurions

IV

While the mutineers had proceeded on their way, strangely oblivious of any impending consequences, and apparently forgetful of any world beyond their own, Tiberius had taken active steps to deal with them. His son Drusus, with a staff of experienced officers, and two cohorts of picked Prætorian guardsmen, as well as some

Arrival of Drusus

[1] This was the centurion who was known by the nickname of "Another, quick!" (*"Cedo alteram"*). All centurions carried, as part of the insignia of their rank, a vine-wood rod, which they were entitled to use upon citizen-soldiers. Lucilius got his nickname from his habit of breaking rods over the backs of his men, and calling for "Another, quick!" Furneaux, note to Tacitus *Ann* I. 23. Ramsay, p. 38, note 1.

German cavalry, set out for Pannonia. His Chief of Staff was a man of whom we shall shortly hear more— L. Aelius Seianus, son and coadjutor of the prefect of the Prætorians. The instructions of Drusus were to act as might seem best in the circumstances.

He arrived to find the summer camp shut and picketed. Drusus arranged to meet the mutineers in a public conference. He entered the camp with a small party; the gates were shut behind him and sentries placed. He took his place on a tribunal in the centre of the camp, and the mutineers assembled in a crowded audience round the platform.

There was much interruption and disorder. As soon as he had obtained sufficient quiet to allow him to be heard, he proceeded to read a letter from Tiberius promising to refer their demands to the Senate. In the meantime (said the letter) he was sending his son in person to make such concessions as could be granted at once.

The meeting replied that Clemens Julius had charge of their demands: namely, discharge after sixteen years' service, with gratuities; pay at one denarius a day: and veterans to have immediate discharge. . . . Drusus argued that he had no power to grant such demands as these: they were within the competence only of his father and the Senate. . . . This—especially, it would seem, the reference to the Senate—provoked a storm. Why had he come, then? Let him consult the Senate every time a man was punished or sent into the fighting line. . . . The meeting began to disperse as a mark of protest.

From a debating point of view, the mutineers had

rather the better of the exchanges. The references made by Drusus to the Senate were, of course, nonsense; the Senate had no control over the Army, and no voice in its administration. The men were not fools: they regarded this attempt to drag the Senate into the controversy as tantamount to a refusal of their demands. . . . But Drusus and Tiberius were not quite fools either; and we are left wondering whether the introduction of the Senate's name may not have had some meaning which it is now difficult to discern. Was it a hint that Senatorial intrigue lay behind the mutiny?—an ironical promise that those who had stirred up the trouble might take a share in stilling it? . . . If so, it is clear that the majority of the men were unaware of any such influence at work among themselves. . . . The shot may have reached its mark, however, among individuals such as Percennius and Vibulenus, and given them some uneasy twinges of apprehension. . . . Whatsoever the intention may have been, we can only guess at it. Yet some definite meaning it certainly had.

The dispersal of the meeting was accompanied by some angry show of feeling. Threatening gestures were made towards members of Drusus' staff, and altercation and violence followed. Lentulus, after a heated exchange of words with the men, found it more prudent to beat a retreat. He was followed by an angry crowd inquiring sarcastically whither he was going?—to the emperor?—or possibly to the Senate? . . . They made a rush at him, and he had to be rescued, battered and bleeding, by the Prætorians. . . . Drusus retired to consider what steps it was advisable next to take.

It breaks up with violence

V

There was every prospect that the events of the night would be serious. A conference evidently took place in the tent of Drusus. His staff had not accompanied him, we may be sure, merely for ornamental purposes. It contained men who were expert judges in military questions. They may have been able to form a pretty shrewd estimate of the real inwardness of the situation; and it is no unreasonable surmise that the reception given to those peculiar references to the Senate had enabled them to ascertain how far intrigue was really at work, and how far the trouble was the product of mere inconsequent unrest. . . . The resolutions which were acted upon a few hours later were probably already taken in substance, when an unexpected event hastened them to their conclusion.

At about three in the morning the moon, shining in a clear sky, began to be eclipsed. An effectual distinc-

The Eclipse Sep. 26th. A. D. 14

tion was suddenly created between the educated men who knew that an eclipse is a natural phenomenon, and those country-bred men who still lived in that folk-world in which eclipses are supernatural events. . . . The folk-philosophers began a clashing of brazen vessels and a blowing of horns and trumpets—brass being well known the world over as a sovereign remedy against eclipses. Then shadow came over, and the moon was swallowed up; and the folk-philosophers knew that the gods were averting their faces with horror from the crime of military mutiny.

The eclipse, which in this way produced an unexpected pause and hesitation in the minds of men, was too good an opportunity to let slip. Action was at once set going. Drusus sent for Clemens Julius and for all other reliable men who were known to be trusted by the troops. They were hastily instructed and were dispatched as propagandists. They were soon talking with the pickets; the familiar, ever-old, ever-new stuff that sways the popular mind. Who (they asked) were Vibulenus and Percennius? Were they going to set themselves up in the places of Tiberius and Drusus? . . . By degrees this language told. . . . In the morning, the pickets had quietly left the gates; the standards, which had been sacrilegiously expelled from their chapel in the prætorium, were unobtrusively restored to their accustomed places. The whole situation in camp was rapidly returning to the normal.

VI

The eclipse lasted until seven o'clock in the morning. Before that, Drusus had already called a fresh meeting for daybreak. He was no orator, but he had the Claudian dignity and self-confidence: a confidence that increased as matters took a more and more favourable turn. He informed the meeting that he was not to be intimidated by threats; but if they approached him in the right frame of mind he would forward their petition to his father with strong recommendation that it should be granted. . . . The meeting preferred a deputation. . . . A deputation to Tiberius was accordingly arranged. It included young Junius Blæsus, Lucius

The second public meeting

Aponius, one of Drusus' staff, and Justus Catonius, a centurion. The deputation set out for Rome.

At this point some divergence of opinion began to manifest itself among the advisers of Drusus. Some were in favour of doing nothing until the deputation should return—trusting, perhaps with wisdom, to the boredom that comes over men with lapse of time, when they are not very deeply interested in the results of their waiting. . . . Others, equally convinced that the mutiny had no deep root in genuine grievances, were in favour of vigorous measures. Drusus finally accepted the advice of the latter.

Arrest and execution of Percennius and Vibulenus

The first step was to summon Percennius and Vibulenus to his presence. They came—and were instantly arrested and summarily executed. The subordinate agitators were then searched for and cut down at sight by the Prætorians. Others were handed over by the men themselves. . . . The eclipse was followed by bad weather. A great storm came up, during which the troops could scarcely leave their tents, so that they had no opportunity for discussion, or for working themselves into any fresh excitement. A general feeling began to spread that luck was against the mutiny. . . .

The mutineers return to duty

The VIIIth. legion went back to duty. The XVth. soon imitated its example. . . . After for some time arguing that they ought to wait the return of the deputation, the IXth. decided to make a virtue of necessity, and also returned to duty. The mutiny was over.

Drusus, seeing that matters were sufficiently forward, prudently left their own officers to deal with them and departed for Rome to report.

VII

The mutiny on the Rhine was, if anything, the more serious episode of the two. It had broken out later than that on the Danube. The whole course of events strongly suggests that the Pannonian mutiny was intended to stampede the Rhine armies, which were the real strategic objective. If any intrigue were afoot to engineer a new civil war and a march upon Rome, it is clear enough that the Rhine armies were the instrument which must be employed. *Situation on the Rhine*

Germanicus was absent in Gaul. The army of the lower Rhine, under Aulus Cæcina Severus, was concentrated at the old Oppidum Ubiorum—the later Colonia Agrippina and modern Cologne. The army of the Upper Rhine, commanded by Gaius Silius, was at Mainz. It was Cæcina's army that mutinied. The mutineers put forward demands curiously similar to those of their Pannonian friends. The organization in this case was not the work of isolated agitators such as Vibulenus and Percennius, nor were the mutineers quite such nervous amateurs as the Pannonians had been, putting their trust in other armies more powerful than their own. The mutiny of Cæcina's army was the real heart of the mutiny. *Cæcina's Army*

The ominous fact was that it was concerted and general. The mutineers acted with order and with discipline. The officers were attacked and "beaten up." One was slain at the very feet of Cæcina, who was unable to save him. Germanicus hastened to the camp.

The interview of Germanicus with the mutineers was of a very remarkable nature, bearing no resemblance whatever to the dealings of Junius Blæsus with his Pannonian legionaries. Germanicus was warmly welcomed. The mutineers at first refused to form up in military order,[1] but after he had reasoned with them he got them to do as he wished. He then addressed them with a fatherly rebuke for their conduct. Uproar instantly broke out. A number urged him to march upon Rome.

A melodramatic and rather peculiar scene followed. It is of course possible that Germanicus was really shocked at the suggestion, and felt that there was wisdom in dissociating himself from it as emphatically as the circumstances allowed.[2] At any rate, he sprang down from the platform, drew his sword, raised it high, and cried that he preferred death to treason. . . . His friends, who stood conveniently near, hastened to restrain him from plunging it into his own breast; and we are certainly not told that they experienced any very great difficulty in doing so. . . . Tacitus himself admits that certain lewd fellows of the baser sort treated the episode with a scepticism which causes the historian surprise and pain. Several voices—and even actual persons close by—derisively recommended Germanicus to go on and smite; and a soldier, so real that he can be named—Calusidius—cynically offered him his own sword, with the probably quite true remark that it was

The Scene with Germanicus

---

[1] They wished to receive him as citizens and electors, not as soldiers.

[2] The very fact that Germanicus was the legal heir to the empire gave him a strong interest in discountenancing unconstitutional precedents of this kind. But there is very little reason to suppose that Agrippina would have been shocked by such a suggestion.

sharper. . . . The troops, Tacitus assures us, thought this remark a most cruel and inhuman one. It certainly cast a douche of cold water on the emotions of the meeting. In the pause which ensued, Germanicus was hurried away to his tent by his friends. . . . It was very sure indeed that he was not going to march upon Rome.

VIII

The situation was (as the panegyrist of Germanicus truly assures us) very difficult. Every possible course seemed equally hazardous. That

> ". . . tangled web we weave
> When first we practice to deceive."

was proving as tangled for the amateur revolutionists on the Rhine as for their brethren in Pannonia. After discussion, it was resolved to write a letter in the name of Tiberius, granting to the mutineers discharge after twenty years' service and partial release to men of sixteen years' service; gratuities to be doubled and paid in full.

The mutineers had, no doubt, not expected this. Their understanding was that they were to march on Rome. Somewhat suspicious, they demanded that these concessions should be immediately executed. The tribunes accordingly made out the necessary discharges. The mutineers were assured that the gratuities would be paid when the army went into winter quarters. The Vth. and XXIst. legions declined to accept the assurance. They refused to move until the money was paid. This was embarrassing. Germanicus and his staff finally

Conces-sions

clubbed together and paid the gratuities themselves—
a step which must have entertained Tiberius to the depth
of his soul when he heard of it! It is unlikely that they
ever got their money back.

IX

Germanicus now went to meet the Upper Rhine
army. The IInd., XIIIth. and XVIth. legions promptly
took the oaths of allegiance to the new emperor without
any trouble. The XIVth. legion hesitated a little, so was
at once granted the discharges and gratuities without
having asked for them. It must have been much surprised at this unexpected windfall; but it did not mutiny. Possibly it felt that such a proceeding would be
superfluous.

**The army
of Silius
remains
loyal**

There was, in fact, no mutiny whatever in the army
of Gaius Silius: and this circumstance made it absolutely
certain that the Rhine mutiny would not succeed.

Tiberius has been adversely criticized for not proceeding in person to the seat of trouble. His own explanation—that he thought he could do more good by remaining in Italy and keeping control of the whole situation
—was disbelieved at the time and has not received much
credit since; possibly because of its obvious and humdrum common sense. He had sent Drusus to Pannonia.
To the Rhine he sent a commission headed by Munatius
Plancus. The arrival of the commissioners at Cologne
was the signal for a fresh outburst.

The army of the Lower Rhine seems to have entertained some suspicion of the sincerity of Germanicus
and his colleagues, for it had no doubt that the Com-

missioners from the emperor brought unwelcome decisions. . . . It chased Munatius Plancus, who had to
seek refuge in the chapel of the standards, where the
standard-bearer Calpurnius protected him. At dawn he
was rescued from his predicament by Germanicus, who
sent off the commissioners with a cavalry escort.

The advent of the commission, however, brought matters to a head. It became necessary for Germanicus
squarely to face the fact that the army of the Upper
Rhine was loyal, and was available for use to put down
the mutiny of Cæcina's troops. For some time he hesitated. If he himself had had any share in stirring up—
or in profiting by—the mutiny, he might well pause
with an uneasy conscience before employing force to
suppress the dupes who had been deceived and en-
trapped. Agrippina—always strong—did not wish to
leave him. It may, as Tacitus alleges, have been her
courage; or it may have been her conscience. Nothing
would happen while she remained. At last Germanicus
had to make up his mind. The women and children were
sent away.

Historians, for reasons best known to themselves, have
loved to depict the touching emotions of pride and
shame which stirred the troops when they saw the procession leaving the camp, Agrippina carrying in her
arms the little Gaius ("Caligula" as they had fondly
nicknamed him) much of whose life had been spent
with them in camp: how they fell on their knees to
Germanicus and besought pardon. . . . It is certain
that Germanicus did send the women and children away
with careful publicity and pointedness. But the emotions of the troops were very different from those al-

leged. They recognized that the procession headed by Agrippina was the first preliminary of the advance of the legions of Gaius Silius. . . . They threw themselves in her way and stopped her. . . . Germanicus was glad enough to escape the necessity imposed upon him. He spoke to them: a florid Italian speech which carried conviction to men already convinced of the error of their ways. They gave in. They did fall upon their knees. The legions of Silius were not called upon to act. All was over.

X

The
court of
inquiry

If we need any confirmation of the suspicion that Germanicus knew rather more about the mutiny than appears upon the surface, we may obtain it from the subsequent proceedings, which were only too clearly designed to shield the real ringleaders. The investigation into the identity of the guilty parties rapidly became an amusing farce, though a grim one for its victims. The alleged ringleaders were passed before a jury of the whole army, and were condemned or acquitted by a massed tumultuary vote. The army soon entered into the humour of the occasion, and enjoyed itself. It is highly improbable that this democratic court condemned the true agents of the mutiny, but very probable indeed that a large number of unpopular persons suffered a fate which they had not deserved.

An investigation was also held, on somewhat similar lines, into the question of the centurions. . . . Whatsoever else might be uncertain, there could be no doubt that the centurions were in many cases bitterly hated.

Before the army went back to its normal duties, it was afforded an opportunity of objecting to any centurion whose conduct it considered oppressive. The opportunity was embraced with ardour; and these two jury courts of the whole army did something, perhaps, to smooth over the feelings excited by the mutiny. . . . No one at any rate could accuse them of being the packed tribunals of a tyrannical government. Their chief fault was that they were a little too much the arbitrary voice of irresponsible democracy.

Such were the external events of the great military mutinies on the Rhine and the Danube frontiers. There were certain events not so obvious, but capable of being discerned by their results.

We have no detailed knowledge of the instructions given to the commission which visited the Rhine, nor of the communications that may have passed between Tiberius and Germanicus. We only know that in the meantime Germanicus had received authority to proceed with the conquest of Germany, in defiance of the policy of the *Brevarium Imperii*. The military chiefs, as soon as their policy was endorsed from Rome, seemed to find it singularly easy to restore discipline.

Germanicus authorized to invade Germany

It is very necessary, in view of the subsequent relations between Tiberius and Germanicus, to note the strong hint implied in these events that Tiberius had been overborne by the threat of force. . . . Tiberius had excellent reasons for entertaining profound scepticism as to the good faith of Germanicus. The latter was, after all, more than an isolated individual. He was the head of a party—Julia's party, for he was married to Julia's daughter. The senatorial party looked to him as to a sympathizer; and they presumably knew what they were about in doing so.

The historical tradition is that Tiberius was jealous of Germanicus. Such an assertion tells us very little; for jealousy is a general term covering a large range of emotions of varied character, from that of the Lord our God, who is a jealous God, down to the pettiest feelings that lurk behind Nottingham lace curtains in the back streets of a manufacturing town. . . . But the war between men of the type of Tiberius, and those of the type of Germanicus, is universal and eternal. Every man who has fought his way to the front, and has a solid appreciation of the duties and responsibilities of leadership, resents the existence of those men who, without real ability, seem able to command the enthusiasm of the world—because they flatter it and do what it wishes, and embody its own superficial folly and represent its own ignorant desires. . . . And there is such a thing as political jealousy. Germanicus never gave Tiberius the stern devotion which Tiberius had given Augustus, reserving himself free of all interests and affiliations for the service of his master. The eye of Tiberius was fixed upon a danger-spot, a centre of political disaffection.

Relations of Tiberius and Germanicus

XI

The principles which Tiberius proposed to uphold and defend are visible in his attitude to the military mutineers. The concessions which had actually been made to the mutineers on the Rhine he immediately, with his usual sense of justice, extended to the Panno-

Tiberius and the concessions

nian troops. But he steadily refused to endorse them as permanent changes for the future. Moreover, the demands of the men had taken a shape not unknown in later ages. In order to remedy particular grievances they demanded changes in the general rules which had been abused. Tiberius declined. He was willing to see that the regulations were carried out with justice, but he would not alter them in the way desired. . . . Instead of diminishing the length of military service, he actually increased it. . . . It does not appear that the discontent in the army was deepened by his attitude: in fact, we hear no more of it. The truth probably was that it was the maladministration of the rules, not the rules themselves, that created the discontent.

Here, incidentally, we touch on a very delicate and curious point in the relations between men and their governors. It is much easier to alter a rule than to ensure that it shall be administered with justice and good sense. A regulation may be changed every time it is applied unjustly: but if it is never applied justly, no number of changes will make it satisfactory. Tiberius took his stand on the principle that good administration is the secret of satisfactory government. *The principle involved*

His success and failure as a ruler is a tolerable index to the amount of truth in this principle. He was not prepared to shape his actions according to the wishes of those he governed. . . . The surprise he sprang upon the Roman world—the trap and pitfall he constituted for many zealous but misguided men—the foundation of the tragedy he was to play out to its finish, were all alike due to a personality which it is necessary to have vividly before our eyes before we proceed: and this is the clue to it.

Augustus had been physically a frail and delicate man. Nothing is better attested than the physical health and strength of his successor. Tiberius could crush an apple in his left hand, and take the skin off a man with a fillip of his finger. . . . At first waking he could see in the dark, as a cat does, though the power faded after a few minutes. He was a long-headed, square-browed, fair-skinned, aquiline man, walking with a slow stride, holding himself very erect, but with his head bent and his eyes veiled; silent, deliberate in speech, with a mordant, rather baffling humour, which sometimes he meant to be baffling; patient, reserved; one of the proud eccentric Claudians. This Claudian quality is the key to Tiberius. He was an aristocrat to the finger-tips, full of fastidious likes and dislikes, iron inhibitions and inexorable tabus.

The personality that explains it

He had none of the personal tastes of the parvenu. He never built himself a staircase of solid gold, nor decorated himself in gorgeous raiment. His habits were simple to the point of austerity. He was precise, careful, economical: a man too accustomed to money either to be intoxicated with it or to neglect it. His mental build was somewhat similarly restrained. He never used the title Imperator. He called himself "Augustus" only in foreign correspondence. He dryly and persistently refused the somewhat Pecksniffian title of "Father of his Country." He would not allow anyone save men of servile status to address him as *Dominus*, Lord. He remained simply Tiberius Cæsar. . . . This tendency to snub alike servility and pomp was a marked and permanent feature in his character. He did not like men who stood off from him, nor men who ran too quickly to him. He liked obedience; he disliked servility. He set little store by the decorative. His attention was fixed upon the real qualities of things: on brains and character in a man, on justice and good sense in an action. . . . And a man such as this is little likely to inquire what men at large wish him to think or expect him to say. He was prepared to take the responsibility of leadership.

The right to command belongs naturally enough to a ruler: but much depends on the source from which he derives it. The problem resolves itself into the question whether he derives it from the knowledge that his followers will agree to the command, or from the intrinsic rightness and wisdom of the command itself. . . . Tiberius clearly believed that the validity of a command depended on its own intrinsic rightness.

XII

The view he took of his duties as head of the state was therefore austere. He treated his subjects as he had treated his Illyrian army—that is to say, with real thought for their practical welfare. He was a good governor, as he was a good officer. And similarly, he was not prepared to admit that they knew better than he what was to the general good. . . . The art of government comes by no gift of divination. . . . Digging the ground or hammering horseshoes gives a man no more insight into statesmanship than fighting Germans

His view of his duties

or bridging rivers. There is only one thing that the ordinary man can tell his governors—and that is, that all government ought to be based upon justice and directed to the common good. . . . And who were they, to tell Tiberius Cæsar such a thing as this? Was he some idle fat man who thought his own glory and prosperity the purpose of government and the ends of the state? And when, like Tiberius, a man has been trained through a long life in all the processes of government, he needs little kind advice from those who have neither his knowledge nor his skill.

With a strong and able man, there is validity in this; for the weakness of the opposite point of view is that it regards the truth and the right as being, not objective, but dependent on what men feel and imagine. This last doctrine goes to the weak, the ignorant and the lost, not with strength and knowledge and rescue, but with the profession that they may have what they want—power, if they know what it is, and the way home, if they know where it runs. . . . But a consensus of lost sheep is seldom much guide to a shepherd.

This sense that his power was a right and a just power —and a wise one—underlay all the actions of Tiberius. On this ground he defended it against all attacks. He was never driven to that point at which a selfish and self-indulgent man finds his sub-conscious mind automatically admitting the truth by compromising. There never came a time when he suggested splitting the difference with his foes. . . . He had none of that secret doubt as to the abstract rightness of command which plagues a modern man.

His faith in himself

On such foundations as these his policy was built. He faced realities to a far greater extent than Augustus had ever done. He had not pretended to accept the principate for a term of years only. One of the last traces of the old popular government was the election of magistrates in the assembly of the people. The transformation of the ancient party of the *Populares* into the imperial military guild made these assemblies a very empty show. The candidates were nominated by the princeps, and the election chiefly consisted in the candidates expending large sums of money on a more or less imaginary electoral campaign, the results of which had been fixed, within narrow limits, beforehand. . . . Tiberius abolished this by nominating exactly as many candidates as there were offices to fill: so the result was absolutely pre-determined, and they could save their money. The legislative action of the assembly was confined to the bestowal of the tribunician power. . . . These changes made no difference to anyone. They were merely realism, and their motive was economy.

His realism

The old assembly had long been superseded by the powers which he himself wielded; but the Senate, which retained its old constitution, he treated with consideration, because it was still a reality. He consulted both its dignity as a House, and the dignity of its individual members. He declined to test the qualifications of the candidates for office whom it proposed to him for nomination. Under his government the Senate gained rather than lost. It established its position as the principal court of criminal law, subject only to the right of appeal to the imperial court.

The good
shepherd

He himself said that the duty of a good shepherd was to shear his sheep, not to flay them. He kept a firm and formidable hand on the provincial governors. Means of redress against oppression were made as easy as he could make them, and prosecutions on this ground were frequent. It has been said that this in many cases was shutting the stable door after the steed was stolen; but Tiberius had not invented the system of Roman government, and was not prepared to suggest a better. He could only work it as well as it could be worked—and he certainly did so. . . . The provinces under his control were better governed than those under the Senate; so much so, that the transfer of a province from the Senate to the imperial government was equivalent to a reduction of taxation. He never raised the rate of taxation. For a short time he actually reduced it. By careful economy he accumulated immense reserves, which enabled him to meet unforeseen contingencies, as we shall see. The provinces flourished; and yet there had never been a Roman Government which possessed such reserve sums. . . . The existence of these funds may have attracted the careful thought of many who would have liked to handle them.

XIII

The
response

The testimony to the soundness of Tiberius' government is general; and it comes no less from the evidence of his own actions than from the words of historians. Like all good government, it was singularly unsentimental. It was distinguished by an almost mordant realism. He appealed more to his subjects' pockets than to their hearts. And he can hardly have been unconscious that he secured the safety of his power by the methods in which he exercised it. . . . From the day of his second meeting with the Senate he must have been aware that if he were to hold his own he needed backing; and he obtained this backing from the immense multitude of ordinary people whom his rule benefited. Step by step his position grew firmer. It became at last almost impregnable. But there is no mystery about the reasons. His policy was to support the small capitalist, the small farmer—the class of men who from the first had constituted the main strength of the *Populares*. And they supported him.

But this very fact brought him into collision with the members of the old Senatorial oligarchy. He was faced with a coalition of parties which presently we shall have occasion to inspect with the interest it deserves.[1]

---

[1] The testimony to the character of Tiberius is quite clear and emphatic, and is sufficiently detailed and illustrated by examples to make it fairly certain that it is accurate. Dion Cassius LVII. 7–12; Suetonius *Tiberius* XXVI.–XL.

Tiberius himself contributed, as his view of the relations of government and governed: "No man willingly submits to government. Men accept it as a regrettable necessity. They take pleasure in getting out of it, and they enjoy being against the government." (Dion Cass. LVII. 19.) See also Tacitus: *Annals* I. 54.

CHAPTER VIII

GERMANICUS

I

GERMANICUS crossed the Rhine in the early autumn, and the second attempt to conquer Germany was begun. It was too late in the season for a long campaign, but he seems to have wished to make the invasion an accomplished fact forthwith, and to record his right to the mantle of Drusus. He had excellent excuses for prompt action. It seemed wise to employ the troops and to obliterate from their minds the memory of the recent troubles.

Invasion of Germany A. D. 14

His appearance was unexpected. Setting out from Castra Vetera, he pushed up the Lippe Valley, the main entrance into western Germany. The Marsi, one of the four tribes implicated in the attack on Varus, were surprised, and received very heavy punishment. Their land was ravaged with fire and sword, and the sanctuary of their god Tamfana was destroyed. The Marsi called up their allies. The united forces of the Bructeri from the north and the Usipetes and Tubantes from the west joined with the Marsi to catch the Roman force on the way back. It cut its way through, and reached Castra Vetera in safety.

Such operations were a preliminary to the serious work which began in the following year. Two invasions of

Germany were designed. They followed—though not in
the same order—the plans of Drusus. . . . Cæcina, with
four legions, marched up the Lippe Valley to hold the
Marsi and the Cheruscan league. Germanicus started
from the middle Rhine at the same time, and attacked
the Chatti. He was on his return march when urgent
messages came to him from Segestes, the Cheruscan
chief.

Second
(double)
invasion
of
Germany
A. D. 15.
Part I

The renewal of the war had found the Germans at
first unprepared: but a rapid change soon took place
which a good deal altered the situation. The younger
men, who had all the prestige of the defeat of Varus,
were quickly in command. There was no method of
dealing with the Romans save the over-riding of the
separate tribal unities, and the concentration of power.
Irmin lost no time in re-establishing the great league
which five years earlier had been successful in expelling
the Romans from Germany. He met with determined
resistance from the elder men. Segestes sent at once for
help from Germanicus. The latter did not fail to re-
spond. He reached Segestes in time. He could not, however, maintain him in power; the utmost he could do
was to rescue him personally and to give him a safe refuge in Gaul. This fact alone was a proof that there
were very serious limitations to the protection which
the Romans could afford to their friends. Segestes carried off with him two of the eagles which had been lost
when Varus fell, and his own daughter Thusnelda, the
wife of Irmin. They were highly acceptable to Germanicus. Irmin, however, remained in power, his influence
increased rather than diminished by an episode which

Changes
in the
German
situation

attracted the sympathy of his countrymen, and which did nothing to damage his practical power.

The course of events, therefore, tended continually to strengthen the German power of resistance. The situation was no longer that with which Drusus had dealt. A rapid process of unification was taking place under the compulsion of necessity; and if the necessity continued long enough, there was every prospect that it would end by the creation of a German kingdom of which Irmin would be the natural head: and this would be a far more difficult problem to grapple with.

Germanicus seems hardly to have possessed the mental equipment for dealing with such considerations as these. There is no sign in any of his actions that he had political conceptions of a very profound nature. He seems to have proposed to conquer Germany by military means alone, without reference to any other considerations. . . . Tiberius knew better than this; but it was not his business to enlighten Germanicus and his friends. They would not have listened. They would have accused him—as they did—of jealousy, and of a wish to prevent what he could not share. . . . It was very much to his interest now to permit an experiment which would end by discrediting a political party opposed to him.

II

The second invasion of the year revived the old plan of Drusus. A flotilla had been gathered. Germanicus passed through the Fossa Drusiana, the great canal that his father had dug to link the Rhine with the Yssel, and reached the mouth of the Ems. His voyage was pro-

Marginal notes:

Unification

Invasion of Germany A. D. 15 Part II

tected by the parallel march through Frisia of a cavalry column under Pedo Albinovanus, while further inland the legions under Cæcina made their way through the Bructerian lands to the upper waters of the Ems. The three forces met on the Ems, and the lands between the Ems and the Lippe were ravaged. All the tribes which belonged to the league which had destroyed Varus had now had punishment brought home to them.

The spot where Varus had fallen was not far off. Germanicus went to visit the place. He found it much as it had been left after the battle, and the scene made a deep impression upon all who saw it. There was the broken ground amid the woods, the half-finished camp with its ramparts not fully raised nor its ditches completely dug; everywhere lay the wreckage of the destroyed legions, skulls and skeletons, heads that had been impaled on trees, even the altars raised by the Germans, on which the principal officers captured had been sacrificed. . . . Survivors of the battle conducted their comrades over the field, explaining the course of events and showing the places in which the various episodes had happened. . . . The ground was cleared, and funeral honours paid to the fallen. A mound was raised and a trophy built—long since vanished, so that the spot cannot now be found.

Visit to Teutoberg

Germanicus performed a highly popular act by laying the first sod of the mound with his own hands.

The luck of that place was not good for Romans; it still, in some measure, held its malign power. Germanicus had hard work to rejoin his fleet. The cavalry column of Albinovanus made its return march in safety:

but Cæcina unmasked the main enemy force, which was hovering on his flank ready to strike at the first favourable opportunity. . . . The blow fell when he reached the "Long Bridges," a narrow causeway where the road was built across a great marsh. Irmin had already occupied the surrounding slopes. It was a situation which needed sound and skilful soldiering; but Cæcina was an old and an experienced commander, with forty years' service behind him. He dug in while the road was surveyed and repaired.

Cæcina at the "Long Bridges"

The first struggle was for possession of the causeway. The Germans diverted into the marsh all the streams on the surrounding heights, and raised the level of the water. The Cherusci had the best of the contest under these trying conditions. The Romans were saved only by the fall of night. It was a very bad night for them, "wakeful rather than watchful"; while the Germans were drinking high, and ready to resume business when the light came. Cæcina saw that he must clear them out of the marsh, and drive them to the heights, if he were to get across. As it happened, there was just about enough space round the edge of the marsh to enable legionaries to take ground. . . . But when at last he slept, it was to dream of the gory ghost of Varus calling him into the marsh, and stretching out horrid hands; but he would not go, and thrust the hands away.

The serious work which began at day-break opened with a disastrous muddle. The Vth. and XXIst. legions, which had been detached as flank guards to clear the Germans from the causeway, went forward instead. There was no possibility of recalling them. The transport train had to be got over the causeway as best it could be. This was not lost on Irmin. He showed great restraint in holding back until the transport train was, as might have been expected, stuck, and a mass of distracted men, bogged vehicles, and wasted orders. Then he came on, whooping his men forward with "Another Varus! We have them beaten again!"

The picked *Comitatus* cut the column in two, paying especial attention to the horses, which were soon slipping, throwing their riders, and stampeding over all that was in their way. Cæcina's horse was killed under him, and he would have been cut off and captured but for the Homeric struggle waged over him by the men of the Ist. legion, who came pouring to the rescue. . . . The surviving *personnel* was extricated, at the price of sacrificing most of the transport train, to which the Germans clung with ardour. . . . By nightfall the legions had won across the causeway and gained firm ground.

The transport train lost

Their situation was not inspiring. Most of their entrenching tools had been lost, but they managed to scrape up sufficient of an earthwork to satisfy the army regulations. There were no tents, and no surgical dressings for the wounded: and their rations showed as distinct signs as they did themselves of having been on German soil. Even heart seemed to have been lost. . . . When a horse got loose, and knocked someone down, the legionaries, their nerves on edge, made for the gates.

But Cæcina was not Varus.

He failed to breast the panic which set in; but he had moral resources. He laid himself and his forty years' service down in the gate-way and defied his men to step

Cæcina keeps his men in hand

across his prostrate body. . . . He calculated quite correctly. They did not step across him. His officers meanwhile went among the men and convinced them that it was a false alarm. Discipline was restored.

III

It was none too soon. Cæcina collected the men and proceeded to address them. He did not conceal that the situation was a serious one. Their only hope was in their arms and their good sense. He then issued his orders, and added some words of manly sentiment of the usual sort that moves honest and uneducated men. By mobilizing the available horses, his own and those of his officers, he improvised a cavalry force out of the best of his men. He then awaited events.

The Germans had been divided in opinion. Irmin was in favour of blockading the camp. His kinsman Yngwe-mar advocated taking it by assault: and finally this view carried the day. As soon as light came, they filled in the ditches, cast hurdles over, and scaled the earthwork, where only a few persons, apparently screaming for help, were visible. As soon as they were on the wall, Cæcina played his cards. The gates were thrown open, and the legionaries sallied out in force. . . . Irmin, as usual, escaped unhurt; Yngwe-mar got off severely wounded. Not until nightfall did the victorious legionaries return from the pursuit, much refreshed by their day's work.

The
Germany
repulsed
from the
camp

At Castra Vetera it was already rumoured that the worst had happened, and that Cæcina and his men were the latest victims of the Germans. It was even proposed to break down the bridge over the Rhine as a precaution against a German surprise. . . . Agrippina did not believe that Cæcina was lost, and would not allow the demolition of the bridge. It is said that she stood her stand on it until Cæcina's column came struggling home safe and sound. . . . She distributed clothes to those who needed them, and looked after the wounded.

Germanicus himself had been none too fortunate. His ships had gone aground in the Frisian shallows. In order to lighten them, he landed P. Vitellius with the IInd. and XIVth. legions, who, marching along the beaches, were caught by one of those tremendous equinoctial tides to which the Romans could never accustom themselves. They reached shore with difficulty, and passed a miserable night. . . . Rumour reported that the entire flotilla was lost; and its safety was believed in only when Germanicus and his troops at last arrived to prove it.

The fleet in difficulties

IV

The conquest of Germany was obviously not proceeding quite according to plan. These campaigns were of very doubtful value. They had been merely punitive expeditions; not one inch of new ground had been permanently occupied; not a single tribe had been permanently reduced. The cost had been great, and the results were nothing.

Tiberius, however, had not yet made up his mind to intervene. If Germanicus and the Rhine army wished to prove still more convincingly that they could not conquer Germany, they were at liberty to carry the experiment to its end. . . . He spoke with praise and commendation of Germanicus, and the Senate granted a triumph. Men at large were sufficiently intelligent to feel some doubt of his sincerity.

Third
Invasion
of
Germany
A. D. 16
If the policy of military conquest which Germanicus represented were to be successful, it must be still more vigorously carried out. The third campaign was carefully prepared and designed on a larger scale. It was intended to crush the Cherusci and to carry Roman arms right up to the Elbe. The Cherusci seem to have had full information of these intentions, for they prepared their resistance with equal care. Gaius Silius opened the campaign by crossing the middle Rhine with the object of holding the Chatti. Lower down, Germanicus started up the Lippe valley from Castra Vetera with six legions. Furthest down of all, the fleet, increased to a thousand vessels, made its way through the Fossa Drusiana to the Ems mouth, where it anchored, and landed its troops. Leaving the ships under guard, the legions advanced south-eastward, while Germanicus advanced northward to meet them. They met on the banks of the Weser, and found the Cherusci and their allies there in force to meet them.

The campaign was more than an attempt to conquer Germany. It had by this time become a political struggle on which vast issues depended. The conquest of Germany meant the supremacy of Germanicus as surely as the conquest of Gaul had meant the supremacy of Gaius Julius Cæsar. Tiberius was watching. He had no doubt as to the significance of the conduct at any rate of Agrippina. But it was the success or failure of Germanicus himself that would decide the issue.

The whole history of these campaigns has been coloured by the political propaganda which was designed to justify them. They were magnified and distorted into a romance of ardent youth and military glory—with Agrippina playing the part of the noble woman in the background—dogged and repressed by the Ogre of Capri. Even over a space of nearly two thousand years this propaganda survives in the pages of Tacitus, and it still reflects upon Germanicus the same magical glow that it cast upon him for the benefit of public opinion in Rome. . . . But public opinion in Rome, with all its faults, was not entirely insensible to the advantages of the policy of Tiberius, who never fought a war he could possibly avoid, and never spent a penny he could possibly save.

Significance of the German War

V

The tale of the battle of Idiaviso opens with a dramatic dialogue between Irmin and his brother Flavus, who was an officer of auxiliaries in the Roman service. Standing on opposite banks of the river, they rehearse the case for Roman civilization or German independence. It ends by the brothers dashing furiously into the water to reach one another, and being restrained by their friends. . . . The tale may be true; but it has in all probability been neatly retouched by a skilled literary hand well acquainted with the eternal taste of the public for romantic drama.

The prologue being finished, the heroic pageant be-

The
battle of
Idiaviso

gins. The Germans had occupied ground on the lower slopes of the hills. An open wood protected their rear. The Cherusci formed the reserve, which was intended to strike at the crucial point when the battle had developed sufficiently far to reveal it.

The infantry of Germanicus made a frontal assault on this position. The cavalry, as soon as the battle was joined, and attention was concentrated with increasing intensity on the infantry struggle, enveloped the German flank and turned the position. They drove out the Germans who were in the wood, while the infantry drove their own opponents into it. The Cherusci descended into this confusion, and were decisively defeated. The victory of Germanicus was complete, and his losses were small.

This is at least the program with which the heroic pageant was intended to conform; but, as often happens, the rehearsal was defective, and it had to be gone through again. The Germans do not seem to have allowed their defeat to be so complete as the program directed. . . . The wily Irmin got away by hard riding. The Saxon auxiliaries knew him by sight, and let him go. Some of the Germans were forced into the Weser; others, caught between the infantry and the cavalry attacks in the woods, climbed trees, whence they were subsequently hunted at leisure. But a considerable body must have effected a retreat. The pursuit is said to have lasted many hours, and to have extended over ten miles, which were marked by the traces of their flight; from which we may deduce that they retired in fairly good order.

The
German
retreat

Such a belief is confirmed by the events which followed. The legions had already saluted Tiberius as Imperator after their victory, and Germanicus had erected a trophy, when it became clear that the Germans were once more in the field. . . . The explanation given is that the trophy enraged them; but their rage, however great and however natural, could not by itself have produced another army in so short a time had their military defeat been as decisive as we are expected to believe.

It was necessary for Germanicus to take the offensive, and to fight decisive battles. Quick results were of the first importance to him; he could not wait, or trust to time. Hence the Germans could choose their own ground, and could fight on prepared positions. They selected a position protected by woods and a swamp, and on the third side by an earthwork.

The main attack of Germanicus was directed against this earthwork. The assault of the legionaries was repulsed, and was withdrawn. Javelin men and slingers, supported by engines, were then employed, and the position carried by Prætorian guardsmen. The defenders were caught at the disadvantage so often fatal to German or Celtic fighting men, packed on a limited front with insufficient play for their weapons. . . . Nevertheless, the heroic pageant remained a failure. The battle was not decisive, and the results required by Germanicus were still to seek. *The second battle*

It was only the middle of summer: there was yet time for further operations: but he began his retreat. He erected a second trophy, with an inscription relating that the army of Tiberius Cæsar, having subdued the nations between the Rhine and the Elbe, consecrated this memorial. . . .

VI

The return of the armies was untroubled. But disaster overtook the fleet. It set sail in excellent weather. Soon after it left the mouth of the Ems, however, it was caught by a hailstorm; a rising sea and violent squalls followed, which produced a panic amongst the troops. Their attempts to help the seamen only embarrassed the latter. The weather worsened. A violent south-easterly storm began to drive the ships out to sea and upon the islands. Anchor was cast, and the intention was evidently to ride out the gale: but at this moment the tide turned, and on an ebb receding with the wind the transports dragged their anchors. Many were shipping water. Horses and baggage animals, and even military stores were thrown overboard to lighten the vessels; but many foundered, and others were driven upon the Frisian islands. Germanicus himself was separated from the fleet, and driven north upon the Chaucian shore. Here he had to stay till the storm blew itself out. He blamed himself bitterly for the disaster, and his friends (who seem always to have exercised great influence upon his conduct) had to restrain him from seeking a penitent and watery grave.

With the good weather, the scattered ships began to return. The first to arrive were repaired, and sent out to search for others. Most of the missing men were rescued. Some had died of starvation and exposure on

Disaster to the fleet

desolate islands; some had been living upon the carcasses of the baggage animals thrown up by the sea. The tribe of the Ampsivarii made a search inland, and recovered many who had been carried off by the Germans. It is even said that some of the missing men had been blown right across the sea to Britain, and were sent back by the British chiefs. They brought back remarkable tales with them, which the Roman historian justly treats with doubt.

There was not much ground for enthusiasm over the results of the great campaign. Some encouragement was found in local successes against the Marsi and the Chatti, and in the recovery of the last of the three eagles that had been lost with Varus. . . . Germanicus saw to it that the sufferers in the disaster to the fleet should be compensated for their losses. The expenses involved could hardly be other than serious.

The campaign unsuccessful

VII

The time had now come when Tiberius could intervene. Germanicus believed—or said that he believed—that one more campaign would achieve their objective. . . . Tiberius evidently took a different view of the probabilities. In a letter which he wrote about this time he observed that he himself had always obtained better results on the Rhine by diplomacy than by arms. . . . He offered Germanicus the consulship for the ensuing year—which, as it would necessitate his presence in Rome, was equivalent to recall: and Germanicus accepted it with a meekness which suggests that he was not altogether sorry to be relieved of an impossible po-

Tiberius intervenes

sition. Tiberius took the opportunity to make important changes. The command of the Rhine armies was definitely separated from the Governorship of Gaul, and the two posts were never again held by the same man. In the year in which Germanicus came back from the Rhine, Drusus took up the Illyrian command.

Germanicus celebrated a magnificent and popular triumph, on the 26th of May, in the year A. D. 17. There was a feeling that he had fallen from power. Tiberius had won a great political victory, and had established himself as undisputed master of the Roman world. He was now, for the first time, free from that haunting threat which had followed him while his adopted son and intended successor held in his hands the immense power of the Rhine command.

The failure of the German campaigns was the failure of the most scientific soldiering which the Roman armies had ever attempted: and it is curious to note that these campaigns, so thoroughly planned, so well conducted, were unsuccessful, when Cæsar's campaigns in Gaul, the magnificent chaos of an inspired amateur, achieved their end. The causes, however, are not entirely mysterious. The Gallic campaigns of Cæsar paid for themselves and yielded a profit over and above. The German campaigns needed to be paid for out of the resources of the imperial fisc.

Causes of the failure

Neither Augustus nor Tiberius were men who contemplated with complacency this tremendous drain on the treasury without any prospect of return. We need not be surprised, therefore, if at the first convenient opportunity the project of conquering the north was turned down for good and never resumed. But there were more reasons than one for such a decision. The Rhine command, in the hands of Germanicus, had become a political danger which might involve the fall of the principate. Germanicus himself was but the stalking horse of more formidable powers. Tiberius was the last man to feel it his business to finance an enterprise intended to give effect at his expense to the tenuous hereditary claim of Julia's daughter, encouraged by a senatorial oligarchy which counted upon political profit by his fall.

But even so, the question always remained whether the conquest of Germany were practically possible. The experience of nineteen hundred years seems to show that the doubts of Tiberius were justified. Even to hold the Rhine frontier at all is possible only under certain conditions. The masters of that frontier must possess either Britain or the alliance of Britain. . . . There is at least no question whatever that Cæsar, the creator of the Rhine frontier, recognized the necessity of dealing with Britain as an integral part of the scheme. It was only the intervention of pressing political events which kept him from completing his plan. That which he knew, he certainly did not fail to record for the benefit of those who followed him. Augustus had allowed himself to be persuaded into a different policy. The invasions of Germany by Drusus and Germanicus were therefore experiments on which important decisions hung. Their failure proved that Cæsar was right. The decision to recall Germanicus was a reversion to the views of Cæsar. It settled a number of historical consequences

Conquest of Germany abandoned

which have deeply influenced the later development of Europe. The inclusion of Britain in the Roman dominion, and the exclusion of Germany, went far to determine the whole subsequent course of European history.

Tiberius had his own plans. The treaty which he had made with Marbod at the time of the Illyrian revolt proved enduring. No military operations against the Suabian king were ever resumed. They were, indeed, not necessary, if the policy of an Elbe frontier were to be abandoned. The policy of Tiberius was to take advantage of the new situation in Germany, and to relieve the pressure on the Northern frontier by allowing free scope on the one hand to the antagonism between the Rhenish [1] and the Suabian elements, and on the other to the internal differences between the old tribal and the new political parties in each.[2] This policy was successful. The Germans became involved in a party strife far too important to allow them to pay any attention to the Roman frontier. It lasted the time of Tiberius, who could leave to his successors the task of completing the designs of Cæsar.

German
policy
of
Tiberius

VIII

The year after the battle of Idiaviso the antagonism between Irmin and Marbod was fought out. The in-

---

[1] Frankish, as they would have been called in later ages. The Cheruscan league, though not identical with the later Frankish league, was constructd of much the same materials.

[2] That is to say, those which men like Harald Harfagr in Norway afterwards encountered.

fluences which were at work in Germany penetrated to and affected the far north, and brought about a re-arrangement of forces that went far to decide the result. The Suabian power of Marbod was split by the defection of the most formidable of the far northern tribes, the Semnones and the Langobardi. The divisions among the Cherusci, which were to have serious results later on, were illustrated by another split in the ruling family. Just as Segestes had gone over to the Romans, so now Yngwe-mar went over to Marbod. But to the latter the gain was no effective substitute for the loss. The principles and ideas at work can be seen by the speeches which Tacitus puts into the mouths of Irmin and Marbod. The former represented Marbod as a satellite of Cæsar: a minor power whose orbit was dependent upon the greater. . . . Marbod contrasted the moral qualities of his own rule with those of Irmin's: his own open and honourable war against the Romans with the hole-and-corner attack upon Varus. But the hard-bitten war-beasts of the far north turned the scale against Marbod. He was beaten, and retired south-eastward into his strongholds. He requested the help of Tiberius. The latter replied that Marbod had scarcely the right to ask for a gift he had never himself given. He sent Drusus to Pannonia, however, to watch events. The young man was best out of the moral atmosphere of Rome, and it was safer to have the armies under the command of someone too close for conspiracy or revolt.

Fall of Marbod

Two years later, a new force appeared upon the scene

—Catualda of the Gotones.[1] He entered the realm of
Marbod, drove him out, and took his palace and the
new trading town which he had founded near it. Marbod wrote a dignified letter to Tiberius, praying for
sanctuary. Tiberius freely granted him permission to
come and go as he would. To the Senate, Tiberius spoke
very differently. Marbod, he said, had been a more serious danger to Rome than Pyrrhus or Antiochus. He
enlarged on the dangerous character of the peoples
ruled by Marbod, and thought that he might congratulate himself at having put so formidable a foe out of
harm's way.

Irmin fell, this very same year, before his domestic

**Assassi-
nation
of
Irmin**

foes, who all along had fought against the introduction
of political ideas and the principle of political kingship.
. . . All the actors were swept off the stage together.
Marbod was in exile at Ravenna; Irmin falling to the
assassin's sword in Germany; the fate of Germanicus
himself we shall see.

Marbod lived in Ravenna for eighteen years. He was
never restored to his throne. He suffered in Roman eyes
by thus surviving his fame and power. But hari-kari
has never been a familiar custom among the northern
peoples. He had the qualified satisfaction of seeing his
enemy Catualda follow him into similar exile at Forum
Julii. The North sank again into the condition of inter-
necine strife and divided counsels from which the policy
of Drusus and Germanicus had temporarily rescued
her. Much water was to flow down the Rhine before

---

[1] It has been suggested that Catualda was a Goth from the Vistula. His
name, however, seems to be "Caedwalh"—which we meet with later in the royal
family of Wessex.

the North grew gradually and naturally into unity. She has, indeed, not fully acquired it yet. The struggle which Marbod and Irmin began is still, after many vicissitudes, proceeding. . . .

IX

The task now was to find some occupation for Germanicus which might be a little less harmful than that of wielding armies. He could not be allowed to remain in Rome, a centre for all who saw in him the hope of an oligarchic restoration.

Germanicus goes to Asia

There was ample work for him to do at a comfortable distance from Rome. Affairs in the East needed the presence of a plenipotentiary of high rank and with full powers. The deposition of Archelaus, the last king of Cappadocia, and his death in Rome, had decided Tiberius to make Cappadocia a Roman province. Antiochus IIIrd. of Commagene also died in the same year, and the country applied for direct Roman government. There was discontent in Judæa. There were difficulties with Parthia and with Armenia. Vonones, whom Augustus had helped to make King of Parthia, had been driven out. He had been offered a crown by the Armenians; and M. Junius Silanus, the legate, had consequently detained him in Syria, in order to avoid complications with the new Parthian King. . . . Most serious of all was the great earthquake of A. D. 17, which involved twelve cities and caused widespread damage in Asia Minor. Tiberius sent 10,000,000 sesterces in relief of the suffering, and as Asia was a senatorial province he arranged

A. D. 17

to pay the taxes himself to the Senate for five years. . . . All these matters required attention.

But the convincing nature of the reasons for appointing Germanicus did not reconcile his friends to his departure from Rome. They wished him there; Tiberius, as decisively, did not wish him there. The resentment they felt, their acute perception of the political reasons which lay behind the appointment, prove those reasons to have been only too well grounded. . . . Germanicus himself, a perhaps too good-natured fellow, does not seem to have shared these feelings. Whatsoever happened, his own position was secure. . . . He was on excellent personal terms with his severe and square-toed cousin Drusus. Most people seem to have been on excellent personal terms with Germanicus. It was a gift he had.

Anger of his friends

Tiberius took his precautions. He had no intention of leaving the friends of Germanicus as free a hand for political intrigue in the east as they had had upon the Rhine. Silanus, the legate of Syria, who was a personal friend of Germanicus, was therefore replaced by a very different type of man, Gnæus Calpurnius Piso. . . . Now Piso was in many respects a remarkable personality. He sprang of the very old and august plebeian Calpurnian house, and he was an excellent illustration of the fact that the old republican temper was very far from dead: a rough, proud, unbending man, very wealthy, very independent, choleric, confident in himself. That he was transparently honest we may guess from his general behaviour. His wife Plancina was a friend of Livia Augusta. . . . This was the man whom

Gnæus Piso as a counterweight

Tiberius sent to Syria as a counterweight to Germanicus. He had evidently good cause for reckoning on Piso as one who would endure no nonsense from elegant young men and their crowds of interested flatterers.

X

The visit of Germanicus was the most important occasion of state which the east had known for a generation past. He visited Athens and Lesbos, and was everywhere received with ceremony. It was all in great contrast with life on the Rhine. On the Euphrates he had an interview with King Artabanus. The King was content with the importance and elegance of Germanicus, and the matters at issue were settled without difficulty. . . . The only difficulty which Germanicus found was, indeed, with Piso; and here a certain divergence of tone and mutual lack of sympathy seem to have been emphasized by the antagonism between Agrippina and Plancina. Neither Livia Augusta nor any friend of hers was an acceptable person with Julia's daughter. Piso took a very independent line. A command to lead Syrian troops into Armenia he simply ignored. Had Germanicus referred the matter to Rome, Tiberius would have been obliged to control his legate; but Germanicus, possibly misled by his friends, refrained from this obvious course.

Dissension between Piso and Germanicus

Matters grew somewhat involved. There was a serious scarcity in Egypt, and Germanicus proceeded thither to examine the situation in person. By releasing grain from the government store-houses, he brought down prices. . . . Wise as this action may have been, he was probably exceeding his authority, and trenching upon imperial prerogatives which Augustus had strictly reserved. In view of the definite and well-known prohibition which restrained men of senatorial rank from entering Egypt without the permission of the emperor, it was an act of imprudence for him to extend his visit in order to inspect the famous archæological wonders. . . . Piso seized the opportunity to assume that Germanicus had left Asia for good: and when the latter returned, it was to find that Piso had cancelled his arrangements, and was making his own.

The makings of a pretty quarrel were contained in these events. Germanicus took his stand on the authority he possessed, and Piso had to give way. He made ready, though reluctantly, to leave for home. Up to this point, Piso had a strong case. At Antioch, however, Germanicus became seriously ill: so seriously, that his friends soon asserted that he had been poisoned. Piso did not realize the situation. On hearing the news, he stopped his voyage at Seleucia, the port of Antioch, and sent messages of sympathy and inquiry. . . . The answer he received was a letter from—or alleged to be from—Germanicus, renouncing his friendship with Piso, and commanding him to leave Syria. . . . Piso accordingly proceeded on his way. Touching at Cos, he heard the news that Germanicus was dead.

The death of Germanicus was a sensational event which shook the whole Roman world. The circumstances surrounding it constitute one of those historical mysteries which can never be cleared up. From the moment when his illness became serious, Germanicus practically disappears from our view, and we are groping

Illness
of
Germanicus

His
death

in a mist of determined controversy and embittered propaganda in which we must grasp the truth as best we can.

The allegations evolved at Antioch were that Germanicus, solemnly declaring himself to be poisoned,[1] gave his friends on his deathbed a commission to bring his murderers to justice. He did not exactly say that Plancina was the criminal; nor did he in so many words declare that Livia and Tiberius had procured her to commit the crime; but he left this to be understood by inference. And his friends were instructed to take back, as the figure round which this cloud of vague accusation against Tiberius was to centre, his wife and children—Julia's grandchildren and Julia's daughter.

The allegations

Such are the allegations.

Gnæus Calpurnius Piso was an extraordinarily unlikely man to have been guilty of poisoning. He would have been far likelier to hit an enemy with a stick. The allegations which were being made at Antioch penetrated but slowly to his intelligence. At Cos he held a conference to discuss the situation. Officers who ar-

---

[1] The account of the death of Germanicus in Tacitus, *Ann.* II. 70–73, including his Last Dying Speech and Pathetic Appeal for Justice, is too much for anyone over the age of twelve to swallow. Tacitus was not present at the event. All he tells us is transcribed from the accounts of authorities whose identity and value are unknown to us, and can only be estimated by internal evidence. . . . Judging by internal evidence, his chapters 70–72 are copied from some political pamphlet of an anti-Tiberius and highly seditious nature. A similar tractate, published today, would land its writers in gaol for criminal libel. . . . It contains not a single definite allegation or plain fact, but is composed entirely of pathos and innuendo, evidently intended for readers who would not worry about such a thing as proof. . . . The remarks in the first part of chapter 73, comparing Germanicus with Alexander the Great, are of the most unblushing effrontery. With the second half of the chapter Tacitus returns to the normal, by the admission that the appearance of the body afforded no proof that Germanicus had been poisoned.

rived from Syria assured him of a welcome if he returned. His son Marcus voted for returning to Rome as the most prudent course. Domitius Celer reminded him that he was the legal governor, and that he had the sympathy of Livia Augusta and of Tiberius, though they might be circumspect in expressing it. "None," said Celer, "so ostentatiously regret the death of Germanicus as those who are happiest about it." Piso finally adopted the advice of Domitius.

He wrote to Tiberius stating the opinion that he had been driven out of Syria to prevent him from interfering with seditious designs, and assuring Tiberius that he resumed his command in the same spirit of loyalty in which he had hitherto held it. . . . On the voyage his fleet met the ships that were bearing Agrippina back to Rome. . . . Both parties stood to arms, but nothing else happened. . . . M. Vibius warned Piso that he would have to go to Rome to stand his trial. . . . "Time enough when the prætor sends for me," said Piso. . . . He did not understand yet.

He reached Syria, to find that Gnæus Sentius Saturninus, an experienced soldier, had been left in charge. Piso proceeded to resume his province by force. Defeated in a battle, he had to take another view of the situation. Saturninus directed him to return to Rome on parole.

Piso sent back to Rome

Piso went, still confident that he had done rightly.

Tiberius, in Rome, saw the second wave of unrest and hostility roll towards him.

CHAPTER IX

JULIA'S DAUGHTER

I

THE arrival of Agrippina at Brundusium was an event which would have attracted the attention of any government in any age. She had stopped for a few days in the island of Corcyra, "to compose her mind," before crossing the narrow sea. . . . The interval, which we may hope fulfilled its purpose, incidentally fulfilled one or two other purposes which may have been even more useful.

Arrival of Agrippina

Tiberius had had some warning of the turn which the occasion was likely to take. The news of the death of Germanicus had been treated as an excuse for demonstrations of loyalty so marked as to be a little bewildering. Business in Rome was suspended. The courts were closed. The Senate heaped memorial honours upon the heir to the principate. It heaped them so high that when a proposal was made to dedicate an especially large golden plaque to Germanicus among those which had been set up to famous authors, Tiberius began to feel doubtful. . . . He observed that a man's literary style was not determined by his rank. It was quite sufficient for Germanicus to be included among the classical authors at all. So the plaque was cut down to the usual size, and Germanicus reigned—officially at least—among the classics, where we now have considerable difficulty in finding him.

If Tiberius had misunderstood the nature of these demonstrations of grief, another incident might have made him aware of his error. It was no doubt unfortunate that Livilla, the wife of young Drusus, should at this particular moment have become the mother of twins. Tiberius was delighted, and for once expanded into something resembling tactless enthusiasm.[1] He pointed out to the Senate that never before had twins been born to a Roman father of similar status. . . . The Senate must have been exhausted by its previous efforts, for it apparently did not share the enthusiasm of the happy grandfather.

The suggestion implied in the words of Tiberius started a train of thought which it might have been safer to leave unaroused. That Drusus was now the obvious heir to the empire was quite true; but it was a reminder that would only add to Agrippina's anger.[2] A fault of tact was so rare in the Tiberius of these days, that we may guess that he, like Piso, had not yet appreciated the full import of what was coming.

II

The delay in Corcyra enabled the forces of Agrippina to be mobilized. Tiberius, naturally enough, had sent

Signs
and
Portents

Reception
at Brun-
dusium

[1] It would seem that Tiberius entertained some special devotion to the Dioscuri; so that the birth of twins would strike him in the light of a specially favourable omen. See p. 126 *ante*. The reference on p. 61 might also be derived from Tiberius himself.

[2] From Tacitus, *Ann.* II. 82, 84, we can see that it was the "family of Germanicus" (i. e., Julia's daughter and grandchildren) who were envisioned as the injured parties. Germanicus himself was a means to an end.

two cohorts of Prætorians to meet the ashes of Germanicus, and had directed the city authorities to accord an official reception. . . . His representatives found at Brundusium not only a full assembly of the friends of Agrippina, but a concourse the presence of which needed a little more explanation. Officers who had served under Germanicus of course journeyed thither. Others turned up out of respect to Cæsar. Others still, who had no particular motive to go, went because everybody seemed to be going; a reason which has its power in all times and at all places. The buildings and approaches of Brundusium were covered with an immense crowd. The cue had been passed. Percennius cannot have lacked surviving colleagues no less eminent in their profession.

Agrippina's carefully staged entry was a highly successful dramatic performance. When, slowly, weighed down with grief, the desolate widow appeared before the spectators bearing in her hands the funeral urn, and accompanied by her two young children, the crowd responded. . . . The note which was struck at Brundusium was sustained all the way to Rome.

Germanicus would have had noble obsequies in the ordinary course of events; but there was skill and subtlety in the way in which they were exploited. Every stage of the route was marked by religious ceremonies and popular gatherings met to pay the last homage of grief to Germanicus. At Terracina the delegation from Rome was waiting, headed by Drusus, bringing with him Germanicus' brother Claudius (afterwards emperor) and his remaining children. The consuls and

The imperial family abstains

senate, followed by another immense concourse, accompanied them. . . . Although the truth became clear, that a huge and successful effort was being made to capture the occasion in the interests of Agrippina, it was not possible to change the official part of the ceremony, which had to proceed to its due conclusion irrespective of any use that was being made of it. . . . By this time, however, not only Tiberius and Livia, but also Antonia, the mother of Germanicus, had withdrawn from any association with the occasion.[1]

Germanicus had owed his elevation not to any hereditary claim, but to co-optation. It is impossible now to estimate how far Augustus, by arranging his marriage of Germanicus and Agrippina, had wisely fortified his arrangements by engaging in their favour the interests of the hereditary line through Julia; or how far he had fatally weakened it by reviving the hopes of candidates for empire who could never permanently have maintained themselves. . . . What Tiberius now faced was a revival, in a new form, of the coalition between the claimants through Julia, and the senatorial oligarchy, which he had faced in the first year of his reign. Neither party to the coalition was strong enough to act alone. Together, they might succeed. The influence of Julia's faction might split the forces of the empire. . . . But if Agrippina could achieve her ends, the first stage of the destruction of the principate was in sight; for none of her sons could have grappled with the task of controlling the dominion of Rome. It would have fallen

The questions at issue

----

[1] Tacitus (*Ann.* III. 3) surmises that Antonia was intimidated. But Tiberius had reason to be grateful to Antonia for her loyalty at a moment even more serious than this. See *post* p. 263.

naturally into the hands of the oligarchy; and then by all precedents the destruction of Rome itself would be at hand.

III

The day of the funeral saw the climax. . . . Rome was thronged. It was a city on the verge of revolution. The Campus Martius was crowded with people who cried that the republic was lost, and all hope had departed. . . . It was Agrippina's hour. The enthusiasm for her was tremendous. She was saluted as the glory of her country, the only survivor of the race of Augustus, the model of ancient virtue. These were highly significant forms for enthusiasm—whether amateur or professional—to take. . . . Prayers were offered that her children might be spared to her and might avoid the snares of their enemies. . . . Placards were posted up: "Give us back Germanicus": and in the evening, these words were shouted about the city by people who took advantage of the dark to remain in the obscurity which still surrounds their identity.

The *funeral*

Tiberius displayed a calm which, if he took these demonstrations at their face value, is truly remarkable. . . . Afterwards, even some of those who took part in them suffered a little from reaction. It was remarked that it was a comparatively poor funeral. . . . The share of Tiberius in the occasion was confined to throwing a little cold water on the patients who suffered under this remarkable delirium over a commonplace young man and a violent young woman. He issued a proclamation which, though it never won him inclusion among the famous authors of Rome, has descended in some of its phrases to us. . . . "Principes mortales: rempublicam æternum esse . . ." it was perhaps his own profession of faith . . . "proin repeterent solennia: et quia ludorum megalesium spectaculum sub erat, etiam voluptates resumerent." Business as usual was resumed.

It remained to be seen whether, in a calmer and more judicial atmosphere, Agrippina could maintain the charges she and her allies had thus broadcast. Although no names were mentioned, it was clear enough that Tiberius was being accused to the whole Roman world of having poisoned Germanicus. . . . The charge was no trifling one. Owing to the circumstances in which he was placed—for which not he but Augustus had been primarily responsible—it was easy to demonstrate that he had an interest in removing Germanicus. . . . Agrippina knew, moreover, in all human probability, that Tiberius had reasons deeper and stronger than any of a personal nature, for profound hostility. . . . The conscience of a conspirator is very quick. And if Agrippina had not systematically and persistently conspired, then words have no meaning and facts no sense.

Propaganda against Tiberius

Tiberius became the more dangerous, the cooler he kept. He might or might not have been the man who was responsible for the poisoning of Germanicus. But suppose it became clear that Germanicus had never been poisoned at all?

IV

The stage was cleared now for the serious business—the trial of Piso.

The case for Agrippina was in the hands of Quintus Servæus, Publius Vitellius and Quintus Veranius, who had put it together at Antioch. Vitellius and his colleagues had requested Sentius Saturninus to send them from Syria a certain Martina, alleged to be a well-known poisoner, and a friend of Plancina. Martina, however, died suddenly at Brundusium on her way to Rome. . . . Poison was found concealed in a lock of her hair, though apparently she had not died of poisoning. . . .What she died of, and what poison was doing in a lock of her hair, we are not informed; but the instance of Martina was to prove a good example of the unsatisfactory type of evidence that was to be brought against Piso.

To Piso, also, the real state of affairs was penetrating by degrees. He sent his son ahead to see Tiberius, who gave him a reception which showed that he did not intend to condemn Piso unheard. . . . Piso himself went to see Drusus in Illyria. Drusus was too prudent to grant a private interview; but he expressed publicly his own hope that the stories which were being spread would prove to be false. . . . On his arrival in Rome, Piso showed no signs of a guilty conscience. He reopened his house, and resumed his usual social activities, much to the indignation of his foes.

The case against Piso

Fulcinius Trio, the well known delator, opened the proceedings by a move of his own. He himself laid

an information before the consuls against Piso. Against
this, which would have had the effect of a modern blocking motion, Vitellius and his friends lodged an objection,
which was sustained. Fulcinius then shifted ground,
Prelimi-
nary
moves and put in an indictment of Piso's previous career, asking for a trial in the imperial court. Piso consented to
this course: and had it been carried out, the whole set
of cases against Piso would have been tried in the imperial court. Tiberius, however, realized that this would
not do, since he was himself practically in the dock
with Piso, and he remitted the case to the senate.

Piso now needed an advocate of senatorial rank. His
search for a suitable defender illustrated old lines of
party cleavage. Among the five senators who refused
to handle his defence were Asinius Gallus and L. Arruntius, whom we have met before. But not all senators
belonged to the oligarchic party. Finally Manius Lepidus, Lucius Piso and Livineius Regulus, who were of
imperial sympathies, offered to undertake his defence
for him.

Tiberius, although he would not touch the case in
Tiberius
opens the
trial his own court, exercised his indisputable right to preside
in the Senate. His opening speech (given at length by
Tacitus) was a model of fairness and judicial temper,
which gives a very high impression of Roman justice.
"No British judge in summing up," says Professor Ramsay, "could put a case before a jury with more admirable precision and impartiality." Trio led off for the
prosecution, but his case was of no importance. He had
never had any purpose in intervening save to get the
trial removed to the imperial court, an object which

he had failed to achieve. The real business began when Vitellius rose to speak for the friends of Agrippina.

They did not rely exclusively on the charge of poisoning. The indictment against Piso was complicated by further counts of relaxing military discipline, condoning illegal actions towards allies of Rome, and injustice towards innocent men. He had used military force against an officer representing the state.

The charge of poisoning Germanicus broke down altogether. It proved a farrago of nonsense which could not for a moment endure the light of a judicial investigation. The allegations were, variously, that bones of dead men had been found in the house which Germanicus had occupied, and sheets of lead engraved with curses—which hardly formed a proof that he had been poisoned; that the condition of the body was consistent with poison having been administered—but here the evidence conflicted; that Piso had sent emissaries to watch the symptoms which Germanicus exhibited—but these were only his inquiries of courtesy. It was alleged that at a dinner, Piso had been seen to mix poison with the food of Germanicus; but no satisfactory evidence could be produced.

The poisoning charge breaks down

Had the case against Piso depended entirely upon the charge of poisoning, he would have got off a free man; but the political charges were more effective; and the evidence made them good. That he had sought to re-enter Syria by military force was indeed unquestionable. . . . Tiberius maintained his attitude of impartiality. He would not exercise his power to condone these political offences. . . . Livia, less interested in such

The political charges proved

matters, began to exert her influence to protect Plancina, who accordingly declined responsibility for the political actions of her husband. . . . Piso began to see that he was isolated, and he could not rebut the political charges. He proposed to abandon his defence.

His sons urged him not to give way, and he re-entered court. But unless Tiberius exercised his power on behalf of Piso, it was useless to proceed: and too much lay at stake for Tiberius to go out of his way. The Senate would almost certainly inflict the heaviest penalty within its power.

Piso went home without giving any sign of his intention. He acted as though he intended to return to court the next day. He wrote various letters and memoranda which, having sealed, he gave to one of his servants; performed his usual toilet and locked the door. . . . They found him next morning, impetuous and decisive to the last, with his throat cut vigorously through and his sword beside him.

Suicide
of
Piso

v

To the shocked and astonished Tiberius the news of Piso's death, and the letters which he had written, were duly delivered. He felt it somewhat as King Charles felt the death of Wentworth. He examined the servants closely as to the circumstances. Satisfied that he could do nothing there, he read aloud to the Senate the touching and manly appeal of Piso that his son should not be involved in any sentence passed upon him; and he now proceeded, since he was set free to do so, to use his power to see that the appeal should not be fruitless,

Young Marcus Piso was discharged from the political indictments; as was Plancina also, though Tiberius duly marked his sense of the difference by informing the Senate that he intervened for Plancina because his mother had asked him to do so. When the sentence upon Piso was debated, Tiberius vetoed the proposal, which could harm no one but his son, to erase his name from the consular fasti; he vetoed any form of sentence that involved the confiscation of his property; and when Messalinus and old Cæcina proposed, the one to set up a golden statue of Tiberius in the temple of Mars the Avenger, and the other an altar to Vengeance, he vetoed these no less decisively. Victories over foreign foes might deserve monuments; those over domestic enemies deserved only concealment.

Messalinus and Cæcina no doubt expected this veto upon their motions; for those motions were, of course, attempts to make the Senate declare, by special resolution, what it could not prove by judicial process—that Germanicus had been murdered. The resolution of Messalinus further attempted to involve Tiberius in this declaration. . . . Defeated in this he had another expedient—he proposed a vote of thanks to Tiberius, Livia Augusta, Agrippina and Drusus for their efforts to avenge the death of Germanicus. . . . This list contained (with the significant exception of Agrippina) only the names of those who had shown very qualified sympathy with the idea that Germanicus had been murdered; and it was a fresh attempt to involve them in an acceptance of Agrippina's point of view. L. Asprenas therefore rose to inquire politely if the omission of the

Tiberius exonerates his son

Manœuvres to involve Tiberius

name of Claudius were intentional. Messalinus accordingly was obliged to include it, with the result of considerably blunting the point of the resolution. . . . Tiberius quashed this too.

The victory of Tiberius was complete, though it had
been won at the cost of Piso. But Piso had no one but
himself to blame for the indiscretion which had wan-
tonly laid him open to charges he need never have incurred. . . . Since it could not be argued that Tiberius
had intervened to save a guilty accomplice, it was rumoured that he had had the accomplice murdered in
order to hide the evidence of their connection. . . .
Those who enjoyed the recreation of arguing in a circle
no doubt believed this rumour, which had the singular
advantage of being incapable of answer. . . .

But it is certain that the guilt of Piso and the complicity of Tiberius over the death of Germanicus have
never been proved; and that no evidence ever was produced which by any stretch of imagination could be
held to prove them.

VI

The death of Germanicus and the trial of Piso mark
the advance of the tide which had begun with the military mutinies on the Rhine and the Danube. It was
certainly an advantage to Tiberius that Germanicus
Advantages should be gone; but only because of the relation which
accruing Germanicus bore towards forces whose puppet he was.
to
Tiberius . . . In other respects it made no difference and brought
him no gain, beyond the freedom which he now pos-
sessed to make Drusus his heir.

We may measure the importance of the death of
Germanicus by the fury it occasioned. No accusation
that rage could invent or craft could level against Tiberius was left unhurled: and when proof broke down
and even coherence grew difficult, recourse was had to
those forms of slander which, since they are not rationally couched, cannot well be rationally refuted.
Anger so great must have had a cause: and the cause
was that with Germanicus vanished the one soldier who
had both the rank and the popularity to carry the army
against Tiberius.

Germanicus himself, of course, had never had anything to gain by revolution. His succession to the empire was assured. But he was very much of a cipher
beside Agrippina, whose interest in the subject has already been touched upon. The danger began with the
coalition between Agrippina with her hereditary claims
and the senatorial party. To this coalition Germanicus
had been indispensable. Like some other ciphers, he multiplied its force by ten. His disappearance meant that
the army would remain an intact *bloc,* and that Agrippina and the oligarchic party must face it with no weapons but intrigue and the appeal to public opinion.

There were difficulties in the way of doing this: and
the difficulties are instructive because they sprang from **Difficulties**
conditions inherent to the situation. The strength of **for**
the principate which Augustus had founded was based **the Sena-**
upon realistic compromise. It was strong, because he **torial**
had deliberately founded it on the fantastic peculiarities **party**
of actuality, and not on the neat symmetry of abstract
theory. It was never approved nor sincerely accepted

by a party which created out of their own imaginations an abstract theory of what the Roman political state had been, and who sought to restore a republic which, in the sense they meant, had never existed. . . . There had indeed once been a republic: but they had forgotten what it was like in the days of its strength.

If representative institutions have no other advantage (and they have many) they perform the invaluable service of constituting an index to public opinion and the strength of parties. In the absence of such an index men are liable to gamble on hazards which they would not otherwise run. Hence, while the power of Tiberius could be estimated with some approach to accuracy, it was impossible to guess the real strength of the oligarchy, which had been slowly recovering itself from the defeat of the civil wars. The new generation, which did not directly suffer from the moral impression of defeat, possessed the old political tradition bathed in a romantic glow which misled them as to its nature.

The deep weakness of the Senatorial opposition lay in that they had no gift of a political sort to give mankind; **Weakness of their position** they did not even realize that political power was based upon its practical utility to men at large. They were appealing tacitly for a support for which they could not pay. The old republican oligarchs had given Rome the hegemony of the Mediterranean, and had extended one inter-connected system of commerce and finance over the whole contemporaneous civilized world. This was a very practical gift to give men. It had added enormously to the potential wealth and prosperity of mankind. But when they had failed to realize those potenitalities, the principate had outbid them with the gifts of order, security, equality before the law, and opportunity for the smaller type of enterprise. . . . The political peril of the oligarchy had only come when it could no longer offer gifts of equal value: its end had come when it could no longer offer any gifts at all, but could only talk about some abstract "right" it supposed itself to possess.

It forgot that it had not enjoyed power on account of an abstract right, but because of the concrete benefits it could bestow. . . . It had, in its day, outbid and overwhelmed the ancient rule of the aristocracy, which had rather more claim to talk of "rights" than its successor. . . . The oligarchy at last, in this strange forgetfulness, fell into the second childhood which seems to attend so many political parties which have outlived their usefulness; and, like a cheap-jack, being no longer able to sell a sovereign for a shilling, proposed to its audience to sell a shilling for a sovereign. Its audience silently melted away.

VII

The reality of the opposition of the senatorial oligarchy can be appreciated if we trace some of its actions. Side by side with those great events which were connected with the military mutinies, conspiracy had been at work upon a smaller scale and from a different source. Particularly serious was the series of events which had centred round the death of Agrippa Postumus.

The death of Agrippa is usually narrated as if it were an isolated action unconnected with any other circumstances. The real facts show it to have been far other than this. . . . Promptly upon the death of Augustus,

an attempt had been made to carry off Agrippa from Planasia. A slave in Agrippa's service named Clemens organized an expedition and set sail for the island. His ship was too slow; Agrippa was slain by his gaoler, and the expedition consequently came to nothing. . . . Clemens, foiled in this project, formed another, so peculiar that it calls for notice.

He bore some personal resemblance to his master. He retired therefore to Etruria, let his hair and beard grow, and began to show himself more or less privately in various towns, preferably at night, spreading the report that Agrippa was still alive. . . . This report was believed in Rome. The pretended Agrippa was welcomed by a great concourse in Ostia. Tiberius was in some doubt whether to treat the matter with contempt or not. Finally, he placed the matter in the hands of Sallustius Crispus, who kidnapped Clemens by night.[1]

Now, it is of little use to maintain, in the teeth of all probability, that this episode was the creation of a mere isolated adventurer. Agrippa was the grandson of Augustus and the brother of Agrippina; he had at one time been co-heir with Tiberius of the principate, and it was arguable that his rights were not extinguished by the decision of Augustus which excluded him. The project of Clemens had been to carry him to the Rhine Army,[2] where, as we know, a mutiny was in progress. Agrippa would have been a suitable figure-head to lead

---

[1] From this episode and the other referred to on p. 129 f. n. *Ante.* it would seem that Sallustius was the head of some kind of special service.

[2] Tacitus, *Ann.* II. 39–40.

the march of the Rhine Army upon Rome, if Germanicus proved too weak. . . .

The actions of Clemens [1] could not have been conducted upon his own responsibility. They needed money, which he could not possibly have possessed. He certainly had accomplices—senators and knights, and even members of the imperial household—who laid the plans and financed the proceedings.[2] When he was put to the question, he would reveal nothing. Tiberius is reported to have asked him how he made himself out to be Agrippa. . . . "Just as you made yourself out to be Cæsar," was the reply. . . . This kind of thing, disheartening in its obstinate unreason, was also a definite hint. . . . Tacitus tells us that the death of Agrippa destroyed Julia's last hope. . . . This spectre pursued Tiberius. It was the hereditary claim of Julia and her children—who had been excluded by the principle of co-optation—that was employed against him. . . . When Agrippina, Julia's daughter, returned to Italy with the ashes of Germanicus, it was once more Tiberius whom they attempted to involve in responsibility for the death of Agrippina's husband. They could not forgive him.

Its backers

But the hereditary principle, however strong, was not quite strong enough in the imperial Rome of that age to explain the whole of these circumstances. An indefeasible hereditary right to a crown was the invention of much later ages. The crown itself moreover had hardly been invented in days when Tiberius was labouring to govern an empire on the principle that he himself

Affiliations of the conspiracy

[1] Dion Cassius says that he went to Gaul, and gained many adherents there. He describes him as marching upon Rome, as a claimant to empire. (LVII. 16. 3.)

[2] This is Tacitus' own assertion.

—as emperor—did not really exist. . . . The impulse came from men with ulterior motives, who backed the children of Julia for their own ends. . . . The crown was coming; but it had not yet come.

VIII

Almost simultaneously with this episode—extending down to the time of the battle of Idiaviso and the last invasion of Germany—some very strange details had come to light. L. Libo Drusus, after having been for some time under observation, was charged with sorcery: that is to say, with illegal and suspicious proceedings which required explanation.

The case of L. Libo Drusus

The case was a queer one. One of the documents seized was a list of Cæsars and Senators with mysterious signs against some of the names. No satisfactory explanation was forthcoming as to the meaning of these signs. Libo himself appeared to be a harmless but eccentric personage who dabbled in what purported to be occultism: but the cultivation of occult science hardly necessitates lists of political persons—at least, not without explanation, and this (though it ought to have been easy) was lacking. The construction which would, in these circumstances, be placed upon such symbols by a prosaic world trained only in exoteric knowledge, would be that they were notes in cipher, and that the cipher, like the names, had a political reference. . . . Libo himself denied having written the document. Very strong suspicions were entertained that his household could give valuable information—though perhaps not on occult science. It was illegal to force slaves to incriminate their master. When Tiberius instructed the executive to circumvent this legal difficulty by purchasing the slaves of Libo individually, Libo slew himself. He may have so acted in order to save them from the question; but the whole case was unsatisfactory.

But Libo had connections. He was not an unknown and unrelated individual. His identity has a certain interest. He was the great-grandson of the Pompeian partisan, L. Scribonius Libo, whose sister Augustus married; [1] he was therefore the cousin of Agrippina, and he was possibly the brother of that L. Scribonius Libo who was Consul in the year A. D. 16—the year in which Clemens was caught. Hence the interest which Tiberius took in him. [2]

Connections of Libo

Tiberius seems to have come to the conclusion that Libo was the dupe of men more cunning than himself, who employed him as a stalking horse: for he remarked that he would have interceded for him, although the man was guilty, if he had not destroyed himself. Of what precisely Libo was guilty never transpired, but the episode certainly pointed to the existence of underground conspiracy and political discontent among the Senatorial party.

IX

The Senatorial opposition thus tended to take that most irritating of all forms—the secret resistance, the

---

[1] See *ante* p. 10.

[2] Although Tacitus (*Ann.* II. 24–30.) describes the incidents in a way calculated to minimize their importance. Suetonius (*Tib.* XXV.) accepts Libo as a genuine revolutionary conspirator. That he confuses him with the consul is perhaps a valuable mistake.

quiet unconquerable hostility of men who had no practical alternative to propose: who did not want things better, but only wanted them different. . . . Their tactics were wrecking tactics. . . . Such oppositions, though not always ineffective, are nearly always an evil. They never correct the faults of the party in power; they invite mere repression, and their barrenness gives a show of justification for ruthless and equally unreasonable forms of severity. A bad opposition can be almost as serious an evil as a bad government. Sometimes it creates a bad government. The Senatorial party assuredly intensified the worst dangers of the military principate. They poisoned the atmosphere with slander, with treachery, with all the elements of doubt and distrust. They caused men, who were always aware of the precariousness of their position as heads of a military order, to feel morbidly conscious of it.

Evil effects of Senatorial opposition

Tiberius would not have admitted that they were seeking to restore a republic. In his view—as in that of Augustus—the republic, the political state, still subsisted. Their hope was to destroy the principate and restore the oligarchy. Their methods were cautious and secret; their advance was always disguised; the only form in which they never appeared was their own. . . . Against this opposition Tiberius began to construct his defence: not, indeed, invisible, but as subtle and as effective. . . . In this process the republic, torn between two forces, was indeed destroyed.

The defences of Tiberius

The two main bastions of his defences were the law of maiestas and the system of delation. Maiestas was any crime that injured the state—the respublica—considered as embodying the common interests of its citizens: it covered, not alone material injury to the state, but (and this was of course a logical and necessary extension of the idea) anything that damaged its prestige and impaired its authority in the eyes of men. The law of maiestas, as it developed under Tiberius, grew from this last conception, and was designed to safeguard the person of the princeps as representing the controlling power of the state.

Certain points are beyond question. It was not a military law. It was not an arbitrary law. It was administered by the recognized courts and the conventional magistrates. It would never have taken the turn it did, had not Tiberius been driven to seek special powers for the defence of his office; and he was careful to avoid any appearance of arbitrariness or despotism in his own actions; he threw upon the Senate itself the responsibility for carrying out the law. . . . But it was certainly not an ordinary law. It gave him the power to take proceedings before any actual or substantial crime could be proved: derogatory or hostile words or gestures came under maiestas, even if their meaning were oblique or constructive. A certain sort of political action must either on principle be left alone, or dealt with in this way; for if once it is allowed to take concrete or substantial shape, it may be too late to stop it.

The law of Maiestas

The answer of the Senate was, in many cases, to execute the law with such meticulous exactitude as to make it obnoxious. The Senate was itself subject to the pressure of public opinion; it could not refuse Tiberius the powers he required, nor decline to execute the law. But it could execute it too well, and throw a reflected odium upon him. To this class of case belongs that of Clutorius Priscus the poet, who having received praise for a poem upon the death of Germanicus, ventured, on hearing that Drusus was ill, to write an obituary poem upon him too. . . . Drusus recovered, and the poet found himself charged with constructive treason. What is worse, he was executed. . . . Tiberius was away when this happened. On hearing of it, he at once provided that no such execution should take place without a definite legal interval during which the sentence might be reviewed and quashed.

Policy of the Senate

Tradition has done less than justice to the Senate. . . . Much of what later ages supposed to be servility was sarcasm.

X

The system of Delation was the means, and the Delators were the men, whereby this law of maiestas was put into practical operation.

Delation

Delation was not expressly created: it grew. Augustus himself was the half-unconscious author of professional delation. The original delators were no more than agents who collected information respecting debts due to the treasury, and supplied it to the officials concerned. The title at last came to cover all who laid informations in cases in which the penalty was a fine. Augustus, having considerable difficulty in enforcing his laws with regard to marriage and divorce, offered payment to those who laid informations on which a court could proceed. As there was no Public Prosecutor, private enterprise was

the only method available. His action had the result
of turning delation into a recognized profession. A delator was a professional private detective, making his
income out of the commissions paid for a successful
prosecution. Original character of the Delators

We can form our own judgment concerning the de-
sirability of any such system as this. Most systems of
the sort are arguable. It would be quite possible to make
a serious defence of delation. The difficulty, taking time
and place and circumstances into account, was to think
of any other workable method; moreover, those who
deliberately break the law are at any rate taking a sporting risk, and must not grumble too much at being
caught. . . . But all we need to keep in mind is that
delation, whatsoever abuses afterwards distinguished
it, was not originally ill-meant. It had an intelligible
principle, and an authorized status.

The turn which Tiberius gave to delation was to
add political informations to the list of remunerative
business done by the profession. He thus engaged on
his side a number of expert investigators who were of
invaluable service; and as their reward depended upon
results, their assistance was free from some of the difficulties by which official detective forces are attended.
He could afford to pay high; for the money, after all,
came out of the defendant's estate. The result was that
all the most skilful delators turned to political work as
their principal stay. They become a politi-cal force

We need not, of course, expect to find the activities
of the delators either warmly appreciated or fervently
praised. The views held of their character by the Sena- Their character

torial party are at any rate a testimony to their professional success. . . . It is obvious that, in order to work at all, some of them must have moved in fairly high social circles, and must have been men of education. . . . Domitius Afer, for one, had the same kind of reputation as a speaker in court which is possessed by the more famous modern lawyers. He was perhaps the finest orator of his generation.

XI

It was after the events attending the death and funeral of Germanicus, and the trial of Piso, that the law of maiestas and the system of delation began to extend themselves and become important. The struggle had shifted from the German frontier to Rome itself. All danger of a civil war had been removed. The contest centred now in the capital, and had become a battle of wits and dexterity—silent, concealed, but a war to the death.

Change in the nature of the struggle

Both parties were equipped for the fray, with all the material equipments of money and organization which a political party can need. It was a fight for the possession of the world. . . . They appealed to their followers, the oligarchy with the romantic dream of a republic which had never been; Tiberius, with his prosaic principle of good administration.

XII

New elements imminent

But meanwhile, something else, which neither of them had foreseen, was advancing quietly towards them.

THE IMPERIAL HOUSE OF CÆSAR

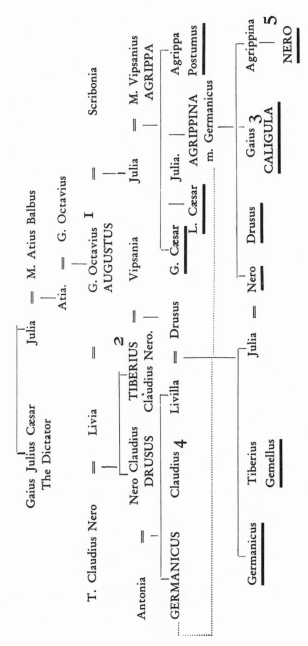

Note: The names numbered 1 to 5 are those of the first five emperors.

CHAPTER X

THE ADVENT OF THE TUSCAN

I

THE death of Germanicus created a situation for which no one was fully prepared. Tiberius was free from a burden which he had borne, and would no doubt have continued to bear, without overt complaint, since it was his duty to bear it; but it was open to him now to follow the somewhat rusty dictates of his own heart, and to settle the succession upon his son Drusus. . . . This very fact contained a trap and a pitfall.

Drusus was Tiberius without the touch of genius. Something of his grandfather, moreover, the great Agrippa, mingled with the Claudian blood in Drusus. He had a square-toed, undecorative sense of duty; but his duty, his affection, his robustness and good sense— and he had all these—seemed to be built of a less seasoned timber than those of his father. . . . He had loved and admired his cousin Germanicus; he took up the task of looking after the welfare of his cousin's children. But no one really loved Drusus. Even the relations of Tiberius with his son were qualified by an element of natural and unintentional disagreeableness.

Where the Vipsanian blood betrayed itself was in a strain of coarseness foreign to the subtler quality of Tiberius. . . . Drusus showed signs of suffering from the opportunities afforded by the imperial dignity of

Drusus the Younger

his father. He drank too much for his own good, and
he sometimes revealed the Vipsanius rather than the
Personality of Drusus Claudius in his cups. . . . Tiberius said, with paternal
candour: "You shall not behave like that while I am
alive to prevent it; and if you are not careful I will see
to it that you have no chance of doing so after I am
dead." . . . Nobody could complain that this was not
plain speaking. . . . What neither of them perhaps
fully appreciated was that the death of Germanicus laid
Drusus open to the attack of forces from which he had
been safe while his cousin lived.

Livia—Livilla, the little Livia, to distinguish her from
the Augusta—could hardly be expected to develop a
passion for her angular husband, who combined most
of the obvious faults of Tiberius with most of the obvious flaws of Agrippa. She was a beautiful, clever and
thoroughly modern woman, with evidently some touch
of that readiness to become the tool of others which her
brother Germanicus displayed. And in this case there
was someone else in the background—Seianus. The personality of Seianus is worth dwelling upon in some detail.

L. Aelius Seianus He was a Tuscan, sprung of that strange, dark and
ancient Etrurian race which seemed to derive many of
its typical characteristics from an older culture than
that of classical Greece and Rome. The Etrurian possessed a start in the virtues and vices of civilization that
the Roman, trained in a later school, never quite recap-
tured: his very mind and temperament, like those of
the Jew, were attuned by a remote historical experience
to the life of populous cities and crowded human society.

Mæcenas had been a Tuscan—that very wise man of the world who never fought nor worked, but, because he lived in a torrent of talk, ruled the men who did so. . . . After all, the art of arriving at an understanding with other men is the whole art of civilization.

Seianus possessed this gift. He had a genius for adapting himself to other men. We may call it genius, for he successfully adapted himself to the mind of one of the subtlest, most discerning, and most difficult men who ever lived—Tiberius.

II

Lucius Aelius Seianus had had, as we might expect, a brilliant career, and most of it had been intimately connected with the Augustan house. We may count him among the earliest of those men who used the military guild of the Cæsars as a ladder to fame and fortune. He was the son of a simple *eques,* Seius Strabo, the commander of the Prætorian Guard during the last years of Augustus. His mother was a sister of Junius Blæsus. After serving with young Gaius Cæsar in the east, he had been attached to the staff of Tiberius, to whom he made himself useful. Seianus became colleague with his father when Tiberius entered upon the principate. We have seen him accompanying Drusus on his mission to the Pannonian mutineers. When Seius Strabo was transferred to the governorship of Egypt, Seianus received the appointment to the sole command of the Prætorians.

Career of Seianus

His ability was by no means imaginary. Tiberius evidently found that he could rely upon it. By all the evi-

His ability

dence, Seianus was a cheering and encouraging person, who jarred on no man's feelings, but dwelt in a pleasant atmosphere of inward confidence and outward success. All the wheels of life revolved swiftly, quietly, adequately, on well-oiled bearings, around Seianus. As Prætorian prefect he had control of the guards on whom the immediate military power of Cæsar depended.

The importance of Seianus, and the convenience of having a man so astute and so capable at the head of the Prætorians, can be appreciated when we consider the circumstances of the first few years of the reign of Tiberius. His alert watch kept guard over the princeps. But it was a watch that was attended at first by no very sensational results. During the first eight years there were but twelve trials for treason; and in view of the crises through which Tiberius had passed, and the omens of trouble that had surrounded him, it is difficult to excite ourselves over this number. As long as the hopes of the opposition were still mainly in a military revolt, we hear little of Seianus.

Tiberius in these days had not lost that sense of republican freedom which had peeped out at Rhodes. . . . Long before he himself ever thought of giving up and retiring to Capri, Lucius Piso, after inveighing in the Senate against the evils of the day, had proposed to depart to the ends of the earth, and had proceeded to do so. . . . Tiberius was greatly disturbed, and Piso was soothed by an immediate mobilization of all available friends. . . . This was the Piso who had the hardihood to go to law with a lady named Urgulania, a friend of Livia Augusta. She naturally defied him, and Livia

Tiberius still comparatively free

invoked the thunders of empire, in the person of Tiberius, upon the head of Piso. As a man ought to obey his mother, even when he is fifty-seven, Tiberius started for court—but with habitual craft he went as a private citizen! . . . There was still a margin of hope when he could walk the streets of Rome like anyone else, his Prætorians hovering in the distance. . . . Matters had not drifted too far when old Lentulus, a mild and ancient Senator, on being charged with treason, could meet the charge merely with laughter. "I am no longer worthy to live if Lentulus hates me," says Cæsar with satisfaction: and the Senate disperses in perfect love and harmony. . . .

III

But all this was perhaps bought with a price, and the price was paid later on. Part of it was no doubt due to the unsleeping watch of the Tuscan. Though his watch might be unsleeping, yet never the less he began to dream dreams. He had his own methods of keeping in touch with the ebb and flow of opinion. One of them was to carry on intimate love affairs with selected wives, who furnished much useful information. He possibly extended this method a little further than was strictly necessary for his purposes: at any rate, he included Livilla, the wife of Drusus, in the sphere of his operations.

An intrigue with Seianus must have been an exhilarating experience if he conducted his love-making with the same skill that he showed in other branches of activity. Everything connected with it would go un-

Watchfulness of Seianus

obtrusively right. A young wife, married to a clumsy and angular husband, could scarcely fail to be thrilled by the spectacle of a man as graceful and adequate as Seianus, who could enchant the day and night and fill the sky fuller of stars than mortal eye had ever seen it. And a man like Seianus has the gift of putting square-toed husbands in the wrong. Drusus played his part too well for them to fail in theirs.

Seianus and Livilla

The clumsiness of Drusus rendered him unable to hold his own against such competition. He complained to his father. Something of an instinctive prejudice strengthened his perception: the intuitive doubt which plain men have of those who are too facile and too clever. This man would be their master. . . . Considering his own history, Tiberius showed a surprising lack of sympathy. He did not appreciate—how should he do so?—the extent of the damage. He had, naturally, a strong interest in seeing only virtues in the Tuscan. He had made Seianus and could unmake him. Men do not usually fear the tools they employ. Seianus, able to adjust himself to the nooks and corners of any man's mind, adjusted himself to this view of Tiberius. The Tuscan, in these days, was perhaps the only person who had a private key to that secret and secluded world where sat alone, in his real being, free of all masks and pretences, not Tiberius Cæsar, but the man Tiberius Claudius Nero.

The success of his experiment with Livilla seems to have revealed new and dazzling possibilities to Seianus. Not until he had actually made the experiment could the Tuscan have been aware of the extent to which it was practicable to go. Even if he had entertained hopes and ambitions before—and there is no evidence that he had—they would necessarily have been considerably qualified by the extreme improbability of success. But even half-way through his intrigue with Livilla there must have flashed across him the real and dramatic truth. By such a means he could—what? . . . The answer is, That which, by the allegation of the historians, he did do; that which his actions (if circumstantial evidence be worth anything) show him to have done. He marshalled the whole political strife to suit his private ends. The sheep dog drove shepherd and sheep alike where he wanted—that is, up to a point. There came a point at which the shepherd, late in the day, awoke, and asked himself whither he was going. It had not come yet.

Possibilities before the Tuscan

Drusus, though he realized the situation, was quite unable to deal with it. His warnings, his complaints, his contentions were ignored. He drifted farther into the wrong. Once, it is said, he lifted his hand to strike Seianus. But to strike a Tuscan is dangerous, even for a Roman.

IV

The dissension between Drusus and Seianus was brought to an end in the ninth year of Tiberius' reign by the death of Drusus after a short illness. . . . The public at large was not so surprised as it might have been. Two years before, Drusus, in the course of his

Death of Drusus A. D. 23

progress, had held the consulship with no less a colleague than his father. There were not wanting prognosticators of evil. It was remembered that P. Quintilius Varus had held the consulship in B. C. 13. with Tiberius; and everyone knew what had happened to Varus. And Gnæus Piso had held the consulship with Tiberius in B. C. 7; and everyone knew what had happened to Piso. And Germanicus had held the consulship with Tiberius in A. D. 18; and everyone knew what had happened to Germanicus. . . . When Drusus, the fourth man to hold the consulship with Tiberius, died two years afterwards, the prognosticators wagged their heads. It was not healthy to hold a consulship with Tiberius. Who would be the fifth?

It is possible that Seianus too had observed the singular fate of the consular colleagues of Tiberius. He was to observe it again, later on, in circumstances even more interesting to them both.

Severity of the blow to Tiberius

The blow to the old man was very heavy. The death of Drusus was but one more example of an embittering ill luck which dogged all his simple human hopes. He had been obliged to divorce Vipsania—to marry Julia, the root of his greatest troubles. He had been obliged to pass over Drusus and adopt Germanicus as his heir. . . . Germanicus had died . . . we have seen in what circumstances: and now Drusus had been snatched away. . . . No child of his own would follow him, but some other person, more or less of a stranger, and more or less—but probably more rather than less—indifferent to the methods and ideals of government which Tiberius had at heart.

V

The death of Drusus marked a certain stage in the life and character of Tiberius. He passed it over lightly to the eye of the outside world, [1] and refused to interrupt the business of government by a long period of official mourning. But he was never again quite the same man. The feelings which he repressed gave him a tendency to retire somewhat into aloofness. . . . He appeared in the Senate as usual, and gently deprecated marks of mourning. Without condemning those who acted differently, he had sought consolation (he said) in his work. . . . He may not have thought the Senate entitled to exhibit very marked grief; and possibly the senators felt that, out of mere decency, the less they felt the more they ought to show.

If Tiberius had had any share in the tragedy of Germanicus, he certainly gave no sign of it now. He had already, with the severe impartiality which he always showed, decided to adopt the common sense course of passing over his own grandson, the child of Drusus and Livilla, and to settle the succession on the sons of Germanicus and Agrippina whose age made them fitter candidates. They were accordingly now brought in by the consuls in person, and placed before him. He addressed them in a short speech which reduced the Senators to emotional tears.

The succession reverts to Agrippina's sons

[1] That he did feel it is shown incidentally by the anecdote given by Suetonius (*Tib*. LII). A deputation of citizens from Ilium offered, rather late in the day, their condolences. Tiberius underlined things for them by asking them to accept in turn his condolences for the loss of their late eminent fellow-citizens, Hector!

He told them that when their father died he had placed them in the care of their uncle. Now that Drusus was gone, he prayed the Senate, before their country and their country's gods, to act as guardian of these grandchildren of Augustus. "To you, Nero and Drusus, the senators will take the place of fathers. Born as you have been born, your good and your ill alike are matters which concern the state." [1]

Agrippina was not mollified. If Tiberius hoped that his action would in any way form a bridge to better relations, he was disappointed.

The funeral of Drusus was remarkable for its display of ancestral portraits. Borne in the procession were those of Æneas and all the Alban Kings,[2] as well as those of Attus Clausus and the Sabine ancestors of the Claudian house.

VI

Another couple also came before the notice of Tiberius. Seianus wrote an application for permission to marry Livilla. He had divorced his wife Apicata, so that no legal obstacle stood in the way.

Seianus applies for Drusus' widow

This, however, was going a little too far. Tiberius wrote back in full, warning him that he could not safely marry Livilla. He would not himself oppose anything that Seianus intended to do; but also he would not reveal the plans he had formed for the advancement of Seianus. Nothing was too good for him, and in due time he would hear further.

[1] Professor Ramsay's translation of Tacitus, *Ann.* IV. 8.
[2] These presumably came through the adoption of Drusus into the Julian house.

This letter certainly possesses a diplomatic quality so much out of the common as to suggest that it may be a genuine document.[1] It disturbed and puzzled Seianus, as it may have been meant to do; nor could a modern commentator help the Tuscan to unravel its signif- icance. What precisely was the danger of marrying Li- villa? The letter seemed to hint that Tiberius proposed something better for him. In fact, it was so phrased that it met nearly every possible event. . . . It may have implied no more than that the aristocratic Tibe- rius did not intend to promote his Convenient Instru- ment into the circle of the Augustan family. The Con- venient Instrument retired to think out other ways and means.

Tiberius refuses

Events were now shaping themselves in such a fash- ion as to fend Tiberius away from Rome.

The Tuscan's plan to marry Livilla, and to become the step-father of the emperor's children, had quite mis- carried. With the adoption of the children of Germani- cus as heirs of the empire, the prospect of future power had passed over to Agrippina.

But—casting our eye over the situation in general— there were many factors which might be transferred to the Tuscan's side of the calculation. Tiberius had learnt many lessons, but had he learnt the bitterest of all—that of treachery? . . . To Seianus, of course, the matter appeared in a more rosy light than this. He was propos- ing to himself (as he no doubt saw it) nothing worse

---

[1] A good deal depends on this; for the letter may be interpreted as a hint to Seianus that Agrippina and her party stood in his way. We must remember, however, that so astute a man as Tiberius would hardly leave his own life the one bar between Seianus and empire!

than a very skilful excursion into that realm of high
intrigue of which Gaius Julius Cæsar and Augustus
had been past masters. If he could outwit the craft and
penetration of Tiberius, what law could be adduced to
forbid him? . . .

The position of Agrippina was assailable; and if she
and her sons could be destroyed, it might once more become possible for the Tuscan to reach the end he had in
view. Tiberius could not be turned against Agrippina
by any direct or simple means. Having made her sons
his heirs, he would stick to what he had done. Inter-
mediate stages must be employed. The emperor could
be convinced that the supporters and friends of Agrippina in the Senate were politically dangerous. Agrippina
might be persuaded that a campaign against her friends
in the Senate was intended against herself. The breach
might be assiduously widened until it was beyond re-
pair. . . . And for all that then came to pass as a result, Tiberius himself would in the eyes of all men be
responsible. . . . Seianus could reflect with gracious
irony on the irrefutable truth that he was, after all,
himself but a Convenient Instrument. . . . There
might yet come a day when he could repudiate the acts
of Tiberius, and stand in the position of one who
brings deliverance to the victims of an unreasoning oppression.

VII

And these were no idle thoughts. We should err if
we believed that Seianus invented and devised the po-

litical clash of which he proposed to take advantage.
He used it for his own ends; he used it to discredit Tiberius and to blacken his name; but he did not cause it.

Agrippina was little more than an ignorant and ardent woman who never knew that she was caught in
a political battle of giants, and used as a weapon in a
strife in which she, certainly, could never be a victor,
because she did not appreciate the essential truth of
the position in which she found herself. She needed only
to be enticed to be a little more what she always was—
a little more angry, a little more suspicious, a little more
unreasonable—and she would sacrifice, on behalf of
children who needed no sacrifice, since Cæsar had made
them his heirs, all the concessions which Cæsar had made.
. . . She had already proposed to surrender the empire
into the hands of the senatorial oligarchy. The oligarchy
had welcomed her alliance. It admired the enlightened
patriotism which proposed to sacrifice so much to its
interests. It has commemorated the virtues of one who
consented to be its dupe, in contrast with the vices of
one who did not. . . . And indeed, in the history of
politics it is usually the dupes whose reputation descends
to us labelled with many virtues. Those who have had a
more vivid sense of their own interests have suffered a
harder fate.

Although the clash would have taken place even if
Agrippina had never been, yet it was she who became
the occasion of it. . . . She could not believe in the
sincerity of Tiberius. . . . With her, perhaps, first began that attitude of mind so obsessed with the imaginary hypocrisy of Tiberius, that even if he had killed

Weakness
of
Agrippina

Agrippina
utilized
by both
parties

himself as a mark of good faith, it would have suspected him of ulterior motives.

VIII

The transfer of the centre of contest to Rome itself was marked in many ways. There had been twelve impeachments for treason in the first eight years of Tiberius' reign. In the next six years, beginning with that which saw the death of his son Drusus, there were twenty. Seianus in this year, advised a precautionary step which Tiberius adopted. The Prætorian guard, hitherto scattered in various camps about Rome, was concentrated into one permanent fortified camp at Rome itself. . . . This measure had far-reaching effects. The reasons for it were that it added to the security of the princeps by assuring that adequate military force should always be at hand. It brought with it a possibility which did not become an actuality until many years later— too late for the intelligent diplomatist who first devised the plan. It put Rome, and the princeps too, at the mercy of that military force and the man who controlled it.

The coincidence of this concentration of the Prætorian guard with the death of Drusus, and the events which were closely to follow, is circumstantial evidence of some value respecting the intentions of Seianus. Any one link in the chain, taken alone, might be an accident. All of them, linked together, cannot be an accident. And by the testimony of the historians who wrote the history of those times, they were no accident.

From the time of the death of his son, moreover, Tiberius allowed a good deal of public business to pass

The Prætorians concentrated in Rome

through the hands of Seianus before it came to him. The consuls and magistrates habitually called at his house for audience every morning, to lay their agenda before him; and even personal communications were transmitted through Seianus. Hence the Tuscan became cognizant of all business, and his influence was recognized as supreme.

The discernment of Tiberius was not at fault. Up to a certain point, which was not yet in sight, Seianus was the perfect servant. Exactly how far the discernment of Tiberius penetrated; exactly how far he gauged the position of that point of peril, is a problem beyond our power to answer. . . . Which of the two was the subtler man could only be made evident by events.

If now Agrippina had accepted the olive branch silently held out to her, and had consented to await the natural end of the reign of Tiberius, and the natural succession of her sons, this would be the end of the story, and there would be no more to tell save that they all lived together happily ever after. . . . But she could not trust Tiberius. The pressure to prevent her from doing so was too powerful to resist. The senatorial party was as deeply interested as the Tuscan in irritating and inflaming her feelings. Between the two forces she was swept into a vortex from which there was no return.

New relationship of the political parties

Tiberius would never himself have struck down Agrippina. Her life and that of her sons were his security against such powerful but necessary servants as the Tuscan. While they lived, he was safe, and Seianus could without danger be given full power to deal with the oligarchy. But if they went, the time would come when he would have to look to himself.

Tiberius had, in effect, offered Agrippina and her sons a coalition against the common enemy, the price of which was to be the succession to the empire. . . . It soon became clear that they did not accept the offer, and that their hostility was increased rather than diminished.

Seianus
leads

So far, therefore, success lay with the Tuscan.

IX

The interests of Tiberius and Seianus thus remained close enough to be called identical. To track down the work of Agrippina and her friends was for Tiberius the readiest means by which he could check the party which aimed at the destruction of the principate: while to Seianus it promised the best opportunity of widening the breach between Tiberius and Agrippina. . . . Gaius Silius belonged to Agrippina's party. Cremutius Cordus, the historian, belonged to the other, the senatorial party, the action of which was independent of Agrippina.

The case of Cremutius is the first important case in which a "dummy" charge was used to secure a conviction, and it is also the first which betrays the methods of Seianus. Cremutius was accused of having called Brutus and Cassius the last of the Romans. . . . This was certainly as much constructive sedition as praise of Robespierre would have been under a Bourbon monarchy, or praise of the regicides in the days of Charles the Second. It was argued (and the defence, if true, was a strong one) that Augustus had heard the book read, and had raised no objection. . . . Cremutius, however, saw that Trial of Cremutius Cordus he was about to be condemned, and removed himself by voluntarily abstaining from food. . . . The assertion is made that the real cause of the action against Cremutius was of a more personal nature. When, three years previously, the theatre of Pompeius had been burnt down, Tiberius had especially thanked Seianus for his activity in dealing with the fire, and a statue of Seianus was accordingly set up in the restored building. Cremutius had made one of those airy remarks with which the senatorial party was so free. He had observed that now, at any rate, he could detect the damage done to the theatre. . . . But if this is the best that could be said in defence of Cremutius, even his friends must have admitted that he was surprisingly lacking in discretion.

The trial of Cremutius Cordus shows that the battle was now joined.

That it had been joined to some purpose is illustrated by another trial which took place not long after. The disposition of Tiberius to retire up the stage had been Case of Votienus Montanus sympathetically encouraged by Seianus: and it was still further increased by the case of Votienus Montanus, who was indicted for treasonable slander. Tiberius attended court in person to hear the case. Among the witnesses was a soldier named Aemilius. The evidence of Aemilius, particularly detailed and firmly adhered to, was so scandalous that Tiberius was struck with consternation. He cried out that he must clear his character himself without delay and in that very court. It was necessary for his friends to soothe his feelings; but even the assurances of the entire assembly present did not content him.

Although the evidence of Aemilius has not been recorded for our benefit, the nature of his statements is not difficult to guess. They must have consisted substantially of the charges which have come down to us in certain notorious chapters of Suetonius; for though they are ascribed by that writer to the later years when Tiberius had retired to Capri, we have already seen at least some ground for thinking that their origin is traceable to a much earlier time, and that they were in fact the slanders started by Julia and by her handed down to Agrippina. . . . If this be the case, the feelings of Tiberius are comprehensible. They were certainly strong.

The case of Votienus had considerable and serious effect. Tiberius did not treat lightly the statements he had heard; and if, as Tacitus informs us, he showed from that time forward greater severity, his indignation must have been directed against Agrippina, for she was the chief sufferer from his change of mood.

Case of
Claudia
Pulchra

Although we are not now able to trace it with any certainty, there must be some connection between this case of Votienus and the case of Claudia Pulchra. The trail was by this time running very close to Agrippina, for Claudia was her personal friend. The charges against Claudia included adultery with one Furnius, and attempting the life of Tiberius with poison and incantations. . . . This was a famous and sensational trial in its day. The prosecution was conducted by the delator

Domitius Afer, who founded his fame as an orator by his work in court.

How far we are to accept these indictments as representing the real crimes of Claudia is questionable; the art of obtaining a conviction upon technical charges, when the real ones are difficult or undesirable to prove, is not a purely modern acquirement. They sufficed for their purposes in the skilled hands of Domitus Afer. The trial had the effect of bringing Agrippina to the surface.

As soon as she knew that the verdict against Claudia was a certainty, she had an interview with Tiberius.

X

The interview was a remarkable one.

As the memoirs of Tiberius were never published, the details more probably come from Agrippina herself.[1]

She found him sacrificing to the Divine Augustus, and she told him that it was inconsistent of him to pay respect to Augustus and at the same time to persecute his descendants. The spirit of that divine man had not passed into any image: *she* was his true image and representative. Claudia's sole crime had lain in being her friend.

Agrippina's interview with Tiberius

All this, however true, was hardly tactful. She could not more neatly have stated the underlying principle of legitimism, nor have questioned his title more thor-

[1] Through the memoirs of her daughter, the younger Agrippina, the emperor Nero's mother.

oughly. Tiberius answered with a quotation from a Greek play:

> "My daughter, have I done you wrong
> Because you are not a queen?"

And this was the real issue between them.

She broke down when she heard of the verdict against Claudia. . . . Whatever the real crimes of Claudia may have been, it seems evident that Agrippina felt herself **Deadlock** included in the indictment. Tiberius went to see her. She asked permission to marry again. He left the room without replying. What object, after all, could she have in contemplating a second marriage? It was his turn to be unable to answer without saying that which was better left unsaid.

All this defined the breach and increased it. Seianus took care that nothing should be left undone to prejudice Agrippina still further. She grew convinced—or acted as if she were convinced—that Tiberius was intending now to poison her also. When she dined with him, she pointedly refused to eat. . . . Tiberius would have been more than human if he had not resented so clear a hint. The less the implicit accusation corresponded to the truth, the more serious a view he must take of it. If she did not believe it herself, the case was bad enough. If she did, the case was infinitely worse. . . . Tiberius was dealing with the sister of Agrippa Postumus and the mother of Caligula.

State of Agrippina's mind Some thoughts and feelings, if entertained, devour and destroy like living parasites the mind that is their host. Tiberius might be dealing with a mad-woman—

but she was one who successfully got nineteen centuries
of posterity upon her side.

XI

He was not unscathed. The wear and tear of these
things told upon him. He was driven still further in
upon himself. But the thunder-bolt which drove him
out of Rome, drove him into his second exile and his
second hermitage, came from another quarter. It came
from Livia Augusta.

Since Livia published no memoirs, we are deprived
of the intimate details—real or imaginative—which
Agrippina supplied to posterity. Suetonius himself relies
upon "it is said" for his authority. There were plenty
of good reasons why Tiberius should grow restive at
his mother's attempts to keep her control over him.
Livia disliked Seianus, and was opposed to the adoption
of any strong measures against Agrippina. She may
have distrusted, as mothers do, her son's ability to hold
his own with the Tuscan, once Agrippina and her sons
were gone. Tiberius was willing to take the risk. . . .
But the actual and immediate cause of the crisis was
much more characteristic. She wanted a newly-made
citizen placed upon the roll of jurors.

Tiberius objected. Livia argued the point. He at length
agreed, on condition that the new juror's name on the
register should be endorsed as forced upon the emperor
by his mother. At this adroit twist to the old point of
debate, Livia lost her temper. To prove her contention
that Tiberius was a thoroughly disagreeable person who
could never have achieved anything without her help,

Quarrel
with
Livia
Augusta

she produced some old letters which Augustus had written to her. . . . The blow was more devastatingly effective than she can ever have intended it to be. . . . Tiberius beat a retreat. To judge by his subsequent attitude to his mother, he felt it as a cruel and humiliating blow in the back. . . . This, apparently, was all he could expect in return for the many sacrifices he had made, and for a devotion to duty which few men had equalled! . . . He may not in these days have been his old self. He could not—at any rate, he did not—laugh it off. He very certainly was not a man on whom destiny showered her softer rewards!

He hardly saw Livia again. . . . He beat a retreat not only out of her presence, but out of the presence of all these people who had pursued him with their blind rancour, their hopeless malice, and their ignorant opposition.

XII

He was sixty-seven years old in this year in which he did the strangest, most mystifying thing of a strange and mystifying life. He had dwelt at home so far throughout his reign. Though he had talked of visiting the provinces, he had never gone; he had changed his mind at the last moment as a certain sort of shy, secretive man will do, and had remained at his desk and at the routine of business. Now he set off, ostensibly to Campania, to consecrate a temple at Capua. He was accompanied by one senator, M. Cocceius Nerva, grandfather of the emperor Nerva; by Seianus; and by a group of astrologers and other inquiring spirits. . . .

Tiberius leaves Rome

After consecrating the temple he visited the island of
Capri, that strange romantic rock which Augustus had
bought of the city of Neapolis, and which towered huge
out of the blue Mediterranean beyond the point of the
Sorrentine peninsula. . . . At Capri he remained.

He built twelve villas on Capri, and there settled in
seclusion. The island was guarded against all unauthor-
ized persons. Tiberius had disappeared into the fast-
nesses. From that time forward he became a tradition,
a legend; he ceased to be a man amongst men, and grew
to be an invisible power, proving his existence by his
actions, but by nothing else. It was promptly whispered
in Rome that he had gone there in order to wallow in
debauchery: that he had gone to hide from the eyes   Tiberius
of men his hideous and crime-ravaged countenance,   retires
to
conscious that it deserved to be hidden. . . . To which   Capri
Tiberius made no reply. . . . The world talked, but
silence fell over Capri, where the level waters glittered
around sunlit rocks.

It is not difficult to understand the feelings which
led him to Capri. And he had his reasons. He left the
field in Rome clear for young Nero, the son of Germanicus and Agrippina, who, free from the repression
of his presence, might perhaps learn the ropes of imperial rule more easily. Whatsoever there was of good
in the children of Agrippina would have its fair chance
—or whatsoever there might be of evil. The removal of
Tiberius was a test.

Such reasons walked hand in hand with those of Seianus. If the Tuscan himself had planned it, the retirement of Tiberius to Capri could not more neatly have

fitted in with all he desired. It left the field in Rome clearer still for him: it left him the mouth-piece of empire. . . . Tiberius, after moving up the stage, had passed off the stage altogether: and Seianus remained before all men's eyes, the sole speaker and actor thereon.

Signifi-
cance
of his
retire-
ment

When, by degrees, that prompting voice grew faint—when, at last (from whatsoever cause) it ceased—then Seianus would still remain; the audience would hardly notice that the words he spoke were now his own.

All things which arise from the thoughts of men intellectually powerful have a strange and baffling quality of intricacy, like the moves of an expert chess-player, which at any moment have a hundred shifting aspects, fulfil a hundred purposes, and can be turned to a hundred different possible eventualities. This quality resided in all the simplest actions of Tiberius. It did not reside in those of Seianus. The retirement to Capri could have many events for Tiberius. One event exhausted its possibilities for Seianus. This was the essential weakness of the Tuscan's position. His position was not ringed with the infinitely complex defences which Tiberius, hardly thinking, perhaps never consciously designing, by mere instinct swept around himself in such plenitude.

And while the people of Rome—the well-dressed and the ill-dressed mob alike—fancied that Cæsar had gone to Capri to forget the world, the old man of Capri remembered the world very well. He sat at his desk there, as he had sat at it in Rome; business went through his hands as before. Perhaps he could see the perspective of

things better in Capri, free from the disturbing influence
of Rome and the hostility of Romans.

XIII

That it was no common moroseness towards man-
kind at large that drove him, he proved immediately   Tiberius
after his arrival in Capri. A theatre in Campania col-   still
active
lapsed, with serious loss of life. He returned at once to
Campania to show his practical sympathy, and he made
his personal presence all the more public because his
earlier passage through Campania had been strictly private. He was always his old and usual self when there
was something useful and practical to do.

CHAPTER XI

THE ENTANGLEMENT OF JULIA'S CHILDREN: AND THE FALL OF THE TUSCAN

I

IF the old man had reckoned that his absence from Rome would betray young Nero into showing, whether for good or ill, his true nature, he was right in his calculation. . . . The friends of Agrippina seemed to think the departure of Cæsar a retreat. In the strange freedom of Rome they began with confidence to lift up their heads. But Tiberius had left behind him eyes as keen and as watchful as his own. If Agrippina and her sons elected to wander from the straight path of rectitude, the Tuscan was waiting, and he would not miss that prey.

The tale of the process by which he caught them is a complex one, with dark interludes wherein the modern historian can but grope at large. As the Romans themselves told the story, it began with the delator Latinius Latiaris and three friends, who wanted the consulship. Seianus disposed of the necessary patronage, and accordingly they directed their attention first to him. It is evident that they already possessed private information of a nature which would interest him to the highest degree; and the power of patronage held by the Tuscan was the means by which he secured this information for Tiberius and himself.[1]

Latiaris and his syndicate—which included Fulcinius Trio—were at any rate aware that Titus Sabinus, a friend and devotee of Agrippina, had important schemes on foot. As soon as their price was agreed upon, they set to work upon the case. By suitable advances, Sabinus was induced to talk; and when he had sufficiently revealed his plans, he was induced to commit himself in the presence of hidden witnesses. The evidence was then sent to Tiberius, who communicated it to the Senate.

The news of the arrest of Sabinus had some very strange effects in Rome. The state of panic-stricken distrust and suspicion which immediately followed would seem to show that a large number of important people had only too much reason to fear the inquiries of the delator. An outward show of confidence was restored only when they began to be conscious that their apprehensions betrayed them. Arrest of Sabinus

The account given by the friends of Sabinus is that he was charged merely with having expressed outspoken opinions of Cæsar for his cruel and unfeeling treatment of the unhappy Agrippina. . . . The official communication which reached the Senate from Capri put a very different complexion upon the matter. Sabinus was charged with tampering with the servants of Tiberius, and with conspiracy against his life. . . . Precisely how much Tiberius revealed in his message is The Charge

[1] In view of the status of the persons concerned it would seem at least probable that Latiaris and his syndicate did not care to handle the case without some guarantee for the future, such as the consulship would give them.

uncertain. It was at least sufficient to secure the immediate condemnation of Sabinus: and in the promptitude —even the haste—with which the execution was dispatched by the Senate, there is a suggestion that influential persons were very much afraid that Sabinus, forsaken by his friends, might in despair make further inconvenient revelations on his own account.

Tiberius sent a further message to the Senate. In returning thanks, he hinted that he still feared danger to his life; and though he mentioned no names, the allusion was evidently to Agrippina and Nero.

But how much did Tiberius know? There must have been many men who would have given a good deal to discover that! They found a spokesman in Asinius Gallus, who rose to suggest that Cæsar should confide his grounds of apprehension to the Senate, and allow it to deal with them. This disingenuous proposal that he should disclose, to the very persons most concerned, the full extent of the incriminating evidence in his possession, attracted the angry attention of Tiberius. Seianus diverted his wrath. There were (at any rate, from the Tuscan's point of view) more important issues at stake than the debating points scored by Asinius Gallus during a life and death struggle for empire.[1]

Nero and Agrippina implicated

The truth would seem to be that Nero and Agrippina had both been implicated by the evidence obtained. But to make the real heads of these conspiracies amenable to the law was extremely difficult. Their devoted friends

---

[1] Asinius, having married a half-sister of Agrippina, was related to the latter, and therefore presumably an interested party. Asinius seems to have been unable to cure himself of a certain smartness which can hardly have commended him to a man who loathed smartness in all its forms.

were ready to take the risk of acting on their behalf. Even against Nero the evidence was more circumstantial than direct. To secure the trial of Agrippina and Nero it might be necessary to substitute a technical charge which could be substantiated for the real one which could not be. But this could never be done while Livia Augusta was alive. She remained a firm barrier in the way, and the alienation of Tiberius did not induce her to change her attitude.

II

During the tense interval which followed the execution of Sabinus, the relationship of the parties was strained. It was still impossible to make out how much Tiberius knew. Nero grew somewhat reckless. He spoke openly against Tiberius, and took little trouble to conceal his embittered hostility. The friends of Cæsar treated Nero with mingled coldness and contempt. There were not many who cared to show him any degree of cordiality. Tiberius himself seemed self-conscious, and avoided noticing the extent to which Nero was cold-shouldered by his supporters. . . . The matter could not remain permanently in this condition. The first event which altered the balance of affairs would see a violent crisis.

The interesting feature of the day was the glory and magnitude of the Tuscan. His splendid orb began to eclipse the sun of Cæsar. Which was the sun and which the satellite became, indeed, a problem which troubled the minds of men. The Senate voted altars to Clemency and to Friendship, beside which stood statues

Growing power of Seianus

of Tiberius and Seianus—a novel pair of Heavenly Twins. . . . It solemnly requested them to allow themselves to be more frequently seen. . . . Apparently they split the difference. Seianus was willing enough to shine before men; Tiberius did not see the necessity. So instead of going to Rome, they paid a visit to Campania. . . . Everyone who could go, hastened to wait upon them—especially upon Seianus. Senators, equites and more common persons camped in the fields and besieged the Tuscan's door. But to get at Seianus was difficult. He was becoming accessible only to those who were willing to commit themselves to his cause: and even this could be effected only by buying or fighting or cajoling a way through the crowd of competitors. . . . If Tiberius missed any of this, then the less Tiberius he. The man would have been dull who failed to notice that the throne of Cæsar was being contested by two groups of protagonists. Very ordinary persons were able to perceive it; and many of them thought that Cæsar would readily fall before the victor. . . . Cæsar himself had become the doubtful, the problematic factor. He was, after all, a very old man; he was seventy years of age this year.

The Campanian visit

III

When Livia Augusta died at the age of eighty-six, the principal difficulties were swept from the path of Seianus. The depth of the dissension between her and her son is visible from his conduct. He did not visit her during her last illness. After her death, although he expressed the intention of seeing her, so that they waited several

days in anticipation of his arrival, he did not come, and
it became necessary to carry out the funeral without
further delay. He wrote explaining that he was detained
by urgent public business. . . . Her funeral oration
was spoken by her great-grandson Gaius—better known
by his nickname of Caligula. . . . Tiberius damped the
expression of extraordinary honour towards the wife of
Augustus. The Senate was refused permission to deify
her; the funeral was quiet; he disregarded her will and
left it unexecuted. . . . The Tuscan must have been
happy to observe that Cæsar apparently did not endorse
those views which his mother had held. But precisely
what views Cæsar did or did not endorse had become a
problem perilous to guess at. Death of Livia Augusta

That the Senate was by no means entirely subservient
to Tiberius is visible in its conduct with respect to Livia.
It did not confine itself merely to the program he
recommended. While it politely acknowledged the pro-
priety of putting public business before private grief,
it proceeded to vote a year's mourning and an arch in
her honour—which was a tribute never before paid to
any woman. . . . Tiberius undertook to build the arch
at his own expense. As he never did, the arch was never
erected.

IV

Seianus acted with promptitude: perhaps too great
promptitude. He began to feel himself in control, and
feelings of this kind are always a dangerous luxury. Tiberius was ready to take the step on which such great
issues depended. Immediate action against Agrippina

A message therefore came to the Senate from Capri. Agrippina was charged with insolent language and refractory temper; Nero, not with conspiracy, but with immoral habits. The sensation created by this message was tremendous. It was increased by the absence of any hint concerning the action which Tiberius expected the Senate to take. Like Henry VIII, and for the same reasons, he was determined not to shoulder the entire responsibility for these great measures of state: he intended the Senate to share it with him. But it had many and various reasons for declining to do so. . . . He seemed to be implying that the Senate knew the facts as well as he did, and needed no information! But no one could be sure how much he knew; and to assume the guilt of Nero and Agrippina would be to admit a knowledge which some did not possess, and which others would be the last men to admit that they possessed. . . . Those who were adherents of Agrippina would not readily allow her to be condemned on technical or "dummy" charges. . . . There were others who were of Cæsar's party; but some of these held Livia's views, and they implored the House not to support a policy that Cæsar himself might in the end bitterly regret. . . . When M. Aurelius Cotta, on behalf of Cæsar, rose to move a vote of condemnation, senators took refuge in agitated disclaimers. . . . The old man had presented them with a dilemma singularly difficult to face!

Consternation of the Senate

A popular demonstration was (as it so often is) the only resort. It came to the rescue by parading with the images of Nero and Agrippina, and it provided that useful political speaker, "A voice," to declare that the message of Cæsar was a forgery. Bills were circulated, containing what purported to be resolutions against Seianus moved, or to be moved, by various eminent senators. The result of this test of public opinion apparently proved disappointing. The appeal to public opinion was, indeed, a forlorn hope. The men whose views might have mattered were the rank and file of Cæsar's own armies; and they, who could not be captured on the Rhine and the Danube, could not be swayed from Rome. . . . Cæsar remained unmoved. . . . Seianus, moreover, was stinging in his retort. He counselled Tiberius that his complaints were being treated with contempt; and he made a damaging reference to the imminent appearance of the realities instead of the effigies at the head of this Revolt of the People. . . . Tiberius seems to have agreed; for he sent a second message, in which he demanded that if the Senate felt unable to act, it should leave the matter to his discretion.

The Senate leaves the matter to Tiberius

Once it was put to the test, the whole position of Agrippina and her supporters proved to be built on sand. The Senate surrendered, and humbly replied that it would endorse any action he might take.

v

Agrippina and Nero were tried, therefore, before Cæsar himself: and as few particulars of the trial have survived,[1] it was probably held *in camera*. Among the charges against Agrippina (which were of course denied) was a project of escaping to the army and taking refuge with it. Gnæus Lentulus Gætulicus, the comman-

---

[1] Philo records that Avillius Flaccus was the principal prosecutor.

der of the Rhine army, was implicated. He escaped by one of those bold and manly answers which often went down well with Tiberius: he said that he had done nothing against Cæsar, but if his own life were in peril he thought he could do a great deal. No further action was taken against Lentulus. He was popular with the Rhine army; and after his disclaimer, Tiberius elected to let well alone.

Agrippina had had a long rope; but this was the end of it. No *lettre de cachet* ever swept away a dangerous conspirator more effectively than the judgment of Cæsar swept away Agrippina and Nero. They were removed, she to Pandataria and he to Pontia, fettered, and in closed litters. Their guards prevented any passers-by from even stopping to look. . . . At Pandataria, her mother's place of imprisonment, the fury of Agrippina broke forth. She spoke the whole of her mind on the subject of Tiberius. But she was in the wrong place for that. Here, Cæsar's word went without question. There was violence, in which Agrippina lost an eye.[1] When she went on hunger-strike, she was forcibly fed. Public opinion thought that the voice might be the voice of Cæsar, but the hand was the hand of Seianus.

Two sons of Germanicus still remained: Drusus and Gaius, both of them kept under the eye of Tiberius himself at Capri. Gaius—an unbalanced, degenerate, baby-faced rat—was too cunning for Seianus, and survived

---

[1] What actually happened is too uncertain to be described more explicitly than this. The allegation of Suetonius, that the granddaughter of Augustus was flogged by the order of Tiberius until she lost an eye, is a highly sensational statement to be slipped almost casually into the narrative. Had he told us that she was injured in a struggle with her guards, we could unhesitatingly believe it.

to become the emperor Caligula. . . . But Drusus, after first being used as a means of trapping Nero, was in his due turn caught in the Tuscan's net. Seianus intoxicated Lepida, the wife of Drusus, as he had intoxicated Livilla. On her evidence, Drusus was sent back to Rome. . . . This was not enough for Seianus. At his instigation, the consul Cassius Longinus moved the arrest and imprisonment of Drusus: the second of the name to fall to the Tuscan's wiles. . . . Tiberius surveyed young Gaius. His ominous comment was: "He lives to become the destruction of himself and of other men."

Drusus arrested

The obstacles in the way of Seianus were rapidly thinning. At this rate, they would soon have disappeared. The apparent exemption of Gaius was no more than a respite. A brother of Germanicus still survived—Claudius: but he was considered to be of defective intelligence, and hardly entered seriously into the question of the succession. He was absorbed in the compilation of a history in many volumes. The Tuscan was on the verge of becoming the one man able to take up the mantle of Cæsar, and the time was at hand.

VI

But what thoughts and calculations were in the mind of Tiberius at Capri? . . . The Tuscan's work had been accomplished: the children of Julia, who twice had sought to snatch the principate out of his hands, were gone: the senatorial party, whose hope they had been, was paralysed. He could now at leisure direct his atten-

New position of Seianus

tion to the Tuscan, and survey that remarkable figure with the interest it deserved.

Seianus stood to Tiberius in a relation not altogether unlike that in which the latter had stood to Augustus. But there were differences worth noting. . . . Seianus had not quite given Tiberius those guarantees of fidelity which the latter had given to Augustus. He had never humbly subordinated himself, nor served those years of self-repression which Tiberius had served: he had never retired to Rhodes, nor disinherited his own son for such adopted heirs as Germanicus and Agrippina. A man grows cold with age: and the older Tiberius grew, the less he was likely to relish the strain of lusciousness that marked the Tuscan. Seianus had bloomed with some of the quality of a tropical orchid. He was a man who did not know how to lose himself in his background.

The loyalty of the Tuscan had endured only one kind of test. There had been a famous example of it. Passing through Campania on the way to Capri, Cæsar's party had picnicked in a natural grotto. The place was unsafe, and during the meal there had been a fall of rock and a panic. Seianus had knelt over Tiberius and received on his own shoulders the falling stones which might have killed his master. Such a proof of devotion was gratifying and satisfactory, as far as it went. But how far did it go? It meant nothing more than that the life of Tiberius was essential to the Tuscan while heirs to his power still lived.

The public opinion of Rome cast an instructive light on the situation. It had no doubt who was the master. Tiberius was supposed to be hidden in Capri with his

Problems
for
Tiberius

orgies [1] and his astrologers: the man who swayed destiny was Seianus. His birthday was publicly observed; altars were built to him and libations offered: men swore by the fortune of Seianus as well as by that of Tiberius: he was in separate and distinct communication with the Senate and the people. . . . The old man at Capri might congratulate himself on possessing a distance and perspective that he would not have had in Rome. The very absence of Tiberius threw into clear visibility facts which might otherwise have remained obscure.

There were other alarming features. The Prætorians were as a matter of course at the beck and call of their chief. Worse, his influence affected even the private entourage of Cæsar. The movements and words of Cæsar were regularly reported to him: whereas Tiberius had difficulty in acquiring information respecting the Tuscan. . . . Agrippina was in Pandataria; Nero in Pontia; and if once the slender cord of communication were cut, Tiberius in Capri might be as much a prisoner as they.

Ominous features of the situation

The policy of Seianus was now to gain over by friendly means or by intimidation the party which had supported Agrippina. The next step—if ever he took it—would be to cast upon Tiberius the responsibility for the action taken against Agrippina, and so to stand at the head of a coalition of parties before which Tiberius would be isolated.

---

[1] It is now that we begin to hear of the hideous orgies of Capri. The doubts entertained on this score by recent critics are well founded. It is unnecessary to suppose that Tiberius was ahead of the average morality of his age; but the particular detailed allegations made by Suetonius need not detain us. They were, in all probability, among the offences for which Agrippina was sent to Pandataria.

To an observer, indeed, it might very well seem that the position of Tiberius was weaker and more perilous than it had been at any past time. But the old man knew what he was about. . . . And perfect quiet and silence brooded over Capri.

VII

First moves against Seianus

The calculation of times and moments might be controlled by the occurrence of definite events on which they depended. The crisis would come with the death of Agrippina and her sons. Tiberius held hostages for himself in their persons: for Seianus would never attempt to strike him down in face of the prospect that he might put them in his place. Tiberius thus had every reason for preventing Agrippina from destroying herself.

When Nero died in Pontia, the first moves in the dangerous game began. Tiberius, with a touch of irony, bestowed the widow of Nero in marriage upon Seianus. She was his granddaughter—the daughter of his son Drusus. Tiberius resolved to pay Seianus the honour of holding the consulship in his company. The Tuscan was therefore sent to Rome to take up office on their joint behalf. His influence was now all-powerful. His doors were besieged with callers anxious to register themselves upon the winning side. He enjoyed the sensation of actual supremacy, such as Tiberius had never wielded, and had never sought to wield. Men referred to him as the colleague of Tiberius—and not with regard to the consulship alone. . . . One of the ways of killing a cat is to choke it with cream.

Silence in Capri.

But there a greater and colder and more complex mind than the Tuscan's had glided into motion and had begun, like some vast calculating machine, to work out a subtle and intricate reckoning. Tiberius sat in Capri, thinking. But the machine made no sound to betray its working. In the roar and hurry of Rome were hope and fear, doubt and confidence, feverish energy and worried forethought; but perfect calm brooded over the sunlit rocks and turquoise sea of Capri.

Things came about by slow degrees. They made their next step, perhaps, when Tiberius, after five months, resigned the consulship. Seianus had to follow suit, and two suffecti succeeded in their places. The lead which the old man had now established, he kept to the end. It must have instilled into the heart of the Tuscan just that faint spirit of doubt which spurs men on to haste and self-betrayal. In July, Tiberius saw that L. Fulcinius Trio was made suffectus. Trio was one of the party of Seianus. . . . The old man may, in the world's eye, have seemed irresponsible and capricious, but Seianus was probably better informed. There were omens and portents, some of which, if true, may have been engineered by Tiberius. . . . Tiberius was certainly expert in that art of testing a guilty conscience which has always been a supreme art in Rome. . . . He very gradually shook the Tuscan's nerve. *Development of the contest*

Although Seianus was now free from the engagements involved in holding the consulship, he did not return to Capri. Tiberius said that he himself was coming to Rome. He next raised Seianus to the pro-consular *Seianus induced to conspire—*

power—one of the main powers of the principate. Having thus encouraged him, he deftly undercut the encouragement by the expedient of bestowing the priesthood upon Seianus and Gaius Cæsar simultaneously. This casting of the imperial mantle over Gaius—a proceeding which mollified Agrippina's party, and tended to detach it from the Tuscan—was so ominous that Seianus grew alarmed. He begged permission to return to Capri to see his bride, who was ill. Tiberius blandly replied that they were all of them just about to visit Rome. A little while after came a message to the Senate in which Seianus was briefly referred to without any of his titles, and the payment of divine honours to a living man was prohibited.

This form of moral stream-whipping brought Seianus to the surface. He grew convinced that unless he leaped now, he would leap too late. The arrangements were made. Tiberius was to be assassinated when he came to Rome. The old man in Capri must have smiled to himself. He was not going to Rome!

VIII

Tiberius had not finished yet. His most enticing fly was cast last of all. Only one thing was wanting to place Seianus on the throne beside Cæsar himself—the tribunician power, the second main source of imperial prerogative. It was this at which Seianus leaped, and this with which Tiberius struck his line and hooked his fish.

—but induced to hesitate

But Tiberius did not after all appear in person to bestow this final gift on the Tuscan. All this time he was sending message after message to the Senate, or to

Seianus himself, with the most contradictory news. He was well; he was not well; he was never better; he was at death's door; he succeeded in baffling them all as to his real state of mind, or the purport of his actions. The number of people who prudently sat on the fence continually increased. Seianus was never sufficiently alarmed to retreat, nor sufficiently confident to take some decisive step. Many men began to avoid meeting him, or remaining alone in his company.

On October 1st. Fulcinius Trio was superseded as consul suffectus by P. Memmius Regulus, who was not one of the Tuscan's people. And Tiberius remained still in Capri.

It was only when Seianus, as soon as affairs were stirring one morning, went down to the Senate, that he met Nævius Sertorius Macro. He knew Macro well— one of his own Prætorian officers from Capri, attached to the imperial household. It must have been a distinct surprise to see him. His presence needed at least a word of explanation. Macro was all courtesy and respect. He had a smiling whisper for the ear of Seianus. He was in Rome to see through the business of the day—the investiture with the tribunician power. The Tuscan understood. The great moment had come! Relieved, delighted, yet scarcely daring to believe in his own success until he saw it, he rushed on winged feet into the Senate.

Arrival of Macro in Rome

The Senate sat in the temple of Apollo on the Palatine. All was duly hallowed in. Macro handed a message from Cæsar to the consul Regulus, and went out again. The consul rose with the message in his hand:

and the senators, sitting on tenter hooks of nervous
excitement, hardly knew whither to turn their eyes.
Was this message about to give the Tuscan his life's
achievement? Yes, no doubt! Or—but the alternative
was unthinkable! It was not possible for Seianus to fall
now. Tiberius himself would fall, if the wrestle came!
Regulus unfolded the message of Tiberius. He knew no
more than others did what it might possibly contain,
and he began to read. . . . It was a lengthy document,
written apparently with the fussy circumlocution of
an aged man, but in reality with the astute foresight of
a crafty diplomatist. . . . After its first words, the
more anxious senators began to beam ingratiating smiles
upon the haughty Tuscan. . . . Suddenly they started,
and stopped. . . . A second time they hastened to turn
congratulating faces. . . . And a second time the
cloud came and the smiles froze. . . . And while that
letter is reading, let us look out of the eyes of Macro.

IX

The day before, out of the peace and sunshine of
Capri, Cæsar had quietly summoned Macro: and there
Macro stood, facing the grim old man. . . . Tiberius
had invested Macro with the office of Prefect of the
Prætorians in succession to Seianus, and had given him
definite instructions—as definite as Sherlock Holmes
could have given a deputy, and very nearly as mystifying. What even Macro did not know was that the shat-
tering influence of Cæsar penetrated into every nook
and cranny. . . . Satrius Secundus, one of the men in
the confidence of Seianus, had hesitated, doubted, and

Secret
proceed-
ings of
Tiberius

told the secret to Antonia: and Antonia had taken it to Tiberius, and Tiberius knew.

Armed with his instructions, Macro set out to hold or to lose the new rank which Cæsar had bestowed upon him. He reached Rome at midnight. His first conference was with the consul Regulus. By waiting until Regulus succeeded Fulcinius Trio, Tiberius had made sure that there should be a consul in Rome with power to act, and loyalty to obey the commands of Cæsar. . . . The instructions were that Regulus should convoke the Senate early in the day at the temple of Apollo. The earliness of the hour was a specific feature of the instruction. . . . Regulus carried out his orders exactly, not knowing what they might mean. The messages of convocation were dispatched. . . . The next conference was with Græcinus Laco, the chief of the *cohortes vigilum*. It was arranged with Laco that the approaches of the temple of Apollo should be occupied by military police. . . . The Prætorians were carefully excluded from the plan.

Instructions of Macro

This was what had happened the night before. It is unlikely that Macro had slept between the time he visited Regulus soon after midnight, and the time he met Seianus in the morning. When he left the Senate in session, he had no doubt never removed the clothes in which he had ridden from Capri. He could hardly have had time for more than the hastiest toilet. . . . Finally, in the brief interval between the entrance of Seianus into the Senate, and his own entrance to deliver the message, he had executed the last part of his instructions, and the most dangerous.

It is typical of the craft and thoroughness of Tiberius that he instructed Macro to test the Prætorian escort of Seianus *before* delivering the letter. Had they declined to accept Macro, all would have been lost—but in that case the letter would never have been delivered, and the prestige of Tiberius would have been saved the discredit of a fall. . . . Macro produced his commission and an authority to distribute a gratuity to the guards in recognition of their services. . . . This was the critical moment. All that had gone before, and all that was to follow after, depended absolutely upon the way in which the Prætorians took Macro. . . . But the calculations of Tiberius held good. In the absence of any counteracting force, the name of Cæsar retained its spell. The escort accepted Macro without demur. . . . . He had thereupon given them the order to return to camp. Then after seeing that the military police had taken their places he had entered the temple, delivered the message, walked out again, and with a word to Laco had followed the Prætorians.

Seianus was left isolated in the Senate house.

The Præto-
rians
accept
Macro

X

The reading of the letter went on, while the Prætorians vanished slowly in the distance. By the time they were out of reach and out of earshot, the message of Tiberius, after playing to and fro around the subject, had got to business. It wound up by demanding that action should be taken against Seianus and his accomplices.

Men—Seianus among them—sat stunned. . . . The

Arrest
of
Seianus

consul was taking no chances. He called Seianus to stand forward. . . . The Tuscan had to arouse himself to realize the situation. He had so lost the habit of receiving commands that he could only inquire in a kind of stupor: "Are you speaking to *me?*" . . . At length he stood up, and Græcinus Laco, who had entered, went over to take up a position beside him.

The consul did not adopt the ordinary procedure of asking the vote of each senator separately, nor did he move a vote of condemnation to death. He moved a resolution of imprisonment, put the question to one senator, and on receiving a vote in favour of the motion, declared it carried. . . . He and the other magistrates led Seianus out of the house, after which Laco conducted him to prison. The meeting of the Senate hurriedly adjourned, while every senator watched with anxiety for the possible thunder-bolt that would fall.

None fell. The Prætorian camp, with Macro in command, remained closed. Only the populace paraded in force, to pull down the statues of Seianus and to cheer his downfall. . . . When the senators had sufficiently ascertained that there was no immediate probability that the earth would open and swallow them up, they emerged from their houses and reassembled. The adjourned meeting was resumed, and proceeded to condemn Seianus to death. The sentence was instantly carried out. . . . That morning, the Tuscan had been to all intents the equal and rival of Cæsar. By nightfall his body had been dragged from the Gemonian stairs and was floating down the Tiber.

His family was executed with him. The daughter of

Condemnation and Execution Oct. 18th. A. D. 31

Seianus, that proud and ruthless man, was an innocent young girl who protested against being dragged along by strange and brutal men. Anything she had done, she said, would be punished enough by a whipping. She did not know what that world was, into which she had suddenly fallen. . . . They paused before the fact that a virgin could not, by Roman law, suffer the capital penalty. . . . But they could take no risks. The difficulty was remedied by the executioner, and the daughter of Seianus was strangled and thrown out upon the Gemonian stairs.[1] . . . But Nemesis and the furies were already upon their way.

Cæsar at Capri had entertained no enthusiastic illusions. He, if anyone, knew how far the whole thing was touch and go. A fleet was waiting to take him to the east if his scheme went wrong. He took his own post on the highest cliff of the island, to await the news. . . . When at last it came through by telegraph, and he knew that all was well, he returned home, and the ships were dismissed.

Anxiety of Tiberius

XI

Some of the Tuscan's partisans turned state-evidence. It did not save them, for those whom they involved, retaliated. Tiberius referred all charges to the Senate, as the supreme criminal court.

The charges were serious. P. Vitellius, a prefect of

---

[1] Tiberius was not responsible for this crime. It was done by a senatorial executioner, if not by senatorial order. (Dion Cassius, LVIII, 11, 5, which seems to be the origin of the "young girls" to whom Suetonius, generalizing a single instance, refers in *Tib.* LXI.)

the *ærarium militare*—the army financial board—was charged with having undertaken to employ the military treasury in support of any action Seianus might take. Sextus Paconianus was alleged to have been chosen by Seianus to secure the downfall of Gaius Cæsar. At least three friends of Tiberius were implicated. But out of twenty persons whose names are found in a first rapid inspection of the record, we find that one quarter were acquitted. Some of the accused stood their trial, and defended themselves with considerable freedom of speech. Others, with the aim of preserving their property for their children, killed themselves without facing a trial: for while the estates of men who were judicially condemned were in all cases confiscated,[1] those of men who voluntarily died were usually spared.

Charges against accomplices of Seianus

The investigations into the proceedings of Seianus and his accomplices were lengthy and complicated. Many of the accused persons were detained in prison while the evidence was sifted. Tiberius was determined that everything should be dragged to light. He insisted that the Senate should sit regularly and punctually, at fixed hours. He laid before it all the information he obtained. The sentences were passed by the Senate. Whatever it may have thought or wished, it had no alternative. . . . It is an ironical commentary upon history that though the brilliant partisan pamphlet of

Judicial investigation

---

[1] The property of Seianus himself went, legally, into the senatorial treasury, but Tiberius asked that it might be paid into the imperial fisc. His request, supported by many of the principal senators, was complied with. Tacitus thought this an exhibition of servility, but as most of the property of Seianus must have been derived from imperial grant, it seems reasonable that it should return to the source from which it came. (Tac. *Ann.* vi. 2.)

Tacitus survived, this evidence, over which Tiberius took so much trouble, has very imperfectly come down to us. It seems to have been voluminous, and to have existed in documentary form, filed in the imperial archives, long after Tiberius' day. Many of the accusations against the character of Tiberius himself, subsequently recorded as facts by historians, are thought to have been derived from these very indictments which Tiberius himself published.

But he had not done with the Tuscan yet.

XII

The events which attended the fall of Seianus had been harassing enough to try to the utmost the nerve of a man of seventy-two. The danger, the difficulty, the intellectual exertion, the nervous strain, the tension of those moments when all hung in the balance, the unremitting work and constant concentration—all these must have driven even a robust man to the verge of exhaustion. And now, on the top of this, fell a fresh thunder-bolt: news so terrible, that the worst he had surmised of Seianus seemed a trifle by comparison.

For the revenge of Seianus was singularly complete and successful. His divorced wife Apicata, whom he had put away in order to be free to marry Livilla, must have felt that intoxicated devotion which he seemed able to produce in any woman at will. She had held his secrets—even the secrets which Livilla shared with him. She avenged him now, and herself also. She wrote a letter to Tiberius, and then killed herself. The letter was duly delivered to Cæsar.

Apicata's revelation

By this letter of Apicata the truth stood revealed. Full details were given: details confirmed when the testimony of the slaves concerned was taken.

XIII

Drusus, the son of Tiberius, had not died a natural death. He had been poisoned by Seianus and Livilla.

CHAPTER XII

THE OLD MAN OF CAPRI

I

No one ever recorded how Tiberius took it; what hot and cold fits shook him; what stunning of mind and blenching of spirit made him still and silent. No one tells us of any sleepless nights under the gnawing rage of humiliation and pain; nor of the old man pacing his bed-chamber, full of awful thoughts and dreadful self-doubt. . . . If he felt no such emotions, then he was unlike any other man; for the essence of all was that he had been fooled—fooled, indeed, to the end of his bent. . . . He knew more than we know. He could look back, where we cannot follow him, and perceive precisely how far he had been deluded, trapped into views and actions which we can only guess at now. And this, by a man over whom he had extended the patronizing faith of a master towards a servant: a man whom, at root, he despised!

There are some experiences of bitterness which spread so wide and sink so deep into a man's being, that the whole structure of it is poisoned and changed, and seems to be loosened from its roots in human society. . . . There is no bitterness so bitter as that which springs from the experience of treachery. Man is so made, that it is a spiritual torment to him to know that

Tiberius
completely
deceived
by
Seianus

his friend has taken his confidence, and used it against him: has accepted his heart, and thrown it away. . . . This is multiplied many times when not one man only, but all men are the traitors. There is no more destructive thing in life than to see all men smiling, and to know that every smile is false: to take every man's hand, and to know that it is a right hand of falsehood. . . . But like physical pain, spiritual pain is normally subject to a law of diminishing returns. The last increments no longer give pain at all. They merely poison and paralyse: and what at first was a suffering, becomes transformed into a change of nature. A man learns to accept his isolation, his dreadful separation from the heartening and nourishing fountain of human love and careless trust; he acquires the art of standing alone, enclosed in a shell of individualism: and he learns to watch, to guard, to trace with acute observation the course of the hidden treason: to diagnose it with expert eyes, as a physician diagnoses the symptoms (invisible to any ordinary eye) of some malady: to strike, at the appropriate moment, without ruth or remorse. . . . But to do this involves the loss of all the typically human qualities and happiness. A man so placed and so changed seems no longer human, as we understand the word: he has become dæmonic: he seems possessed of a spirit other than the human. And he is.

Moral results of treachery

Weak men die—perhaps of broken hearts, as we call them; or take to drink, and we find them in obscure taverns, full of a long story of their troubles, in the wild hope of finding someone yet who will understand, and will bring them, however casually, the balm of good-

Effect
on
Tiberius

humoured sympathy and a shadowy affection. But strong men stand fast and become possessed of the dæmon. . . . So did Tiberius. . . . If we look at his portrait as an old man, we see in it the full story. It is lined deep with that dyspepsia which comes of suffering. Children know that moment when they have wept themselves into a mood in which food will not nourish nor drink satisfy. . . . With Tiberius they were inward, spiritual tears, shed invisibly and without hope. He had brushed them away, and dried them, and had regarded the world again with a determination to hold his ground. It is an impenetrable, inaccessible eye, which perceives, but does not tell us what it perceives; a mouth that almost smiles with the scornful content of knowledge.

II

The revelation which followed the death of Seianus seemed to possess Tiberius with this dæmonic quality. It is always dangerous to challenge a man to do his worst. It is so easy for him to do it. It seemed as if all men and all things had conspired together to crush the lord of the world; and the lord of the world set his back to the wall and struck back at all men and all things. It was a quaint logic which made them each other's tyrants and victims. There must have been something wrong about it.

Vengeance

No one really knows the fate of Livilla. Some say she was executed; some, that she killed herself; some, that she was handed over to Antonia, who was given the commission of seeing that Livilla removed herself adequately from the scene. Tiberius was determined to bring to light the whole story. But it was no longer the old Tiberius who did so. It was a new and terrifying man, owning indeed the outlines of Tiberius, but inhabited by a spirit of remorseless and embittered energy.

The truth was torn out. For whole days on end he was absorbed in the task of investigation. So completely was he obsessed by it, that the grim joke was passed round that when one of his old friends from Rhodes arrived, cordially invited by Cæsar to visit him at Rome, Tiberius had forgotten all about the invitation, and ordered him to be put to the question forthwith, under the impression that he was another witness whose testimony was to be examined.[1] Many stories of his state of mind at this time have been preserved.[2] When a certain Carnulus died, Tiberius remarked: "Carnulus has managed to dodge me." . . . To one who begged for a

---

[1] Suet. *Tib.* LXII. Dion Cassius also mentions this story. On the mistake being discovered, Tiberius ordered the man to be executed, in order, Suetonius carefully explains, to prevent him from publishing to the world the wrong done him; but more probably because there was nothing else to do.

[2] That Tiberius was suffering under some almost intolerable stress of mind is clear. His friend M. Aurelius Cotta was involved in the informations. Cotta had used language disrespectful to the house of Cæsar: he had, among other things, called Cæsar his dear little old rag doll (i. e., Tiberiolus meus, which comes to the same thing).

Tiberius roused himself to request the acquittal of Cotta. He wrote that famous letter which began: "If I know what to write to you just now, or how to write it, or what not to write, may the gods destroy me with a worse destruction than that under which I feel myself to be daily perishing." This is probably one of the most remarkable messages ever sent to a court of law: and it is obviously not the letter of a normal man. . . . But he could still write words of robust common sense. He asked the Senate not to construe in a criminal sense words that were twisted out of their natural meaning, and had been uttered without evil intent over a dinner table. The case against Cotta was accordingly dismissed.

Professor Ramsay (Note to Tac. *Ann.* VI. 15, referring also to Suetonius, *Tib.* LXV) thinks that Tiberius was suffering under nervous terrors.

speedy death, he responded: "I have not yet become your friend." . . . This was not a Tiberius whom anyone had heard of before. . . . He showed no sign of failing powers or of intellectual decay. He was never more active nor more energetic. But it was a strange

Demoralization of Tiberius

and dæmonic energy that seemed to be super-imposed upon his normal powers. . . . He had enough wisdom to put an immediate stop to an information lodged by a soldier, and to lay down the rule that no man connected with the army was to turn delator.

All the documents went to the Senate. Even denunciations of his character and charges against him were published. He did not care what was published; all he was concerned with was that everything should come out. . . . Fulcinius Trio (who, though he had hitherto escaped, had a guilty conscience) grew so alarmed at the possibilities that he killed himself. His heirs found his will to contain a wrathful denunciation of Tiberius, who was described as "a senile old man." They tried to suppress the incriminating document; but the "senile old man" ordered it to be read aloud, denunciation and all. No one could understand his motives: and he did not trouble to explain them.

III

The death sentences which the Senate passed fell, however, upon mere agents. The principals—Seianus and Livilla—had already gone. Tiberius sought for some other satisfaction, and he found it in observing the case of Agrippina and her son Drusus.

Tiberius was already aware that Seianus had been deliberately planning to involve and destroy Agrippina and her sons. He knew now what the whole truth was. But although the truth stood revealed, it could not, merely by being revealed, be remedied. Tiberius had no power to extricate himself from the vicious circle. He could not at this stage apologize to Agrippina and Drusus, and put them back where they had been. He could not at any stage have done so. The skill of the Tuscan had been shown in the way in which he induced Agrippina and her sons to give him a complete and irrefutable justification for his action against them. . . . It was this possibility of wiping the children of Julia, with unimpeachable justice, out of the succession to the empire, which had led him to contemplate the removal of Tiberius' son Drusus. . . . It was not unreasonably far-fetched to look upon Agrippina as the original cause of the whole series of events. . . . Those who had egged her on were still more guilty—but they were not directly accessible.

Impossibility of reversing the action against Agrippina

Tiberius could not cancel or eradicate the hate which the children of Julia bore him. That Seianus had used it for his own purposes made no difference. . . . One thing he could do, however—he could drag it to the light. He wished the world to see the unreasoning, implacable hatred working in the minds of Julia's children, that set, persistent obsession that *he* had hounded them and persecuted them—though he had only defended himself against that very conviction on their part. . . . And it is possible that the mere similarity of names rivetted the morbid interest of Tiberius. . . . One Drusus paid for the other Drusus.

His reasons for continuing it

There might be some queer, involved satisfaction in such a theme; for when men are pressed beyond their endurance they find relief in strange forms—superficial likenesses, casual associations of ideas fill the place of real resemblances and unattainable identities. . . . The Senate was filled with alarm and consternation when Tiberius reported to it, in full detail, with a kind of grim satisfaction, the death of Drusus, the son of Germanicus and Agrippina.

Drusus had weakened. It lasted nine days, during which he had gnawed the stuffing of his mattress. Tiberius scornfully called him a weakling as well as a traitor. He produced a carefully posted diary compiled by the gaolers who had watched Drusus die. As if it were some novel of Zola, it described minutely and elaborately the stages by which Drusus had starved to death in his prison; his first fury and terror; how he had abused Tiberius in detail—with, no doubt, all the stock accusations of the friends of Julia—and how they had replied to him, and beaten him back when he strove to tear down the bars of his cell; and then how, giving up hope, he had elaborately and with care called down imprecations on the head of Tiberius, praying that, since he had murdered his daughter-in-law (Livilla) his brother's son (Germanicus) and his own grand-children (the sons of Agrippina) and had deluged his own house with blood, so he might pay the penalty to his name and race in the eyes of posterity. The Senate broke up in disorder, horrified at this story. . . . The old man may have invented it; but he certainly claimed the

Death of Drusus

credit of the crime, and it is not for us to reject his claim. . . . And it had its practical utilities. It underlined, for the benefit of the Senate, the fact that Cæsar was ready to outbid any man; that he would give measure for measure and blow for blow, and that there was nothing he would not cap, and no stake he would not double. . . . Moreover, it disposed of all pretenders and false claimants. The Senate certainly became clearly aware that Drusus was dead.

Agrippina was of stronger nerve. Unconquerable to the last, she retorted by refusing food and starving herself to death, as a demonstration that Tiberius could not frighten her.[1]

Voluntary death of Agrippina

But there was no real satisfaction in all these things. Vengeance is a drug which, like all drugs, will give no permanent rest or satiety: it is a Tantalus-fruit which can never be grasped or achieved. It excites the appetite which it pretends to allay. Tiberius grew weary. He was intelligent enough to recognize these truths, even though he could not place them in the moral scheme. A certain time after the fall of Seianus he found the memory intolerable, and even revenge a fatigue without pleasure. He briefly ordered the execution of all who were detained in prison in connection with the conspiracy of Seianus. They apparently numbered twenty persons.

---

[1] Tiberius tried to disparage her afterwards, but his amateurish attempts at slander (which at any rate prove him to be new to the business) never had any success, and need no attention.

IV

He had lost everything: nothing remained to him but victory. And victory was a trifle in comparison with the things he had lost in achieving it.

V

From this height of crisis, matters began to subside slowly towards the normal. The blow which he had levelled at his foes was followed by a measure which may not have been unconnected with it. Among the legislation of Gaius Julius was a law directed towards restraining the activities of those financial powers which had swayed the political destinies of the old republic. The amount of floating capital which they might hold was limited by the regulation that a certain proportion of their property should always be invested in Italian land. By this means he had prevented the existence of those vast funds of money and of easily negotiable credit which had financed one political revolution after another, and of which he himself had been glad enough to take advantage. Cæsar the Dictator had meant himself to be the last man who should overthrow a government by such means.

In view of the activities of the senatorial party during the reign of Tiberius, we need not be surprised to hear that this law had been very loosely observed. The position which Tiberius had hitherto occupied had been far too precarious to allow strong measures in enforcement of the law. He could not safely have risked the consequences. . . . But the situation was rapidly

Measures against the oligarchy

changing. After the fall of Seianus and the death of
Agrippina, the terrible old man of Capri was no longer
the figure of fun which had patiently borne the insults of the Senate and had been hoodwinked by the
Tuscan.

The delators were set to work. The first legal in- The
formations which they lodged against breakers of the declines
law of Julius were soon fluttering the dove-cotes. The responsi-
cases were carried to the Senate. But the senators were bility
alive to the possible consequences; many of them would
figure in the dock if the informations were systematically laid: and besides, to enforce the law would bring
about a financial crisis. They referred the matter to the
imperial court, and left Tiberius to solve the problem
himself.

He was quite willing to do so, and he had his plan
prepared. It did not meet with universal approval, even
among his friends. His constant adviser, M. Cocceius
Nerva, seems to have been strongly opposed to it. It was
nevertheless authorized. Tiberius informed the Senate
that the law must be enforced, but that eighteen
months' grace would be allowed, during which all accounts might be regularized.

The sympathies of Nerva [1] were with the republican
oligarchy; he did not really care for the atmosphere of
the imperial court, though he had served it with perfect

---

[1] Nerva was a remarkable man, and one of the great figures of contemporary
politics. Not only was he very eminent indeed as a jurist, but he was minister
of works and aqueducts, and constructed that wonderful tunnel, the Crypta
Neapolitana, which connected Puteoli and Naples. It is probable that many
features of the policy of Tiberius in constitutional matters owed much to Nerva.
The political tradition of the family was, however, oligarchic rather than
Cæsarian. Perhaps the family has never quite received the credit it deserved.

loyalty for many years. He too perhaps was worn out and weary with the strain of these years of moral earth-quake and eclipse: a weariness that went beyond mere resignation and retirement. He resolved to die. Tiberius was much concerned. He came and sat by Nerva's bed, and reasoned with him, pointing out how much he himself would feel it, and how much it would damage his reputation in the world's eyes, if his chosen counsellor took this way of expressing dissent from his financial policy. But Nerva was not to be diverted from his resolution. He declined all food and died.

The financial crisis duly arrived. The process of re-arrangement necessitated by the enforcement of the law involved the calling-in of loans; debtors had to sell their estates in order to meet their liabilities; the value of land fell so that many were ruined. . . . Tiberius advanced a hundred million sesterces to the Senate as a loan fund, out of which it could make advances without interest to all debtors who could give suitable security. The plan seems, as far as we can trace it, to have been successful; and the financial situation was reformed into accord-ance with the law without further disaster.

The struggle against Tiberius was now practically at an end. The masked war which for nearly twenty years had been carried on against him was nearing its finish by the gradual arrest of his principal senatorial oppo-nents; and its conclusion was finally ratified by this ad-ministrative step which suppressed the accumulation of free capital by which such a war could be financed.

But when we mark the degree to which the later de-cline of the Roman world was brought about by economic weakness, and when we consider how far economic prosperity is produced by plenitude of free capital, we may wonder whether it was not in these days that the damage was first done. For it is clear that a certain rigidity began to appear in the economic condition of the empire; wealth and productivity no longer expanded with the old vitality; and when, in due time, the stress came, Roman civilization had insufficient resources with which to meet it.

VI

The trouble for Tiberius was the extent of his success. It seemed difficult to restrain senators from wallowing in a desperate and even an inconvenient humility. They could not sufficiently mark their appreciation of the superhuman virtues of Cæsar, or of their own unworthiness. The dawn of a slow smile can be detected in the old man—a smile which, perhaps, betokened, in a reawakening sense of humour, a return to sanity. . . . The tributes which had been cast at his feet were peculiar. Togonius Gallus proposed that the senators should themselves form a bodyguard to defend their beloved friend and protector when he honoured them with his presence: a stroke of humour which cracked the hard shell of the old man's embittered gravity. He discussed the matter with elaborate care, finally deciding that the plan was too comic to be put into operation. . . . It might have led, moreover, to some regrettable accident. . . . Junius Gallio suggested that all Prætorian veterans should be created *ex officio* equites. Tiberius replied by having him turned out of

The Senate crushed

the Senate, remarking that here, evidently, was another Seianus, trying to tamper with the guardsmen. . . . Amid all this, one man's voice had been raised in clear tones. Marcus Terentius, accused of being a friend of Seianus, defended himself as a man should. He spoke the simple words of common sense which, in such circumstances, ring out almost as brilliant paradox. . . . **Exceptions** "Yes," he said, in effect, "I was a friend of Seianus; and so were you and so was Cæsar. . . . Who was I, to investigate the virtues of Cæsar's minister? I crawled, as you all did. It was fame, then, to be known to the hall porter of Seianus, or to his servants. Let plots be punished and conspiracies suppressed; but as for friendship with Seianus, the same argument must clear you, me and Cæsar himself."

Tiberius seems to have liked this, for he made it a case in which "the dog it was that died." . . . The accusers of Terentius received appropriate penalties. Terentius himself went home a free man.[1]

But Tiberius retired still further into remoteness. In this shifting sand of treachery only one thing remained true—the loyalty of the Prætorian guard. While the educated, the wealthy and the distinguished could no longer be trusted, the more elementary instincts of humanity still ran true to type. Uneducated, undistinguished men of the poorer classes still earned their

---

[1] Any mental strain under which Tiberius was suffering seems to have produced singularly little effect on him outside political questions, if one tale is true. The prætor L. Cæsianus organized a show of bald-headed men at the Floralia, which was generally understood to be an allusion to the baldness of a certain distinguished person. He also provided five thousand link-boys with shaved heads, to light people home from the theatre at night. . . . The distinguished person took no notice.

wages, respected the hand that fed them, and obeyed the rules. And they preserved this sense of duty and service towards a hard man who had never flattered them nor cajoled them. Their reward was not yet: but in due time it came.

VII

Then a silence falls upon Capri.

But far away, at the other end of the Roman world, events were moving. What happened in Palestine seemed but a tiny spark compared with the gloom and blaze of the deeds done in Rome—as if, during a volcanic eruption, someone had lit a candle. But at nineteen hundred years' distance the volcano has died to a gleam and a column of smoke, and the candle has grown to a vast light like morning.

The Jewish prophet

The obscure Jewish prophet, Joshua (whose co-religionists Tiberius had expelled from Rome) began his career in the year of Agrippina's arrest, the year before the fall of Seianus; and this year, in which Drusus and Agrippina died,[1] he came up to Jerusalem preaching his remarkable doctrine of the Kingdom of God, with its even more remarkable rules: "Love your enemies, bless them that curse you, do good to them that hate you, and pray for them that despitefully use you and persecute you": and "Take no thought saying, what shall we eat? or, What shall we drink? or, Where-

---

[1] That is to say, calculating by the years on which the 15th of Nisan could have fallen on a Friday. This gives the choice of A. D. 27, 30, 33 and 34, and the traditionally accepted year is A. D. 33. Mr. Sheringham has recently argued for A. D. 30; but for the present purpose, which is merely illustrative, any rough approximation is sufficient.

with shall we be clothed? but seek first the Kingdom of God and his justice, and all these things shall be added." And the crowd followed the candle.

The procurator (who by tradition was Pontius Pilatus) received a deputation of the priests and elders, bringing this man with them. They wished him to be dealt with according to Roman law. Pontius—unconscious that his house had been invaded by the actors in the world's greatest drama, and that he had been roped in to play an impromptu part—pooh-poohed this proposal. What had a Roman procurator to do with the sectarian squabbles of the Jews? They insisted, because this man had preached sedition—a Kingdom that was not Cæsar's dominion. Pontius, living in days when Drusus and Agrippina were dying in their prisons, and when the delators were on the watch for evidence of *maiestas*, may well have rubbed his chin. That allegation, no doubt, altered the question. . . .

Accused of maiestas

He accordingly interviewed the stranger. Did he claim to be a King? . . . Not of this world, answered Joshua. . . . Some kind of King, then? suggested Pontius. . . . The word is yours, not mine, said Joshua. And he added: I was born to testify to the truth. Those who know the truth know what I am. . . . It was then that Pontius unawares took on a sort of immortality by his famous question: What is truth? . . . He got no answer; for truth cannot be defined in words.

Investigation of the Procurator

Pontius was puzzled. Evidently there was no sedition about this Jew: and he said as much. But the charge that the priests insisted on making against Joshua was that he made himself out to be equal to God, and they declined to hear of his release. Pontius, disturbed, went back to interview Joshua afresh. What was his origin? But Joshua would not say. He left it to Pontius to judge. Pontius reminded him that he, as procurator, had power to condemn or acquit. Joshua's answer was: Your power is from above. You are not responsible save to the source from which you derive it. . . . Pontius appreciated this perfectly, and had no doubt as to what he ought to do: but then the priests would not let him do it. . . . They insisted that anyone who made himself out to be a King spoke against Cæsar. . . . So they had their way.

That story is well known: the career of Joshua, his betrayal and his death, and his resurrection and glorification as the founder of the religious society which grew and fought its way through opposition and rivalry until it equalled and then exceeded the empire, and extended its power over lands which had never known the laws of the republic or the legions of Cæsar. . . . Not quite so well recognized are the parallels between the two stories which were being enacted simultaneously in the west and the east. . . . Within the same three or four years both reached their crisis, and determined the subsequent history of the world.

Death of Joshua

VIII

Seianus and Judas Iscariot walked in the same world. The south-easterly wind may have blown to Seianus in Rome the air that Judas had breathed. . . . When we turn from one story to the other, they illuminate one another to a high degree. . . . The story of Tiberius was determined by principles which belonged to a moral world rapidly becoming obsolete; he acted and thought still as a man trained to a narrow and local community; he could not deal with the vast tides which ebbed and flowed around the chair of Cæsar. . . . But the story of Joshua the Galilean was governed by principles belonging to a new world which was just about to issue its appeal to mankind, and to rise to power on the response men made to it—principles which were adapted to a universal application. For the master of Judas knew secrets, wielded a nature and dealt with an experience beyond the range of the master of Seianus. Furthermore, his ultimate object and his immediate duty were also different. . . . About Judas himself we are left in an enigmatical silence. No express forgiveness was ever offered Judas. His crime, too, was of an awful and fundamental nature. But it was permitted to be successful. It was not contested by any such deep counter-plot as that which circumvented and over-threw Seianus; it was never visited by any hurricane of vengeance; it left behind it no such corroding poison as that which ate into the heart and destroyed the soul of Tiberius. . . . The Galilean showed no sign of spir-itual injury: he met, checked, transmuted and annihi-lated that poison, as a physician might administer to himself the antidote to a snake-bite; and he went to his death, not without some ominous occasional silence, and some disquieting warning to others, but, in effect, still cordial, still confident in his firm attachment to the world of grace and loyalty and vivid life. He had communication with that world by another way. His

Another
philosophy
of
treachery

resources were not exhausted by the failure of humanity. He was not distorted by other men's evil. He knew
the means by which to neutralize its effect upon the
world and its results upon himself. . . . But these
things were beyond the horizon of Tiberius.

IX

Sunset.

Little remained, save to look over the calm sea of
Capri and to decide, leisurely, about the future. Tiberius had no enthusiasm on that score. He had seen
the family dissolve round about him; the wreck that
remained was not such as to inspire any man with hope,
and he had none. "The sky can fall when I am gone!"
he once remarked. . . . But habit and temperament
held him from maintaining this mood. He almost automatically fidgetted with the pieces of wreckage, and began to place them in speculative order.

*Tiberius
determines
the
Succession
afresh*

His nephew Claudius he seems to have rejected as
out of the reckoning. Claudius was half-witted. That
misjudgment of character which Augustus had displayed about Tiberius, Tiberius showed towards Claudius. The latter was destined to sit in the seat of the
Cæsars, and to be by no means the worst or weakest of
his house. Yet the misjudgment was not altogether complete. Augustus had been partly right, and so was Tiberius.

There was his grandson Gemellus, the son of Drusus.
Perhaps Tiberius would have preferred him. He was
neither strong nor clever, and moreover his birth was
suspect in his grandfather's eyes. He belonged to that

hateful and horrible time when Seianus was paying court to Livilla. It was a very moot point whether it were worth while to place him in a position which he might not be able to maintain. On the other hand, it might be even more imprudent to place him where his competitors had him at their mercy. Tiberius ended by deciding to give Gemellus a run for his money. Let the boy sink or swim as he could. The strong probability was that he would sink. That could be left to prove itself.

Gaius Cæsar

Gaius remained as the likeliest candidate. He was the sole surviving son of Germanicus, and the attitude which Tiberius adopted towards him is in some ways a decisive test of the old man's real motives and past actions. Had the enemies of Tiberius been wholly right, he would have sent Gaius with some promptitude to join his mother and his brothers. Far from doing this, he showed once more the impartiality which had always marked his views and conduct. He did not like Gaius. If the boy were the survival of the fittest, it was as the fittest to survive in an atmosphere of doubt and suspicion in which nothing sincere could live. . . . With the cunning of some primitive organism, he had taken on a protective coloration and had burrowed into the soil. The old man's terrible eye, straying to and fro, could still see nothing to fear from Gaius. . . . There the little reptile was, obediently burrowing. . . .

It was a very queer result of the struggle for survival, that the survivor should be—this! Yet so it turned out; and no argument could more perfectly prove that it is the nature of the competition which determines the value of the victory. . . . So Gaius was to be the fruit of all that had been done! It was exceedingly strange!

Tiberius made his will. He was seventy-six years old. Gaius and Gemellus were to be his joint heirs. . . . Rome, obsessed with the purely romantic notion that Germanicus had belonged to the Golden Age, and that a son of his would bring it back again, was glad. . . . These are the embittering fantasies of mankind. What virtues had Germanicus ever really shown? . . . That passion for the decorative which fills the heart of mankind perhaps sincerely prefers the aspect to the substance, the show to the reality: it would always rather have its gold fairy gold. . . . While the philosopher will see no reason for quarrelling with this choice, the moralist occasionally finds some ground for doing so.

Will of Tiberius A. D. 35

X

Macro saw how the tide set in this evening light. The will of Tiberius meant practically that Gaius would be his successor: for Gemellus would not count for much. Macro was prompt to take Gaius in hand. His wife saw to it that Gaius should be kept amused. . . . All of which the old man fully appreciated.

"You leave the setting to court the rising sun," he said. He gibed; but it made no difference to Macro.

Whatsoever adventures Tiberius might meet with in his personal life, he was little changed in his character as a ruler. It may be that, as with many another man, his personal life, his hopes, fears, ambitions, and affections, his sufferings, his triumphs, were much less his own than that official life of business and administra-

Official life of Tiberius his true life

tion in which he was truly himself. The former at least had a quality of doubtfulness and instability about it— it changed, varied, crept and paused—that is in striking contrast with the well-ballasted even run of his personality as a statesman. . . . He had steadily declined the title of Father of his Country. He remained without doubt its watchful guardian, always ready to dip his hand into his pocket to meet emergencies. . . . The year after he had made his will, a great fire broke out on the Aventine in Rome, and did great damage in the poorer quarters. The old man, who had waded unhesitatingly through the blood of his political foes, in the interests of the imperial power, came to the rescue of the sufferers. Out of his careful and economical exchequer he produced another hundred million sesterces.

Strangely enough, as time narrowed, and it became ever clearer that the days of Tiberius could not have very long to run, there were those who faced without pleasure the prospect of his departure. It was Lucius Arruntius who expressed the apprehensions which the wiser men entertained. . . . Arruntius was one of the defendants in a case in which Albucilla, the wife of **Views of** Satrius Secundus the delator, was concerned. The Senate **L.** regarded the case as unsatisfactory. The documents **Arruntius** which came before it were not endorsed by Tiberius, and the Senate doubted whether they were in order. It was believed that Macro might have put them through without proper authorization. . . . Arruntius wearied of these things, and made up his mind to free himself from the trouble they involved. Before making his exit from the scene, he made a speech to his friends. He expressed his sense of the hopelessness of the future. There was little to which they could look forward with any expectation of improvement. . . . He spoke, of course, from his own point of view. . . . Tiberius, he thought, had been demoralized by the possession of supreme power, and had degenerated from his natural character into that of a tyrant. . . . This also, of course, was his own point of view. Tiberius might have seen things from a somewhat different angle. . . . But Arruntius was on surer ground when he pointed out that a moral strain which had warped Tiberius would not be without effect on Gaius. He preferred not to suffer the days coming when a worse and weaker man sat in the chair of Cæsar. . . . To which, of course, Tiberius might have replied that they should have thought of that before.

Arruntius was not far wrong; and his words formed, in some respects, the verdict of the wiser men in the Senate on the rule of Tiberius. They had elected to go further; and they were going to fare worse.

XI

Tiberius was certainly failing in health. He had al-ways been a vigorous man, who had never needed a doctor; and even the gradual physical weakness which began to creep upon him could not master the mental energy which had been the main source of his strength. But he needed now to force his energies.

Tiberius fails in health

Early in the year A. D. 37 he set out on his travels, driven by that spirit which sends the dying beast forth to prospect for the heavenly home from which it has dreamt it came. He journeyed slowly along the Via Appia towards Rome. That, to all appearance, must be the place. But the auspices told a different tale. Driven back by adverse omens, he turned away from the distant prospect of the towers and domes of the eternal city—turned away for ever from it and all that it implied. . . . He had reigned there; he, the man Tiberius Claudius Nero, had dwelt there as supreme governor of the Roman world, very nearly the governor of all known mankind: and now he was setting his face in another direction. He was never to see it again. If men are immortal, and the soul of Tiberius still lives, perhaps on his journey his face is still turned away from Rome.

He goes to Misenum He went down to Campania again. At Astura he had fallen ill, but recovered somewhat, and continued his journey to Circei. He insisted on attending a military review which, though he concealed the fact, left him exhausted afterwards. He went on to Misenum. His strength was slowly sinking. It was ebbing steadily, naturally, by degrees. He preserved his austere dignity to the last. He did not admit his weakness; he held up an unconquered, disagreeable face; if his head were bloody (though not so much so as his hands) it was certainly unbowed. At the villa of Lucullus at Misenum he paused in order to rest. It was to be a longer rest than he chose to admit.

He had no regular physician. From time to time he accepted advice from Charicles, the most famous physician of his day. It was probably not altogether a coincidence that Charicles was present at Misenum; but Tiberius would not be doctored. . . . The information which could not be obtained by direct means, Charicles obtained by stratagem. On leaving Cæsar, the physician respectfully took his hand, and was able to judge his pulse. . . . The old man was too keen to be hoodwinked. Recognizing the trick, he ordered another course to be served, and sat at table longer than was his usual custom. . . . Charicles, however, had learned all he needed. He informed Macro that the old man was sinking, and could not last more than two days.

Verdict of Charicles

Hurried consultations were instantly held. The armies were at once notified of the impending event. In the villa of Lucullus, Tiberius slowly sank. He may have thought of that gallant and adventurous gentleman of the old republican time, whose millions and whose profusion were still a wonder-tale for the imaginative credulity of sight-seers. Lucullus had been an artist in the pyrotechnics of luxury: and what an artist! What fireworks he had made of it! . . . Amid those rooms and corridors Tiberius may have taken his last feeble austere meals, reflecting over the simple mind which can really enjoy these childlike things. A great happy baby, this Lucullus! . . .

Well—it was over seventy-seven years since Livia, in the consulship of Plancus, and the year of the battle of Philippi, bore the child Tiberius Claudius Nero in that little house on the Palatine hill: seventy-six since she carried him in her arms in wild flight from their foes in the dark days of civil war, when the daughter of Pompeius Magnus had given him that little cloak which was still carefully preserved in Capri. . . . And one event at last confounds the weak, the strong, the loved,

Death of Tiberius. March 16th A. D. 37

the hated, the good, the bad, the wise man and the fool.
So there, where Lucullus had walked and talked, amid
the splendid gardens, Tiberius died.

The whispers would not let him alone even then. It
ran like wildfire that Macro, seeing the old stalwart re-
vive, had smothered him with the bed-clothes: but the
cold smile of Tiberius Cæsar could not be broken now.

CHAPTER XIII

THE LEGACY OF TIBERIUS

I

THE world of Rome, rejoicing to be free from the old man of Capri, hardly noticed the legacy he left to succeeding ages. It scarcely knew what he had portended, or what he remitted to them. Part of it was his deliberate deed; but part of it was what men call accident and fatality and destiny—part was scattered episode of isolated wreck—part a tangled and involved chain of the logic of events, terribly connected and continuous, coherent with an awe-inspiring coherence, arresting because there is meaning in it, but not a meaning that was ever created by, or due to, or enshrined in a human mind. We see this non-human rationality, and we recoil from it because we fear to behold a reason and a system that, alike in the worst things in the world and in the best, is born of no human ancestry. But it was there; and from a safe distance we may inspect it and debate its nature.

A definite product

II

The product of that tremendous war between the old man and his foes was the principate of Gaius Cæsar, the queer, rickety, abnormal, baby-faced son of Germanicus

The successors of Tiberius

295

and Agrippina.[1] The world went into holiday to welcome him as if he had been an angel of heaven. But Gaius had another name: he was called *Caligula*. And Caligula shot his bolt in a meteoric career of crime and incredible fatuity, and fell to the sword of Cassius Cheræa. . . . Then they pulled Claudius, the brother of Germanicus, to light; and he stepped upon the stage with his voluminous history and his reformed spelling and his wife Messalina—whose name is a proverb—and his freedmen Pallas and Narcissus, who ruled the world for Claudius and made themselves the richest men on earth. . . . And then, unable to find anyone else, they made way for Lucius Domitius Ahenobarbus, whom men remember as "Nero," the son of Agrippina the younger. . . . These were the rulers who were the Nemesis of Rome; these were the men she suffered, because of the deeds she had done to Tiberius. . . . And as one of their contemporaries said, men gnawed their tongues for pain but repented not of the evil. They did not know what they had done; so they could not repent of it.

The
Monarchy
remains
elective

There was logic in this. Two results sprang from it. The failure of Augustus to found a hereditary monarchy opened upon the world all the difficulties and dangers of government by a military guild with an elective head.

---

[1] Tiberius seems to have had his doubts when the moment came. He could not make up his mind to give Gaius his signet ring, and replaced it on his finger, probably relapsing into unconsciousness. Believing him to be dead, Gaius drew off the ring; and everyone left the room. While they were acclaiming Gaius, Tiberius revived, missed the ring, and rose out of bed, but fell upon the floor and died there. The frantic message that he was still alive scattered the meeting like chaff; but when Macro got back to the room, Tiberius was certainly dead. Macro may probably enough have pulled the clothes off the bed and covered the body until the attendants came: which would be quite enough to start a rumour that he had smothered him. Tac. *Ann.* VI. 50. Suet. *Tib.* LXXIII.

That in which Augustus had failed was never successfully achieved by any of his successors. . . . And the
oligarchy was compelled in the end to make a compromise with the force it had thus doomed to remain a
perpetual danger. . . . Rome hovered between two political principles, neither of which she could completely
accept. She could neither retain her hold upon the principle of the elective magistrate, nor seize the principle
of the hereditary succession which might have controlled
the military guild. Having fought with so deep and intense a bitterness to establish one or the other, she had
as a consequence neither; and she bore the brunt of that
disaster.

The power of the principate was strengthened rather
than weakened. The very fact that its headship remained elective ensured on the whole that there should
be none of those minorities, or those long periods of
government by incapable princes, which, under a hereditary monarchy, are the opportunities for weakening its
power. By seeking to destroy the empire, the senatorial
oligarchy had rivetted it around their own necks in its
most oppressive and enduring form.

III

The opposition to the empire, prolonged for genera-
tions by the senatorial order, began, after its defeat at
the hands of Tiberius, to drift away from its old stand-
points. In its new form it found its most coherent ex- The new
pression in the Stoic party. Its association with a philo- opposi-
sophical, rather than a strictly political theory, marked tion
a gradual change in its purpose. Stoicism became the

last refuge of the old Roman spirit. The ancient *gravitas,* the ancient equality found their best expression in Stoicism because Stoicism very happily provided a platform on which they might be displayed without the embarrassment of other old Roman virtues. To be stern, severe and opposed to tyranny became a luxury which could be indulged in without the awkward necessity of producing practical results. The Stoics neither conquered worlds—it was fortunately unnecessary—nor did they demonstrate in any other way the art of government which the old Roman spirit had shown. They did not demonstrate anything except their own virtue.

But in an age, and among a class of men, in which even the merely decorative virtues were growing rare, these virtues made their possessors the heads and representatives of their class. Even to strike a Catonic pose was wonderful in the eyes of men who had forgotten how to achieve even that much of the Catonic.

The decadence of a class is always shown in the disappearance of its ability to produce practical results. The power to move men, the power to create, was passing utterly away from the Roman oligarchy. It could not conceive what it wanted; it could not put before **Political** itself a definite aim or purpose; it could not stand with **bankruptcy** men in the market place and tell them what concrete **of the** **oligarchy** human good it proposed to bestow upon them. . . . It had nothing to give them. . . . The most ragged Christian could promise the Kingdom of God and eternal life; the lords of the world could promise nothing. They did not know what men wanted, because they did not know what they themselves wanted.

There are certain well-worn military maxims which are almost moral proverbs. "Attack is the best defence" is a principle which holds good in more spheres than that of war. The economic rulers of the Roman world never grasped it. They failed because they organized for safety, for leisure and for comfort; and they left no margin for the catastrophes which wait upon human life. A continuous expansion, a continuous vital activity exploring every possible opportunity for change and im- provement, is the only condition under which men may safely count upon holding their own. . . . And such things depend upon the ideal which is continuously held up before men by the religion in which they believe. Fetish-worshippers have a habit of waiting for something to happen by magic. . . . But Stoicism was itself a negative doctrine—a theory of endurance rather than a theory of action. Its effect was to make men imper- vious to evil, not to make them powerful for good: and yet suffering is the price men pay for power. No creed evolved from the philosophical, the intellectual basis, could give them the power of action. Stoicism could not do so. And therefore it did not succeed in restoring to power the republican principle in politics.

Its economic failure

IV

But had the Stoics absolutely no gift of a political sort to give mankind? There is one indirect gift which perhaps they did succeed in giving: and they gave it in peculiar circumstances not without an instructive side to the onlooker. The very fact that the republican opposition took the shape of an ethical theory rather

Stoicism a moral criticism

than that of an alternative policy subjected the empire to a moral criticism more useful than any political criticism could have been.

A military guild such as the imperial Roman army, in which ability is the sole road to success, is liable to develop characteristics of an alarming nature. We can see the deep, the fatal fault that resulted from its headship remaining elective: the atmosphere of internal competition which issued in continual intrigue and conspiracy. . . . As long as the last of the aristocratic houses endured, they managed to stave off the worst of the effects by monopolizing the higher commands. But even under Augustus and Tiberius there were signs that this barrier might not last long. The men from below were already knocking at the door. They brought with them an atmosphere of fierce, deadly, unrelenting, unremitting competition, in which every man's hand was against his neighbour, and every weapon was legitimate in the strife. The prize was the supremacy that placed the whole world in their hands. Men like Seianus and Macro were a new type.

The master of the Roman world thus needed not only to struggle with his external foes, and with the external opposition which questioned his title, but to hold his position against his own friends. . . . Never for one **Difficulties** moment could such a man as Tiberius sleep, or take his **of** disport, or lean his weight on any loyalty or any love. **elective** His watch must be more terrible than that of any wise **monarchy** virgin: a perpetual, wakeful, unvarying distrust. He could never forget himself or others. . . . And this watchfulness, inhuman and abnormal (for in every nor-

mal man's life there must be whole realms he never need
doubt, and many hours in which he can freely forget
that he possesses a back to be stabbed in) could only
end in the spiritual destruction of the men subjected
to it. The wonder is that they were so good.

It was long after the days of Tiberius that this evil
rose to its greatest magnitude; but he was the man who
felt the first force of the tide.

To a less degree the evil ran a considerable way back
into the main body of the army, ceasing only when it
reached the rank and file—men who were trained, for
twenty five years of their lives, as no other men, to trust
their backs to their friends in the hour of danger. There
cannot have been an officer of any considerable rank
who did not, in his place and to his degree, share the
watch of Cæsar.

Against this, at any rate, as against the cowardly dis-
union in their own party, the Stoics set an adamantine
face. In such a world of mutual suspicion and mutual
competition there was something great in the man who
briefly held the doctrine that external circumstances
were of no importance. He declined to watch or to
struggle. He took only moderate and reasonable precautions. He went to death with indifference. . . . The
existence of the Stoic was a silent comment on the
moral tension of Cæsar's palace. It did not ultimately   Compro-
fail of its effect. When Nero had at last fallen, and   mise
Galba, Otho and Vitellius had followed him in the struggle which took place over his body, Vespasian, the survivor, represented a distinct movement towards the
senatorial position. Slowly, a compromise began to work

itself out. After Titus had veered towards the Senate and Domitian had backed away from it, the foundation was laid, in the person of Nerva, for an accommodation which gave the empire four great rulers in succession, of a very noteworthy type. They represented a new orientation towards the Stoic: culminating in M. Annius Verus—the emperor "Marcus Aurelius" —whose Stoicism is too obvious to need mention.

But this moral victory of Stoicism was won only at the moment when it ceased to have any connection with oligarchic politics of the old sort. Stoicism had no real connection with any political theory. It could be as heartily entertained by an absolute monarch as by the most confirmed republican. But when all had been said and done, it formed the bridge by which some of the earlier Roman virtues had been carried over to a new era.

Robbed of its philosophy, the oligarchy continued to become less and less of a political power. . . . It diminished, became misty, and its republican principles dissolved into the intangible atmosphere which never left Rome.

V

Destruction of the compromise

The compromise between the Senate and the empire, which was established by Nerva, gave the Roman world eighty-four years of peace and prosperity. It was broken up under Commodus; and thenceforward the contest was renewed on fresh ground. The real weakness of the Senatorial party disclosed itself by degrees. While it represented the elements of civil and economic life, its members were unable to maintain the world in economic prosperity. They could not organize the production of wealth. Power was torn from them by fierce and hasty soldiers. The struggle terminated in the accession of the Illyrian emperors and the political reorganization of the state as an absolute monarchy, in which the Senate was practically abolished. . . . But the military power could not maintain itself when the economic foundation was crumbling beneath its feet. The effort only hastened the end. There came a time when Roman armies were fighting the barbarians of the north upon no more than level terms. In western Europe the great military guild at last sank and vanished in the slough of economic collapse.

Collapse of the military guild

It was only in the last period of this struggle that the State resorted for help to the new religion which was the expression of its unity and universality. The possible results which might have followed from the quick perception and early adoption of the principles of that religion are illustrated by the wonderful reformation and restoration which they brought about in the eastern provinces, where the empire was given another thousand years of useful life. . . . To the west, they came too late. . . . Men, not being entirely wise nor completely free, are able to see and to act only when the force of circumstances lends its driving power. History is the tale of the blindness and the blunders of mankind far more than (as Edward Gibbon thought) of its crimes and catastrophes.

Christianity was the survivor of a struggle which included a number of competitors. The old Roman religion

—the system we roughly indicate by the general term "paganism"—the old system of local cults and primitive customs, roughly and imperfectly universalized by
a process of identifying the principal figures in its various mythologies, and veneered over with Greek philosophy and literary tradition—this perished with the oligarchy, leaving only traces of its more elementary forms in the popular customs of the peasantry. It was, in its last days, no more than a literary tradition—passionately kept, like the love letters of a lost mistress, but as much a matter of past things and bygone glories. It belonged, in reality, to the days of the independent city-states. With their fall, it had ceased to have meaning. . . . The Egyptian worships and some of the Asiatic cults had more vitality. But the worship of Isis remained too local in conception; its external power of appeal was limited; its inward philosophical structure was suited to a type of mind which fell behind and dropped out of the battle when life became a desperate fight against odds. . . . Mithraism, in some respects the closest competitor of Christianity, was the particular cult of the army. It largely perished when the army dissolved. Many of its adherents of the higher grades probably fell on the field of battle during the numberless civil wars and frontier struggles of the last days.

The power of Christianity rested, of course, upon its extraordinary catholicity. It brought into integration a far larger number of elements than any of its competitors. It was a wine-press into which went harvests of the most diverse intellectual effort, spiritual experience and social tradition. The result was something which did not shield men from pain nor guard them from catastrophe, but braced them to action. . . . Anything is possible to men if they will suffer and act.

The theory that persecution makes men great is a very doubtful one. Persecution is frequently—perhaps usually—successful. The world is strewn with the dust of unprofitable martyrs. Persecution will wipe out anything except the truth. It was the element of truth, the element of life and vitality, that brought the early church—a mixed, often ragged, sometimes disreputable, occasionally magnificent army—struggling through to success.

The battle it fought against its external competitors it carried on also within its own ranks. The form it finally took was one which gathered together in alliance the men who were ready to suffer and prepared to fight.

VI

The degree, as well as the nature, of the influence which could be exerted on the Roman state by the Christian church, was profoundly affected by the structure of the two bodies.

There was but one source from which the organization of a Christian Church could spring—the still unorganized, untapped residuum of population which had not yet been drawn into the circle of authorized Roman institutions. The reason why that Church arose from the humble and the weak, not among the great men of the world, is accordingly clear enough. The social organization of the upper and middle classes could not be converted or twisted or in any way transformed to suit objects and ideals which it was never designed to fulfil: there was no means by which any man, or any minority of men, could effect such a transformation from within. The men who founded the organizations of Roman society had seen to that. They had so arranged its structure that it could only be destroyed—it could never be changed. Hence, when the time came for change, it could not change, and was therefore destroyed.

This result was not to the benefit of anyone. It put back the progress of humanity, delayed its march, and cost it an untold penalty in the destruction of life and wealth and the frustration of happiness. It did not save a single valuable interest; it did not subserve even the lowest ends, let alone the highest.

There was no fresh organization ready to step into the shoes of the old. The old organization had taken care to have no rivals. Like an oriental monarch, it had removed all its natural successors. The church was not an organization adapted for the conduct of ordinary secular life. It was a religious institution alone. It could not take over the work of the landlords and bankers and merchants of the Roman world. It could do no more than nourish and inspire the labours of those who refounded civilization.

Christianity;— Laws of its development

The beginning and the subsequent growth of the church conformed to the rules which govern the formation of all great social institutions. It began—as the rule is—with one man; and that man—as we should expect—had attributed to him a pedigree which classes

him with the kings and aristocracies of the world. His
first helpers and successors were—and here again the
rules hold good—free men accustomed to liberty and to
self-sufficing independence. The organization grew: and
if it grew by the assimilation of men from the lower
and unorganized section of the community, it was only
because the other classes were already bound tight in
the bonds of mutual association—so tight, that to get
free of them was almost an impossibility. Even so, there
were recruits from those other classes, who either took
the risk of discovery or anticipated it by boldly sacrificing their positions. And—pursuing those rules which
govern such institutions—the church acted not by col-
lecting the views of its servile recruits and striking an
average of opinion and doctrine, but by submitting
them to the training of a discipline determined by
men of a very different stamp. The slave learned not
alone to act, but also to think and to be on the model
of that mighty man who was descended from the Kings
of Judah.

This was something of a nature much more significant than could be shown by any of the class-organizations of the Roman civilization. It went nearer to the
roots of reality. All the class-organizations of Rome were
by comparison overburdened with mere custom, subject
to mere drift—were out of control and victimized by
their own incoherence and inchoateness. . . . None of
them could get free from the dreadful drag that is constituted by the necessity of conforming to an average of
opinion.

Christi-
anity:—
not an
"average
of
opinion"

VII

It is worth while to remind ourselves of one particular aspect of the rise of Christianity. In the reign of Tiberius took place a process which consisted in the gathering together, in one brief set of principles, handy and convenient for propaganda, of the whole results of the social experience of the civilization of the ancient east—a civilization older then than our own is now—and its grafting upon the civilization of the Mediterranean. . . . Four thousand years and more of struggle, of success, of failure, of hope, of fear, of passionate aspiration and steady faith, culminating in one brilliant century as pregnant in its religious significance as the age of Pericles was in art, or the nineteenth century in scientific discovery; this human experience was brought into contact with the Roman world until its vitality began to run through the veins of that world and to change its nature. . . . Rome had some seven hundred years of experience, most of it political and legal. Greece had perhaps four times as much: and its complete form was artistic and commercial—consummated in ideas of artistic expression and intellectual conception. But the east had a longer experience still, and the form into which she threw it was religious. . . . Now, religious thought is much the most concentrated form of thinking possible to the human brain. It gives—as nothing else does—a set of values which can determine the relations of all other thoughts. . . . What we need to appreciate, before all else, is the vastness of time, the immensity of the human experience, which went to form

Christianity:—
its
derivation

the set of values that entered the western world under
the name of the Christian faith. . . . When it constructed around itself, as a means of expression, a ritual
gathered from the familiar customs of mankind, a the-
ology largely taken from Greek philosophy, and a canon
law not free from the influence of Roman jurisprudence,
it transformed all these things and gave them a coherence they had never before possessed, by reorientating
them according to one definite scale. . . . Beside this,
the ancient religion of Rome was a trifling thing which
could not hold the attention or the affection of men.

VIII

Before the full results of the Christian movement
could affect the Roman dominion, that dominion, as
far as western Europe was concerned, had collapsed into
wreckage, and the Church, whether knowingly or not,
was launched on a fresh pilgrimage to reconstruct an- Social
other and a more comprehensive world. This is not the result of
                                                        the
place in which to follow it. Let us return to the legacy legacy of
of Tiberius; for there are yet one or two items in the   Tiberius
account which must be reckoned up.

The struggle between Tiberius and his foes, involving
as it did the destruction of the house of Cæsar and the
paralysis of the senatorial oligarchy, influenced the subsequent development of the Roman world in ways which
deserve more particular description in detail.

The root problem of that contest was the impossibility of discovering any effective reason for halting
in it. Neither moral obligation nor material interest was
sufficient to supply an adequate cause. It was on this

problem that the Roman polity, like the Greek, came to grief. To push a social struggle beyond a certain point is to disrupt or corrupt civilization; but where is this point?—by what means is it to be discovered?—and what motives can be found to compel men to pause when they perceive it? A modern man is not free to take up any attitude of superiority on this question. Our greater wisdom still remains to be proved.

Civilization is not simply based upon compromise; it is itself, in its own nature—like marriage—a compromise, continually in being, continually renewed from hour to hour. On the effective construction and maintenance of this compromise depends the continuance of civilized life. It is easy not to make it; easy to follow ideas to their extreme logical conclusion; but in that case both victors and vanquished have lost all and gained nothing. There must be a "Consent to Lose." In the absence of this amicable arrangement there is no alternative but to construct society so rigidly that competition is altogether excluded. But it is highly questionable whether this cure is not as bad as the disease. Hence we are confronted by an apparently baffling and insoluble problem, which can only be circumvented by attacking it from a totally different quarter: namely, by turning our attention to the creation of an actual change in men's minds themselves—not a change in the way we educate ourselves, but a change in the selves we educate.

One of the essential doctrines of Christianity was the possibility of this change in ourselves. There never was any question but that the number of men capable of it is small; but these are the salt of the earth, who preserve

Problem of Party Struggle

Does every civilization end in deadlock?

it from destruction. That we cannot change human nature is a principle that few will dispute. But if a certain
number of men cannot empty themselves of the motives and aspirations of the ordinary sensual life, then
we must be prepared to contemplate the possibility
that every civilization ends in a dead-lock.

But in the absence of such a solution the ready resort
is to rigid organization. The defence of the military
emperors forced this rigidity upon Roman life: it slowly
destroyed the vitality of Roman industry and commerce,
and this in turn undermined the foundation on which
the power of the military order was built. . . . To a
certain extent the Roman empire shared this rigidity
with all its fore-runners. The necessity of control forced
upon all of them alike the same tendency to a system
of caste—the same isolation of one class from another, Rigid
the sharp division of professions, the system of regu- organiza-
lated and closed guilds in industry. . . . This question tion the
is not one of theory. We are not arguing an abstract dangerous
case. Control by the central government was forced alterna-
upon ancient civilization by the most practical neces- tive
sities; competition, attrition, and the survival of the
strongest left in existence those that heeded the necessity
of control, and wiped out those that neglected it. . . .
The Roman state was a victor tottering up to the winning post out of a large field of starters.

The danger of such rigidity is that the state which is
so organized can be easily, and sometimes quite suddenly destroyed. To make a serious breach anywhere in
the fabric is liable to bring the whole structure down
bodily. And this is in fact the fate that befell the civili-

zation of later Rome. It never recovered from the catastrophes of the third century. It could not recover; for a
rigid system of social organization has no generous reserves of intelligent amateurs. . . . When the Irish and
the English got their first grip on Roman Britain by the
simple expedient of destroying whatsoever they could
reach, and then waiting until the body-politic bled to
death, they were following a method which the Turks
afterwards applied to the Byzantine empire. In both
cases, it succeeded but too well.

IX

The policy of Tiberius upon the Rhine frontier—influenced in part, as the story has shown, by the political
struggle—was wise as far as it went; but it left many
issues outstanding. . . . The conquest of Britain must
have become a fixed intention with the Roman army
chiefs after the recall of Germanicus. The condition
of domestic politics, however, made it necessary that a
generation should pass before such a design could be
realized.

**Rhine
policy
of
Tiberius**

Some ten years after Germanicus left the Rhine, the
Frisians were provoked to revolt, and made good their
independence. It was after this that we can trace the
first beginnings of a movement which was destined to
go far and have vast consequences. The Chauci began
a little raiding. In A. D. 47 they came down to the coasts
of Gaul under a leader named Gannascus, a deserter from
the Roman service and by race a Frisian Canninefate.
. . . They had found—or rediscovered—the sea-way
south, which Drusus and Germanicus had so graphically

demonstrated for their benfit. Gnæus Domitius Corbulo repressed their piracies, and once more reoccupied Frisia.

It was Corbulo's intention to stop these raids at the source; but to do this would have meant the crossing of the Ems, and such a re-opening of the German question was a matter for the imperial government, which proceeded to consider the whole subject. The policy of Drusus and Germanicus, stopped by Tiberius, was now reversed, and a return made to that of Gaius Julius Cæsar. Corbulo was recalled from Frisia, and the northern bank of the Rhine, although it remained under Roman supervision, was definitely evacuated. Attention was turned from inland Germany to the North Sea.

The conquest of Britain marked the next stage of a change which developed at first very slowly, but afterwards with increasing rapidity. The raid of the Chauci in A. D. 47 indicated the start of an era of ship-building in the north, and the gradual transference of the main strategic problems from the land to the water. Two hundred and fifty years later, the Chauci had grown into those sea-faring Saxons against whom southeastern Britain was ringed with fortifications as it never was ringed against the Spaniard and the Frenchman in later days. . . . Africa had found no answer to the Roman legionary. Asia had found a partial answer—the mounted bowman. Northern Europe found the complete and effective answer—the sea-going ship. Britain became, and for ages remained, the chief advanced base against the northern fleets—the central strategic point for which they fought, and the possession of which determined the seat of power.

Conquest of Britain

The occupation of Britain was thus no casual episode. It was a serious measure of policy, thoroughly executed from the first, and permanently maintained. How much Gaius Julius definitely foresaw, or how far he judged by the pure instinct of the born strategist, we can never know; but he was in any case right. Whatsoever opinions may be entertained respecting the motives which led the Roman government to occupy Britain, one thing is certain—it gave Rome the secure possession of the Rhine frontier, which was never wrested from her until Britain was lost again. On many occasions that frontier was broken, and Gaul and Spain, and even Africa were over-run: but as long as Britain was held, the line was again restored.

Significance of the conquest of Britain

The Saxons never won Britain. Not until the Angles took over the task was the project successfully achieved, in those days when Theodoric the Ostrogoth was trekking into Italy with ox and wagon, and the Vandals were reigning in Africa, and Chlodovech the Frank was busy trying ineffectually to set up some sort of minor kingdom along the Rhine. . . . The success of the Angles—none too complete at first, but sufficient—resulted in the unpinning of the whole scheme of defence in the western provinces of Rome. The empire was strong enough to wipe out the Vandals, and to reconquer Italy from the successors of Theodoric; but Gaul was never recovered. . . . Chlodovech was a man inferior to a score of fore-runners who had failed. He is not for a moment to be compared with such men as Irmin and Marbod. Nevertheless, with Britain in English hands he succeeded in founding the Frankish king-

Britain a determining factor in history

dom which was to play so great a part in subsequent history.

X

To sum up: the reign of Tiberius, and the events which then took place, determined much subsequent history. That age saw the beginning of a new scheme of social values in the foundation of the Christian faith; and though it did not see the conquest of Britain, it saw the way to it prepared by the definite abandonment of the attempt to absorb Germany into the Roman world-state. It was during the reign of Tiberius that the attempt to found a stable hereditary or co-optative monarchy for Rome broke down, so that the monarchy remained in principle elective. Out of these three elements grew some of the determining forces that have moulded the modern civilization in which we live. For the first provided the basis of a new and wider civilization; and the second secured the strategic military position which was to give this new civilization the power of maintaining itself and of spreading across the globe; and the third made sure that the old civilization of Rome should come to a deadlock and perish. . . . These results cannot quite be called accidental. They grew by an almost terrifying logic out of the precedent circumstances, and the relationships of men.

General results

But the failure of Drusus and Germanicus affected the future almost as profoundly as their success would have done. They had shaken the North out of its tribal institutions. . . . Dominance passed into the hands of barbarian monarchies which had learnt from the Romans the art of politics, and which based the beginnings of the modern national state upon the principle of the military guild which Gaius Julius Cæsar had founded. The stability and survival of these states was for the most part due to a very simple advantage—they could rely upon royal families which produced, generation after generation, men of a sufficient standard of robustness and intelligence to do the work of government and to give it continuity. The whole history of the political state in Europe, for close upon two thousand years past, has been intertwined with this problem of the succession of the head of the state. . . . The house of Theodoric the Ostrogoth could not maintain its quality, and the Ostrogothic Kingdom in Italy perished; the Visigoths of Spain could not maintain it, and the Gothic Kingdom fell; the Franks struggled up to power on the genetic virtues of the Merovingians and the Arnulfings; the English, when the robust Anglian house of Mercia dwindled, barely survived through the weaker line of Wessex.

Importance of hereditary succession

No greater error could be made than to imagine that this question of succession is artificial or unimportant. It is a problem on which depends the continuity of the creative control of the state—and that is the actual identity of the state itself. It first comes before us when we see the Roman state endeavouring to remodel itself by the active exercise of creative intelligence; we see that endeavour repeatedly fail with a gradually decreasing degree of failure through the fall of Gaius Gracchus, the abdication of Sulla, and the assassination of Gaius Julius Cæsar. We can see it take on definite meaning when

Augustus bends his mind to give continuity to the principate; its full significance dawns upon us with the problems of Tiberius and the struggle he waged.

The lives and happiness of hundreds of millions of human beings have hung upon it; the rise and fall of States has hung upon it. For if it were nothing else (and it was often much more) it was the power which controlled, or lost control of, the awful forces of party and interest. Men at large are not their own masters. They are not isolated individuals. They move in vast bodies, which are not self-determined, but are drawn and swayed by the tidal forces of opinion and interest. It is only when the control gives way, and lets these forces free, that men realize one fact about themselves—that they are swept passively into social and political catastrophes by forces which they cannot stop, divert, or change, and before which they, their feelings, their hopes, their wishes, and all the kindly habits of civilization, are straws.

Problem of creative control

THE END

INDEX

OTHER COOPER SQUARE PRESS TITLES OF INTEREST

AUGUSTUS
The Golden Age of Rome
G. P. Baker
378 pp., 17 b/w illustrations, 8 maps
0-8154-1089-1
$18.95

HANNIBAL
G. P. Baker
366 pp., 3 b/w illustrations, 5 maps
0-8154-1005-0
$16.95

HISTORY OF THE CONQUEST OF MEXICO &
HISTORY OF THE CONQUEST OF PERU
William H. Prescott
1330 pp., 2 maps
0-8154-1004-2
$29.95

AGINCOURT
Christopher Hibbert
176 pp., 33 b/w illustrations, 3 b/w maps
0-8154-1053-0
$16.95

THE DREAM AND THE TOMB
A History of the Crusades
Robert Payne
456 pp., 37 b/w illustrations, 11 maps
0-8154-1086-7
$19.95

THE LIFE AND TIMES OF AKHNATON
Pharaoh of Egypt
Arthur Weigall
320 pp., 33 b/w illustrations
0-8154-1092-1
$17.95

T. E. LAWRENCE
A Biography
Michael Yardley
308 pp., 71 b/w photos, 5 b/w maps
0-8154-1054-9
$17.95

GENGHIS KHAN
R. P. Lister
256 pp., 1 b/w illustration
0-8154-1052-2
$16.95

THE WAR OF 1812
Henry Adams
New introduction by Col. John R. Elting
377 pp., 27 b/w maps & sketches
0-8154-1013-1
$16.95

WOLFE AT QUEBEC
The Man Who Won the French and Indian War
Christopher Hibbert
208 pp., 1 b/w illustration, 4 b/w maps
0-8154-1016-6
$15.95

MAN AGAINST NATURE
Firsthand Accounts of Adventure and Exploration
Edited by Charles Neider
512 pp.
0-8154-1040-9
$18.95

Available at bookstores; or call 1-800-462-6420

Cooper Square Press

150 Fifth Avenue
Suite 911
New York, NY 10011